MICROSOFT® VISUAL BASIC® 2005 BASICS

Todd Knowlton
Alfred C. Thompson II
Brad Hunt
Stephen Collings

D0151905

THOMSON™

COURSE TECHNOLOGY

Australia • Canada • Mexico • Singapore • Spain • United Kingdom • United States

THOMSON
™
COURSE TECHNOLOGY

Microsoft Visual Basic 2005 BASICS

by Todd Knowlton, Alfred C. Thompson II, Brad Hunt, Stephen Collings

Executive Editor:
Nicole Jones Pinard

Senior Acquisitions Editor:
Jane Mazares

Product Manager:
Jodi Anderson

Senior Marketing Manager:
Kim Ryttel

Marketing Coordinator:
Julie Schuster

Development Editor:
Rose Marie Kuebbing
Custom Editorial Productions, Inc.

Production Editor:
Kelly Robinson

Compositor:
GEX Publishing Services

Printer:
Banta Book Group—Curtis Reed

How to Use This Book

What makes a good text about Visual Basic? Sound instruction and hands-on skill-building and reinforcement. That is what you will find in *Microsoft Visual Basic 2005 BASICS*. Not only will you find a colorful and inviting layout, but also many features to enhance learning.

Objectives— Objectives are listed at the beginning of each lesson, along with a suggested time for completion of the lesson. This allows you to look ahead to what you will be learning and to pace your work.

Step-by-Step Exercises—Preceded by a short topic discussion, these exercises are the "hands-on practice" part of the lesson. Simply follow the steps, either using a data file or creating a file from scratch. Each lesson is a series of these step-by-step exercises.

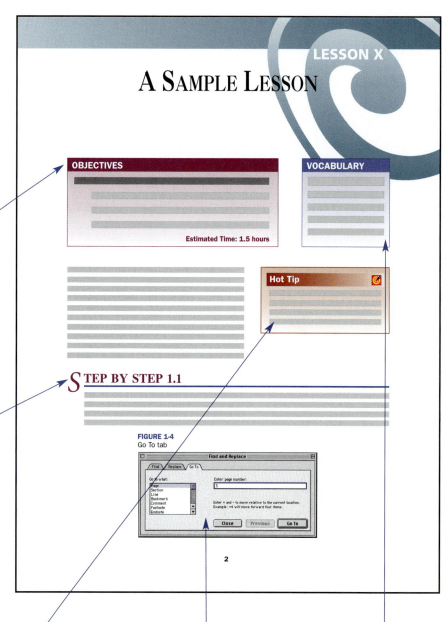

LESSON X

A SAMPLE LESSON

OBJECTIVES

Estimated Time: 1.5 hours

VOCABULARY

Hot Tip

S TEP BY STEP 1.1

FIGURE 1-4
Go To tab

Marginal Boxes— These boxes provide additional information for Hot Tips, fun facts (Did You Know?), Computer Concepts, Internet Web sites, Extra Challenges activities, and Teamwork ideas.

Enhanced Screen Shots—Screen shots now come to life on each page with color and depth.

Vocabulary—Terms identified in boldface throughout the lesson and summarized at the end.

How to Use This Book

Summary—At the end of each lesson, you will find a summary to prepare you to complete the end-of-lesson activities.

Vocabulary/Review Questions—Review material at the end of each lesson and each unit enables you to prepare for assessment of the content presented.

Lesson Projects—End-of-lesson hands-on application of what has been learned in the lesson allows you to actually apply the techniques covered.

Critical Thinking Activities—Each lesson gives you an opportunity to apply creative analysis and use the Help system to solve problems.

End-of-Unit Projects—End-of-unit hands-on application of concepts learned in the unit provides opportunity for a comprehensive review.

Lesson **X**   Unit Sample   Intro Excel   **1**

SUMMARY

VOCABULARY_Review_

REVIEW_Questions_

PROJECTS

CRITICAL_Thinking_

REVIEW_Questions_

PROJECTS

PREFACE

Microsoft® Visual Basic® 2005 is one of the most exciting programming languages in use today. With Visual Basic, you can create professional-looking applications and run Windows programs in minutes using a minimal amount of programming code.

This book will introduce you to Visual Basic and the fundamental features that are required to write useful Windows programs. In the first lesson, you will play a game written in Visual Basic. Later in the book, you will learn how to create the game you play in the first lesson. You will also enhance the game yourself. In the lessons in between, you will learn all the essentials of programming in Visual Basic while you create multi-disciplinary projects.

The lessons in this book do not assume you have any previous programming experience. You do need to have knowledge of basic operations such as how to use a mouse and how to manipulate windows and menus in Microsoft Windows. The concepts learned in this book will prepare you to learn other programming languages, such as C++, C#, and Java.

This tutorial is 30 to 40 hours in length and is designed for use with Microsoft Visual Studio 2005.

Instructional and Learning Aids

This instructional package is designed to simplify instruction and to enhance learning with the following learning and instructional aids:

The Textbook

- Learning objectives listed at the beginning of each lesson give users an overview of the lesson.
- Step-by-Step exercises immediately follow the presentation of new concepts for hands-on reinforcement.
- Illustrations, including numerous screen captures, explain complex concepts and serve as reference points.
- Case studies allow students to learn from completed Visual Basic projects and give them the tools to enhance the program.

End of Lesson

- Lesson summaries provide quick reviews reinforcing the main points in each lesson.
- True/false and written questions gauge learners' understanding of lesson concepts and software operations.

- Projects offer minimal instruction so learners must apply concepts previously introduced.

- Critical thinking activities stimulate the user to apply analytical and reasoning skills.

End-of-Unit Review

- Review questions provide a comprehensive overview of unit content and help in preparing for tests.

- Unit applications for reinforcement ask the user to employ all of the skills and concepts presented in the unit.

End of Book

- The Glossary is a collection of the key terms from each lesson.

- A comprehensive Index supplies quick and easy accessibility to specific parts of the tutorial.

Other Components

- The data files necessary to complete the exercises, activities, and applications in the book are available on the Review Pack (student data CD). You can also download these files from *www.course.com*.

- The Instructor Resources CD-ROM contains valuable supplements that aid in teaching Visual Basic 2005. The CD includes:

  - Data Files for Students: files necessary to complete the exercises, activities, and applications in the book.

  - Solutions to Exercises: solutions to all of the exercises and review questions throughout the book.

  - Instructor's Manual: contains lesson objectives, preparation suggestions, lecture notes and teaching tips, technical notes, "Quick Quizzes" to aid in classroom discussion, and key terms.

  - ExamView Test Bank and Test Engine: ExamView lets you quickly create paper, Internet, and online (LAN-based) tests. You can enter your own questions and customize the appearance of the tests you create. With its many unique features, such as the QuickTest Wizard, you can create and format a test in minutes.

  - PowerPoint® Presentations: ready-made PowerPoint presentations that correspond to every lesson in the text; perfect for a classroom setting.

  - Figure Files: all of the figures in the text, in .bmp format, for use in creating presentations or transparencies.

Acknowledgments

We (the authors) thank all those at Course Technology and Custom Editorial Productions, Inc., who were involved in this project, including Rose Marie Kuebbing, Jodi Anderson, and Kelly Robinson. The authors also thank Cal Zant who helped us all in one way or another to get the lessons and other materials completed.

Brad Hunt:

I would like to thank my co-authors for allowing me to be involved with this project. Thanks also to my wife and children for giving me time away to write.

Stephen Collings:

I thank my lovely wife, Melissa, and my two sons, Nicholas and Nathan, for their love and support throughout this project.

Alfred Thompson:

I thank my wife, Thelma, for her continued patience and support of all my work. I also thank Professor Wally Roth, Taylor University, who is responsible for me being involved in computer science in the first place.

Todd Knowlton:

I thank my co-authors for their work on this project. I also thank my wife Melissa and my daughters Kaley and Amy for keeping life fun. Finally, I owe a personal and individual thank you to my friend Cal Zant. I could not have done my part of this project without him.

START-UP CHECKLIST

This book was written to be used with Microsoft Visual Studio 2005.

The minimum hardware requirements for Visual Studio 2005 are as follows:

✓ Microsoft Windows Server 2003 SP1, Windows XP Pro SP2, XP Home Edition SP2, 2000 Pro SP4, Windows 2000 Server SP4, or Windows Vista

✓ 192 MB RAM minimum (256 MB or more recommended)

✓ 2 GB space required on installation drive (without MSDN)

✓ 1 GB space required on system drive (without MSDN)

✓ Minimum 800 x 600, 256-color display

The Visual Studio 2005 debugger requires that users be members of the Administrators group or the Debugger Users group. The Debugger Users group is created when Visual Studio 2005 is installed. The accounts used by students should be added to this group. The ability to use the Visual Basic debugger is the only access this privilege provides.

TABLE OF CONTENTS

UNIT 1 YOUR FIRST VISUAL BASIC PROGRAM

UNIT 2 CALCULATIONS AND DATA

UNIT 3 DECISION MAKING

UNIT 4 LOOPS AND ARRAYS

UNIT 5 MULTIPLE FORMS, MENUS, AND PRINTING

YOUR FIRST VISUAL BASIC PROGRAM

Unit 1

A First Look at Microsoft Visual Basic

OBJECTIVES

Upon completion of this lesson, you should be able to:

- Explain the purpose of Microsoft Visual Basic.
- Start Visual Studio 2005.
- Open an existing Visual Basic project.
- Explain the purpose of the components on the compiler screen.
- Run a Visual Basic program.
- Position a form in a Visual Basic program.
- Exit Visual Studio 2005.

Estimated Time: 1 hour

VOCABULARY

Controls

Integrated Development Environment (IDE)

Objects

Project

Properties

Properties window

Software development tool

Solution

Solution Explorer

Standard toolbar

Toolbox

Introduction to Microsoft Visual Studio 2005

Microsoft Visual Studio 2005 is a *software development tool*, which means it is a tool that allows you to create computer programs. Visual Studio 2005 allows you to use a variety of programming languages, including Visual Basic.

Visual Studio 2005 combines a graphical interface and programming code to make program development as rapid as possible. With Visual Studio 2005, you use common graphical tools to create the user interface for your program. An easy-to-use programming language helps you create the "behind the scenes" functionality for the program.

You will learn much more about Visual Basic and Visual Studio 2005 as you progress through the lessons in this book. In this lesson, you will take a quick tour of Visual Studio 2005, identify the components of the Visual Studio 2005 environment, and run an existing Visual Basic program.

Starting Visual Studio 2005

Like other Windows programs, Visual Studio 2005 can be started from a shortcut on the desktop (if one is installed) or from the Start button and All Programs (or Programs) menu.

Visual Studio 2005 is an integrated development environment or IDE. An *integrated development environment* is a program that includes tools for creating, testing, and running computer programs.

STEP-BY-STEP 1.1

1. Click the **Start** button.

2. Position the mouse pointer on the **All Programs** (or **Programs**) menu. The Programs menu opens.

3. On the Programs menu, position your mouse pointer on the menu that leads to Microsoft Visual Studio 2005. This menu will probably be named *Microsoft Visual Studio 2005*. A submenu will appear, showing the software installed under Microsoft Visual Studio 2005.

4. From the submenu, click **Microsoft Visual Studio 2005**. The Visual Studio 2005 IDE starts, and the Start Page opens. Your screen should appear similar to Figure 1-1, although your boxes may be sized differently and may contain fewer or additional items. The Start Page may show a list of *Recent Projects*. Clicking on any of these projects will open them. Leave Visual Studio 2005 open for the next Step-by-Step.

FIGURE 1-1
The Visual Studio 2005 compiler starts with the Start Page

Opening an Existing Visual Basic Project

Visual Studio 2005 stores programs in a group of files called a *project*. The main project file has a VBPROJ extension. There is also a file with the same name as the main project file, but with an SLN extension. The SLN file is a *solution* file. In Visual Studio 2005 terminology, a solution is one or more projects. Visual Studio 2005 is capable of grouping more than one project into a larger collection, which it calls a solution. In this book, you will not create applications that involve multiple projects. But every project you create in Visual Studio 2005 will have an SLN file, even if it has only one project in the solution.

To open an existing Visual Basic project, click the Open: Project/Solution link on the Start Page in the Recent Projects information area, then open the SLN file that corresponds with the project you wish to open. In single-project solutions, you can achieve the same result by opening the VBPROJ file. You should, however, develop the habit of opening the SLN file. Figure 1-2 shows the icons for each type of file.

FIGURE 1-2
Visual Studio 2005 saves
a project file and a solution file

STEP-BY-STEP 1.2

1. On the Start Page, click the **Open: Project/Solution** link in the *Recent Projects* section of the page.

2. Click the down arrow in the *Look in* drop-down list box to open a list of available drives and folders.

3. Click the up or down scroll bar arrows to scroll as needed, then click the item that identifies the disk or drive that holds the data files for this text. A list of files and folders contained on the disk appears in the dialog box.

4. In the data files for this lesson, locate the **Step01-02** folder and double-click it to open it. Open the **SnakeGame** folder. Inside you will see the VBPROJ file and the SLN file, both named *Snake* (see Figure 1-3). Your screen may not display the file extensions. Refer to Figure 1-2 to identify the icon for the SLN file if necessary.

5. Click **Snake.sln**, then click **Open**. Leave the project open for the next Step-by-Step.

> **Note** ☑
>
> If the Start Page did not appear when you started Visual Studio 2005, choose **Open Project** from the **File** menu.

> **Hot Tip**
>
> The way in which icons appear will be different if you are using Windows 2000 versus Windows XP. In either case, you may find it easier to locate the proper files based on their file extensions. If the file extensions are not displayed, you can set the folder view to show them. Open a folder, click the **Tools** menu, select **Folder Options**, and click **View**. Deselect the checkbox beside **Hide file extensions for known file types**. Click **OK**.

FIGURE 1-3
The VBPROJ file and the SLN file both appear in the Open Project dialog box

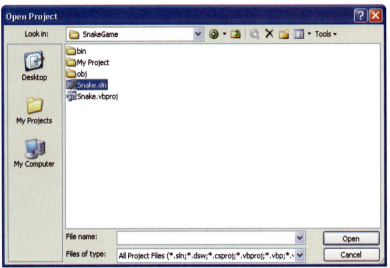

Components of the Compiler

W hen you first run the Visual Studio 2005 programming environment, it looks similar to other programs you have run in Windows. The screen includes a menu bar, toolbars, and various windows. There is even a toolbox with tools that allow you to draw command buttons, scroll bars, and much more.

Figure 1-4 shows the components of the Visual Studio 2005 screen. Do not be concerned if your screen does not show all these components at this time.

> **Note**
>
> Depending on what user customizations have been made on your system, you may see either a blank screen next to the toolbox, or you may see the Snake form. In some cases the Start Page may remain visible. If the Snake form is not displayed, you will learn how to open it later in this lesson.

FIGURE 1-4
Visual Studio 2005 has components that are similar to other Windows programs

Title bar

Standard
toolbar

Toolbox tab

Toolbox

Menu bar

Solution
Explorer

Properties
window

Menus and Toolbars

The Visual Studio 2005 menu bar has some menus found in other Windows programs (such as File and Edit) and some menus that are unique to this programming environment (such as Project and Debug). Like some other Windows programs, Visual Studio 2005 has more than one toolbar available. The toolbar that appears by default and that has the standard toolbar buttons is, appropriately, called the *Standard toolbar*. Items on the toolbar may vary slightly.

Hot Tip

For help identifying the toolbar buttons, position the mouse pointer on the toolbar button and pause. A *tool tip* will appear with the name of the button.

STEP-BY-STEP 1.3

1. Click **File** on the Menu bar. The File menu opens, as shown in Figure 1-5 (the items on your screen may vary). Notice that many of the commands in this menu (such as New, Open, Close, and Exit) are similar to File menu commands of other Windows programs.

FIGURE 1-5
The File menu has many commands similar to those of other Windows programs

2. Click **File** again. The File menu disappears.

3. Open the other menus from the Menu bar and look at some of the commands that are unique to Visual Studio 2005.

4. Position the mouse pointer on the first button of the Standard toolbar. A tool tip appears below the button with the name of the button, as shown in Figure 1-6.

STEP-BY-STEP 1.3 Continued

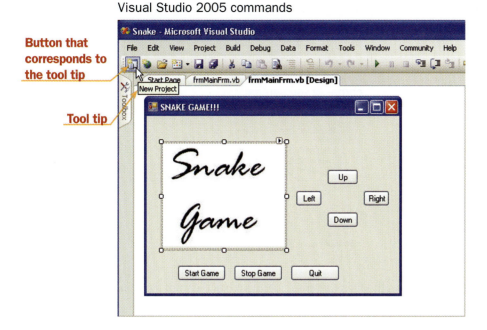

5. Position the mouse pointer on each button on the Standard toolbar and read each tool tip. You will notice that, like the Menu bar, the Standard toolbar contains many common Windows commands. Leave the project open for the next Step-by-Step.

The Solution Explorer

Another important component of the Visual Studio 2005 screen is the Solution Explorer. The *Solution Explorer* allows you to see the forms and files that make up your program. You will use the Solution Explorer to access the forms on which you want to work.

Did You Know?

A form is an object that holds buttons, boxes, and other objects that make up the program's user interface. In this lesson you will work with an existing form. In later lessons you will create your own forms.

STEP-BY-STEP 1.4

1. Click the title bar of the Solution Explorer window. The Solution Explorer window becomes active, as shown in Figure 1-7. If you do not see the Solution Explorer window, choose **Solution Explorer** from the **View** menu.

FIGURE 1-7
By default, the Solution Explorer window is docked at the upper-right corner of the screen

2. The Solution Explorer shows the files that make up the project. A form file is indicated by an icon that looks like a small Windows form, as shown in Figure 1-8.

FIGURE 1-8
The Solution Explorer uses an icon to show which files are forms

Form file icon

3. Your screen should look similar to Figure 1-9. If the SNAKE GAME!!! form is not already displayed, double-click the only form in the Solution Explorer list (**frmMainFrm.vb**). This will open the SnakeGame form.

> **Note** ☑
>
> If you cannot see all the command buttons on the form, you can resize the form when you run the program later.

STEP-BY-STEP 1.4 Continued

FIGURE 1-9
The form appears when it is double-clicked from the Solution Explorer window

4. Double-click the title bar of the Solution Explorer window. The Solution Explorer window becomes undocked and is moved to a floating position on the screen, as shown in Figure 1-10.

> **Note** ✅
>
> The position of the Solution Explorer window may vary when it is undocked.

FIGURE 1-10
The windows on the right side of the screen can become undocked by double-clicking the title bar of the window

STEP-BY-STEP 1.4 Continued

5. Position the mouse pointer on the title bar of the Solution Explorer window and drag it back to the right side of the screen, just below the toolbar. The Solution Explorer window becomes docked again. You can also return the Solution Explorer to its original position by double-clicking on the title bar. Leave the project open for the next Step-by-Step.

The Properties Window

The pieces that make up a Visual Basic program are called *objects*. Windows, command buttons, text boxes, and scroll bars are all examples of objects. Objects placed on forms, such as command buttons and text boxes, are also known as *controls*. Each object has characteristics that can be customized. These characteristics are called *properties*. To see the properties of an object, select the object and view the properties in the *Properties window*. The properties of the object can also be changed from the Properties window. The following exercise introduces you to the Properties window. You will learn how to use the Properties window more extensively in the next lesson.

STEP-BY-STEP 1.5

1. Select the SNAKE GAME!!! form (by clicking anywhere on the form except on an object within the form).

2. Click the title bar of the Properties window (by default, located below the Solution Explorer). The Properties window, shown in Figure 1-11, becomes active. If the Properties window is not displayed, choose **Properties Window** from the **View** menu or press **F4** on the keyboard.

FIGURE 1-11
The Properties window displays
the characteristics of the selected object

Extra for Experts

The properties that are shown in the Properties Window will vary, depending upon the object selected. Select different objects on the form and note the different properties that are available with each.

STEP-BY-STEP 1.5 Continued

3. Click the down arrow on the scroll bar of the Properties window to browse through the list of properties. A description of the selected property appears at the bottom of the Properties window, as shown in Figure 1-12.

FIGURE 1-12
The bottom of the Properties window
displays a description of the selected property

4. Click the **Categorized** button in the Properties window. The list of properties becomes grouped by the functions the properties perform, as shown in Figure 1-13.

FIGURE 1-13
Properties can be grouped by function

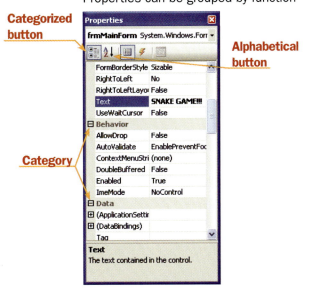

5. Click the **Alphabetical** button. The list of properties becomes grouped alphabetically. Leave the project open for the next Step-by-Step.

The Toolbox

The last part of the Visual Studio 2005 screen to visit is the Toolbox. The *Toolbox* is the collection of tools that allows you to add objects (controls) to the forms you create in Visual Studio 2005. The Toolbox has tools for creating objects, such as command buttons, text boxes, check boxes, option buttons (also known as radio buttons), picture boxes, and scroll bars. You will use the Toolbox in the next lesson to create your first Visual Basic program.

STEP-BY-STEP 1.6

1. Position the mouse pointer over the Toolbox tab. (By default, this will be found on the left side of the screen.) When your mouse hovers over the Toolbox, it opens to show a list of controls. For each control you will see an icon and the name of the control that the tool creates, as shown in Figure 1-14.

FIGURE 1-14
Each tool is shown with an icon and a name

> **Note**
>
> If you click the pushpin icon on the top of the toolbox, the toolbox will stay open. Click the pushpin a second time to use Auto Hide for the toolbox. (Auto Hide will cause the Toolbox to automatically close when you click somewhere else within Visual Studio 2005. When you need the Toolbox, you can re-open it by holding your pointer over the Toolbox tab.)

STEP-BY-STEP 1.6 Continued

2. Scroll the contents of the toolbox to move through the list of tools and read their names. Use the + and – signs to open and close the different categories of tools. Leave Visual Basic open for the next Step-by-Step.

Running a Visual Basic Program

To run a Visual Basic program, click the Start Debugging button from the Standard toolbar.

During development of a program, it is run in what is called Debug Mode. Once a program is completed and fully tested, a production version can be created and distributed to others. The difference between the debug version, which we will use in this book, and a production version is that a debug version can be stopped and examined in the IDE. We will look at features in the IDE that use this information in upcoming lessons.

> **Hot Tip**
>
> The IDE opens a window called Output that shows the results of the build. The information in this window is useful for understanding any problems that may prevent the program from compiling and running.

STEP-BY-STEP 1.7

1. Click the **Start Debugging** button from the Standard toolbar. The SNAKE GAME!!! program appears on the screen, as shown in Figure 1-15. If you cannot see all the command buttons shown in Figure 1-15, drag a corner or side of the SNAKE GAME!!! window to resize it.

FIGURE 1-15
The SNAKE GAME!!! program running in debug mode

2. Click the **Start Game** button. A box appears on the screen, and a line (the snake) begins growing toward the bottom of the box.

3. Before the line reaches the bottom of the box, click the **Right** button. The line will turn to the right and continue toward the right edge of the box.

STEP-BY-STEP 1.7 Continued

4. Continue to click the **Up**, **Down**, **Left**, and **Right** buttons to steer the path of the line. When the line hits the edge of the box or crosses its own path, the game is over.

5. When the game is over, click the **OK** button to dismiss the Game Over message.

6. Click the **Quit** button to exit the program. The Visual Basic IDE is now in Design mode and no longer in Debugging mode. Leave Visual Basic open for the next Step-by-Step.

Exiting Visual Studio

As you now know, Visual Basic is part of the Visual Studio 2005 environment. So exiting Visual Basic requires that you close Visual Studio 2005. Like other Windows programs, you can exit Visual Studio 2005 by choosing Exit from the File menu, or by clicking the Close box at the right side of the Visual Studio 2005 title bar.

STEP-BY-STEP 1.8

1. Choose **Exit** from the **File** menu.

2. If you are asked if you want to save the project and form files, click **No**. Visual Studio 2005 will close.

SUMMARY

In this lesson, you learned:

- Microsoft Visual Studio 2005 is a tool that allows you to create Windows programs. Visual Basic is a language you can use in Visual Studio 2005 that allows you to easily create complex programs.

- Visual Studio 2005 can be started from a shortcut in the All Programs (or Programs) menu or from the desktop.

- A Visual Studio 2005 project is made up of several files. Information about a project is stored in a file with a VBPROJ extension. A collection of projects is called a solution. Information about a solution is stored in a file with an SLN extension. To open a Visual Studio 2005 project, you simply have to open the SLN file.

- Visual Studio 2005 has some menu items found in other Windows programs and some menu items that are unique to Visual Studio 2005.

- The Standard toolbar appears by default and contains buttons for frequently used Visual Studio 2005 commands.

- The Solution Explorer allows you to see and open the forms and other files that make up a project.

- The Properties window lets you view the characteristics, or properties, of the objects that make up a Visual Basic program. The Properties window also allows you to make changes to those properties.

- The Toolbox holds the tools that allow you to add objects, such as command buttons, to a form.

- To run a Visual Basic program, click the Start Debugging button from the Standard toolbar.

- Exit Microsoft Visual Studio by choosing Exit from the File menu or by clicking the Close box on the Microsoft Visual Studio title bar.

VOCABULARY*Review*

Define the following terms:

Controls	Project	Solution
Integrated Development	Properties	Solution Explorer
Environment (IDE)	Properties window	Standard toolbar
Objects	Software development tool	Toolbox

REVIEW*Questions*

TRUE / FALSE

Circle T if the statement is true or F if the statement is false.

T F **1.** Microsoft Visual Studio 2005 allows you to create programs.

T F **2.** Unlike other programs, you cannot start Visual Studio 2005 using a shortcut on the desktop.

T F **3.** Visual Studio 2005 stores programs in groups of files called projects.

T F **4.** The Properties window allows you to add objects to the forms you create in Visual Studio 2005.

T F **5.** The Standard toolbar appears by default.

T F **6.** Positioning your mouse pointer on a toolbar button will produce a list of properties for that button.

T F **7.** You cannot change the properties of an object.

T F **8.** An object's properties can be displayed alphabetically and categorically.

T F **9.** A scroll bar is an example of a property.

T F **10.** The Start Debugging button on the Standard toolbar runs your program.

WRITTEN QUESTIONS

Write a brief answer to each of the following questions.

1. What is the purpose of a software development tool?

2. What file extension is given to Visual Studio 2005 project files?

3. What file extension is given to Visual Studio 2005 solution files?

4. Which window lets you modify the characteristics of an object?

5. Which window lets you view the files that make up a project?

6. Which icon shows properties grouped by the functions the properties perform?

7. What is contained in the Toolbox?

8. Which command in which menu is used to close Visual Studio 2005?

9. How do you undock a window?

10. What is one way to exit a program that you are running?

PROJECT

PROJECT 1-1

1. Start Visual Studio 2005 if necessary.

2. Open the project named **LoanAnalysis** from the **Proj01-01** folder in the data files for this lesson.

3. If necessary, click the + in the Solution Explorer to show all the files, and then double-click the form file.

4. Click some of the objects on the form and view two or three properties of the objects by clicking the property names in the Properties window.

5. Click the **Start Debugging** button on the Standard toolbar to run the program.

6. Enter the following values in the three fields across the top of the window.
   Loan Amount: **1000**
   Annual Rate (in %): **9**
   Years: **5**

7. Click the **Calculate** button. Values appear in the *Payment, Total Interest,* and *Total of Payments* fields at the bottom of the window similar to Figure 1-16.

FIGURE 1-16
The LoanAnalysis program shows calculated values

8. Click the **Exit** button.

9. Exit Visual Studio 2005. Click **No** if you are asked to save any changes.

CRITICAL*Thinking*

Suppose you want to buy a new car for $20,000. The loan will be for a period of five years at an interest rate of seven percent. What will the monthly payment be, and how much interest will you have paid at the end of five years? How much will you actually end up paying for the car?

Open the **LoanAnalysis** project from the **Proj01-01** folder in the data files for this lesson. Run the program and use it to answer the questions in the previous paragraph.

FORMS, CONTROLS, AND PROPERTIES

Creating a New Project

In Lesson 1, you started Visual Studio 2005 and ran an existing project. To create your own Visual Basic program, however, you must create a new project and begin building your program.

When you start Visual Studio 2005 and select the New Project option from the File menu or click the Create New Project link on the Start Page, the New Project dialog box appears, as shown in Figure 2-1. The Visual Studio IDE allows you to create programs in several programming languages. The project types and language choices shown may vary, depending on what options have been installed on the Visual Studio IDE.

> **Computer Concepts**
>
> The other options in the *Visual Studio installed templates* section of the Templates box allow you to more easily create a variety of specialized programs. For example, the *Console Application* helps you create a complete program without Windows features that can be used from the DOS prompt or in command files. On some versions of Visual Basic, other options allow you to create components, such as *ASP .NET programs* for Web pages, or programs for smart devices like Pocket PCs or SmartPhones.

FIGURE 2-1
The New Project dialog box

For now, we are only interested in the Visual Basic Windows Application project type.

STEP-BY-STEP 2.1

1. Start **Visual Studio 2005** from the **Programs** (or **All Programs**) menu. After Visual Studio 2005 starts, click **New Project** on the **File** menu. The New Project dialog box opens (see Figure 2-1).

If the New Project dialog box does not show a *Location* field, use the **Options** item from the **Tools** menu and select the **Projects and Solutions** line. From the Projects and Solutions page, check the option to **Save new projects when created**.

Warning

Depending upon choices made during the installation of Visual Studio 2005, your File menu may contain different items. You may need to click the **File** menu, select **New**, and click **Project** to open the New Project dialog box.

2. Select **Visual Basic** under *Project types* if it is not already selected.

3. Select **Windows Application** under *Visual Studio installed templates*. A default project name is provided, such as *WindowsApplication1*.

4. Change the name to **MyVBProgram**.

5. Click **Browse** and change the drive and folder to the location where your instructor would like you to save your files. Click the **Open** button to return to the New Project dialog box once the location has been selected.

6. Click **OK**. A new project named **MyVBProgram** is created. The project includes one blank form by default, as shown in Figure 2-2. Leave the project open for the next Step-by-Step.

STEP-BY-STEP 2.1 Continued

FIGURE 2-2
A standard new Visual Basic project includes one blank form

Blank form

Forms

The project created by selecting the Windows Application template consists of only one object: a blank form. Remember that objects are the pieces that make up a Visual Basic program. In Visual Basic, *forms* become the windows and dialog boxes when the program runs. Every program has at least one form because all other objects must be contained within forms. For example, a program cannot consist of a command button alone. The command button must be on a form.

There is no functionality in our program, except for the functions common to all forms. In the case of the default blank form, when the program runs, the user will have the ability to move, resize, maximize, minimize, and close the displayed window. These functions are common to all forms.

> **Did You Know?**
>
> If the Solution Explorer, Properties, and Form Layout windows are not displayed, click the **View** menu and click the appropriate window names. If a form file is not displayed in the Solution Explorer, click the **+** sign next to the program name in the Solution Explorer. If the form and a list of properties are not displayed, double-click the form file icon.

S TEP-BY-STEP 2.2

1. Click the **Start Debugging** button from the Standard toolbar (or the **F4** function key on the keyboard). A blank form window appears, as shown in Figure 2-3. This blank window is created as a result of the blank form in your project.

FIGURE 2-3
The form appears when the Start Debugging button is clicked

Close button
Maximize button
Minimize button

2. Click the **Maximize** button on the form. The form fills the screen, as shown in Figure 2-4.

FIGURE 2-4
The window generated by your program can be maximized

Title bar

Restore
Down button

3. Click the **Restore Down** button. The window returns to its original size and position on the screen.

STEP-BY-STEP 2.2 Continued

4. Position the mouse pointer on the title bar and drag the window to the upper-left corner of the screen below the Standard toolbar.

5. Position the mouse pointer in the lower-right corner of the window. The pointer becomes a double-headed arrow.

6. Drag the corner of the form until it is approximately 2 inches from the right edge of the screen and 2 inches from the bottom of the screen. (Exact sizing of the form is not important.)

7. Click the **Close** button in the upper-right corner of the Form1 window. The form closes, and the Visual Studio 2005 compiler with the default blank form is active again. Leave the project open for the next Step-by-Step.

Saving the Project

Visual Basic will save your project, using the name and location you gave it when you created it, whenever you compile and run the program. There are times, however, when you may make changes, but want to exit Visual Studio 2005 without compiling your program. You should always save your work before you exit. The most convenient way to accomplish this is to use the Save All button on the toolbar. You can also use the Save All option from the File menu.

Viewing and Modifying Properties

As you saw in Step-by-Step 2.2, a form has certain characteristics. One of the advantages of programming in Visual Basic is that so much functionality can be achieved without writing programming code. These characteristics of Visual Basic objects are called properties. Every object in Visual Basic has properties. You learned in Lesson 1 that the properties of objects could be viewed in the Properties window.

The Properties window allows you to easily alter the properties of objects. For example, as you will see in the next exercise, you can alter the property that controls whether the window has Minimize and Maximize buttons.

STEP-BY-STEP 2.3

1. Click the **Form1** object to select it, if it is not already selected. Sizing handles will appear around the border of the form when it is selected, and the title bar will be darkened, as shown in Figure 2-5. (Do not be concerned if you see fewer than three handles; you could resize the form to see more handles, but it is not necessary now.)

FIGURE 2-5
An object must be selected in order to alter the object's properties

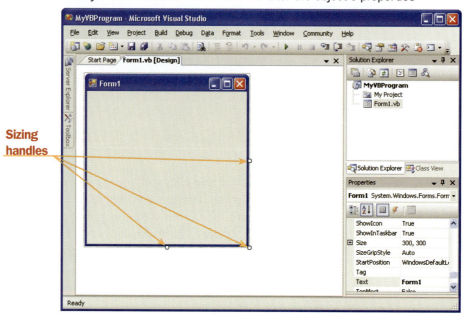

2. Open the Properties window, if necessary. Move the slider in the scroll bar in the Properties window until you see the MaximizeBox property. Click the **MaximizeBox** property. A down arrow appears at the right edge of the MaximizeBox property field. An arrow at the right edge of a field indicates that there are predefined options from which to choose.

3. Click the down arrow at the right edge of the MaximizeBox property field and select **False** from the drop-down menu. Notice that the Maximize button on the form becomes inactive (dimmed).

4. Click the **MinimizeBox** property from the Properties window and set its value to **False**. Notice that the Maximize and Minimize buttons on the form disappear.

5. Click the **Start Debugging** button from the Standard toolbar to run the program. Notice that there is no Minimize or Maximize button on the window when the program is running. The Close button is still on the form.

6. Click the **Close** button on the form window.

7. Click the **Save All** button (no dialog box will appear since the project has already been named). Leave the project open for the next Step-by-Step.

Hot Tip

It is always a good idea to manually save a project. The settings that save a project when it is run can be turned off, and you should never assume that a file is saved unless you saved it yourself.

Two of the most important properties of a form are the Text and Name properties. The Text property allows you to specify the text that appears in the title bar of the form. The Name property has a less visible, but very important, purpose. Each object has a name. The name of the object becomes very important when you begin writing Visual Basic code to manipulate the objects.

When naming objects, you should use names that are meaningful and which describe the object you are naming. Many programmers use names that describe the object and specify its type. To identify the type of object, a prefix is added to the name of the object. Table 2.1 shows some of the common prefixes and sample names.

TABLE 2-1
Common object naming prefixes

PREFIX	TYPE OF OBJECT	EXAMPLE
cmd	Command button	cmdClose
frm	Form	frmPrintDialogBox
pic	PictureBox	picLogo
lbl	Label	lblPrompt
txt	Text box	txtWidth

STEP-BY-STEP 2.4

1. Click the **Form1** object to select it if necessary. Sizing handles will appear around the border of the form when it is selected.

2. Scroll through the Properties window and select the **Text** property. Click in the Text property value field.

3. Key **My VB Program** as the new form title. The title bar of the form will not change until you are finished entering the new value in the Text property.

STEP-BY-STEP 2.4 Continued

4. Press the **Enter** key to exit from the Text property box. The title of the form is changed, as shown in Figure 2-6. Changing the Text property only changes the title bar of the form. The name of the form is a separate property and is not changed to match the title.

FIGURE 2-6
The title bar of the form is changed after the Text property value is changed

Form Text property changed

No Minimize or Maximize buttons

5. Click the **(Name)** property from the top of the Properties window.

6. Key **frmMyForm** as the new name, then press **Enter** to exit from the (Name) text box.

7. Click **Form1.vb** (the name of the form file) in the Solutions Explorer. The properties for the form file will appear. Click the File Name property in the Properties window.

> **Hot Tip**
>
> The Name property appears in parentheses to force it to appear at the top of the properties list when it is alphabetized.

8. Key **frmMyForm.vb** as the new file name, then press **Enter** to exit from the File Name box. This changes the name of the file on the disk. The name of the file and the name of the form do not have to be the same. However, using the same file name and form name makes keeping track of forms easier when a program has more than one form.

9. Save the changes using the **Save All** button and leave the project open for the next Step-by-Step.

Creating Controls

A blank form is not very exciting. To build a blank form into a custom program, the first step is to add controls to the form. *Controls* are the command buttons, text boxes, scroll bars, and other objects that make up the user interface. Like forms, controls have properties that can be customized to suit your needs.

One of the most common controls is the command button. A *command button* is a standard pushbutton control. The OK and Cancel buttons that appear in many dialog boxes are examples of command buttons.

To create controls, you must access the Toolbox. To save screen space, the default location of the Toolbox is docked on the left side of the screen, where it remains hidden until you need it. Figure 2-7 shows you where to look for the docked Toolbox. By mousing over the area on the left of the screen where the word Toolbox appears, you will cause the Toolbox to appear over the area where you work with your form. Alternately, you can choose Toolbox from the View menu to make the Toolbox appear.

FIGURE 2-7
The expanded Toolbox

Command Button tool

Mouse over to expand Toolbox

To create a command button, use the Button tool on the Toolbox (see Figure 2-7). You can double-click the tool to create a command button on the form or click the tool once and draw a command button on the form by dragging the mouse pointer in the area you want the command button to appear. The command button you create can be moved and resized if necessary.

Did You Know?

Command buttons are named automatically as they are created. Generic names, such as Button1 and Button2, will appear on newly created command buttons.

STEP-BY-STEP 2.5

1. Access the Toolbox by mousing over the area on the left of the screen where the Toolbox is docked. If you have trouble with this method of expanding the Toolbox, choose **Toolbox** from the **View** menu. Double-click the **Button** tool on the Toolbox. A command button appears in the upper-left corner of the form. (You may need to close or collapse the Toolbox in order to see the button.)

2. To create another command button, click the **Button** tool on the toolbox one time to select it.

3. Position the mouse pointer in the lower-right corner of the form. Notice that the pointer changes from an arrow to a crosshair.

4. Click and drag the mouse pointer to create a second command button that is approximately the same size as the first command button, as shown in Figure 2-8.

FIGURE 2-8
Command buttons placed on a form

5. Save the changes and leave the project open for the next Step-by-Step.

Setting Properties of the Command Buttons

Command buttons may seem simple at first. Like other objects, however, command buttons have many properties that can be set. The Name and Text properties, discussed earlier, are among the most important. As stated earlier, be sure to give command buttons meaningful names. The Text property of a command button specifies the text that the user sees on the command button. Make sure that this text is clear and meaningful to the user of your program.

STEP-BY-STEP 2.6

1. Click **Button1** to select it (sizing handles will surround it).

2. In the Properties window, click the **Text** property, key **Show Image**, then press **Enter**.

STEP-BY-STEP 2.6 Continued

3. Click the **(Name)** property, key **cmdShow**, then press the **Enter** key.

4. Select **Button2**.

5. Change the Text property to **Exit** and change the (Name) to **cmdExit**. Press **Enter**.

6. Save the changes and leave the project open for the next Step-by-Step.

Moving, Resizing, and Deleting Objects

The objects in Visual Basic can be moved and resized using techniques that are common to most Windows programs. Thus, command buttons can be moved and resized easily. You can delete an object by selecting the object and pressing the Delete key.

When you select and move an object, colored lines, called *snap lines*, appear to help you line objects up with one another. Blue snap lines show how an object lines up with other objects. The pink snap lines show how the text inside an object lines up with the text in other objects. This way you can line up objects so that either their outside edges or the text in the objects line up properly with other objects on the form.

> **Hot Tip**
>
> Visual Basic allows you to be imaginative with the size and position of objects. However, keep the Microsoft Windows standards in mind. Your programs will have a more professional appearance if the command buttons and other objects in your programs have similar sizes and placements as those in other Windows programs.

STEP-BY-STEP 2.7

1. Drag the **Show Image** button toward the upper-right corner of the form. The blue snap lines help you line the button up with the Exit button below it.

2. Click the **Exit** button that you created. Sizing handles appear around the border of the command button to indicate that it is selected.

> **Hot Tip**
>
> If any of the handles are missing, you can drag to reposition the Show Image button again.

STEP-BY-STEP 2.7 Continued

3. Position the mouse pointer on the upper-left handle and drag it up and to the left until it forms a box about the size of the one shown in Figure 2-9.

FIGURE 2-9
The handles are used to resize controls

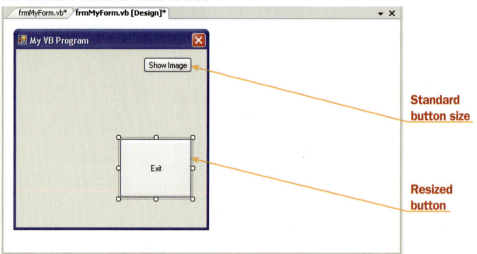

4. If it is not already selected (surrounded by sizing handles), click the **Exit** button again.

5. Press the **Delete** key. The Exit button disappears.

6. Double-click the **Button** tool from the toolbox.

7. Change the (Name) of the button you just created to **cmdExit** and change the Text to **Exit**.

STEP-BY-STEP 2.7 Continued

8. Drag the Exit button to the lower-right corner of the form. The snap lines will help you get objects lined up with each other. Your form should appear similar to Figure 2-10.

FIGURE 2-10
Command buttons can be resized and moved on the form

New Exit
button
created with
default
properties

9. Save the changes and leave the project open for the next Step-by-Step.

Understanding Focus

As you create programs that consist of controls (command buttons, scroll bars, and other objects) in windows, the concept of focus becomes an important one. As you have used programs, you have probably noticed that only one window at a time is active on the screen. You may have also noticed that within the window, only one control is active. For example, the cursor (blinking line) can only be in one text box. The object that is currently active is said to have the *focus*.

To see the focus move from one control to another, you can repeatedly press the Tab key while a dialog box is active. Each object in the window will get the focus in a sequence called the *tab order*. The tab order can be changed by changing the TabIndex property. The Tab order determines which object the users are taken to when they press the Tab key on the keyboard. It is a good idea to have the Tab order take the user in a natural and expected sequence. Changing the Tab order is often easier than moving the objects themselves.

STEP-BY-STEP 2.8

1. Open the **File** menu. Choose **New Project**. (If necessary, point to **New**, then click **Project**.) The New Project dialog box opens.

2. Press the **Tab** key. Notice how the focus moves from one control to another.

STEP-BY-STEP 2.8 Continued

3. Press the Tab key repeatedly until the **Cancel** button is selected and then press **Enter**. The New Project dialog box disappears. Pressing the Enter key activated the command button that had the focus, in this case, the Cancel button. Leave the project open for the next Step-by-Step.

The project you are working on has two command buttons on the form. When the program runs, the focus will alternate between the two command buttons as the Tab key is pressed.

Setting Additional Properties

Other properties that are commonly set when creating Visual Basic programs are the BackColor property and the properties that accurately set the position and size of objects.

Setting the BackColor Property

By default, forms have a gray background. The BackColor property can be changed to display a color other than gray. When setting the BackColor property, you can select from a palette of colors that is accessible from the Properties window.

There are three different collections of colors available. The System colors are based on specific system objects. These colors are set by the color scheme selected for the computer system-wide. This means that, if you select a System color, the actual color the user sees will depend on the color scheme on their computer.

The Web colors are colors and color names that are used by standard Web browsers. Web colors are primarily for use with interactive Web pages.

The Custom colors allow you to specify exactly the colors to display. The custom colors are used when the object does not fit into a system standard object and for when the color displayed should not be dependent on the system color settings. You should use the Custom colors when you want to control the exact color that appears regardless of the computer system being used.

> **Hot Tip**
>
> Color should be used sparingly in your programs. The more your programs have the color and appearance of standard Windows programs, the more professional your work will appear. Additionally, overusing colors can also make text in your programs more difficult to read.

STEP-BY-STEP 2.9

1. If **frmMyForm** is not already selected (surrounded by handles), click on it.

2. Click the **BackColor** property in the **Properties** window.

3. Click the down arrow at the right edge of the BackColor property field. A window of color options appears for the BackColor property, as shown in Figure 2-11.

STEP-BY-STEP 2.9 Continued

FIGURE 2-11
The BackColor property can be easily altered from the Properties window

4. Click the **Custom** tab. A selection of colors appears.

5. Click the white box located in the upper-left corner of the color palette. The form changes from gray to white.

6. Save the changes and leave the project open for the next Step-by-Step.

Setting the Top and Left Properties

Often you can use the mouse to size and position objects, such as command buttons. The snap lines, which have been added for Visual Studio 2005, make this much easier than in previous versions of Visual Studio. However, if you want precise placement, or if you want to move or place an object under program control, you can use the Location property to specify the location of the command buttons. The Location property is a point with X and Y values that locate the object at a distance from the upper-left corner of a form. The Location's X property specifies the distance the upper-left corner of the command button will appear from the left edge of the form. The Location's Y property specifies the distance the upper-left corner of the command button will appear from the top edge of the form. By default, the unit of measure for the X and Y properties is pixels. A pixel is the smallest dot on a screen that the computer can address.

> ### Did You Know?
>
> There is a Left property that corresponds to the X value of Location and a Top property that corresponds to the Y value of Location. These properties can only be read and written using code executed inside the program. They are not available from the Properties window.

STEP-BY-STEP 2.10

1. Click the **Exit** button to select it.

2. In the Properties window, scroll down and click the **+** sign next to the **Location** property. The X and Y values appear. Select the **X** value, key **200**, and then press the **Enter** key.

3. Select the **Y** property, key **200**, and then press **Enter**.

4. Click the **Show Image** button to select it.

5. Change the X property to **200**, and then press **Enter**.

6. Change the Y property to **10**, and then press **Enter**.

7. Start the program. Click the **Exit** button. The Exit button has no functionality yet, so the program does not exit. In the next lesson, you will add that functionality.

8. Click the **Close** button to end the program.

9. Save your changes and choose **Exit** from the **File** menu to exit Visual Studio 2005.

> ### Hot Tip
>
> If your buttons are no longer visible when you change the measurements in these steps, experiment with smaller measurements or drag to resize the form. Even when an object is hidden or not easily found on the form, you can access it in the Properties window by selecting it from the drop-down list of objects.

SUMMARY

In this lesson, you learned:

■ To create your own Visual Basic program, you must create a new project. The Windows Application project template allows you to create a program from scratch.

■ Projects created using the Windows Application template begin with one blank form. Forms become the windows and dialog boxes when the program runs.

■ Every program has at least one form. All other objects must be contained within forms.

■ Visual Studio 2005 will save your project whenever you compile the program.

■ A window created from a Visual Basic form has certain functionality by default, such as the ability to be moved, resized, maximized, minimized, and closed.

■ Properties are the characteristics of Visual Basic objects. Properties can be modified in the Properties window.

■ The Text and (Name) properties are two of the most important properties. The Text property controls what the user sees in the title bar of a form and in other objects, such as command buttons. When we add programming code later, the (Name) property allows us to refer to the object using a meaningful name. Programmers often use a naming standard when naming objects.

■ Controls are the command buttons, text boxes, scroll bars, and other objects that make up the user interface.

- A command button is a standard pushbutton control that commonly appears in dialog boxes. Command buttons can be moved, resized, and deleted like other Windows objects.

- Focus refers to the active status of one of the objects in a window. Only one object can have the focus.

- The BackColor property controls the background color of a form.

- The Location property can be used to accurately position objects. By default, the X and Y point values of the Location property use a measurement called pixels.

VOCABULARY *Review*

Define the following terms:

Command button	Form	Snap line
Control	Pixel	Tab order
Focus		

REVIEW *Questions*

TRUE / FALSE

Circle T if the statement is true or F if the statement is false.

T F **1.** The Console Application option helps you create a complete program with standard Windows features already included.

T F **2.** Every program must have at least one form.

T F **3.** Visual Basic Windows Application programs have some functionality without writing any code.

T F **4.** The btn prefix is commonly used when naming command buttons.

T F **5.** The OK and Cancel buttons that appear in dialog boxes are examples of command buttons.

T F **6.** A text box in a dialog box is an example of a control.

T F **7.** An object can be deleted by selecting the object and pressing the Delete key.

T F **8.** The inactive controls on a form are said to have focus.

T F **9.** Selecting the Background property will allow you to change the background color of a form.

T F **10.** The project name and location are defined when the project is first created.

FILL IN THE BLANK

Complete the following sentences by writing the correct word or words in the blanks provided.

1. When the Windows Application option is selected from the New Project dialog box, _____ appears.

2. The _____ object is always created as the default object by the Windows Application project template.

3. When an object is selected, _____ appear around the object.

4. _____ describes the characteristics of Visual Basic objects.

5. The _____ property determines what value will appear in the title bar of a form.

6. The naming prefix _____ is generally used when naming a form.

7. _____, _____, and _____ are three examples of controls.

8. The _____ is the unit of measurement Visual Basic uses for the X and Y Location properties.

9. _____ is the term that describes the sequence in which the controls in a window become active as the Tab key is pressed.

10. The _____ button on the Standard toolbar is used to save a program.

PROJECT

PROJECT 2-1

1. Start Visual Studio 2005 and create a new project named **MyVBProgram2**.

2. Change the name of the form file to **frmMyForm2**.

3. Change the (Name) property of the form to **frmMyForm2**.

4. Change the Text property of the form to **Lesson 2 Project**.

5. Add a command button to the form.

6. Change the Text property of the command button to **Exit**.

7. Change the (Name) property of the command button to **cmdExit**.

8. Drag the Exit button to the lower-right corner of the form.

9. Draw a new command button on the form that is approximately the same size as the Exit button.

10. Change the Text property of the new command button to **Go** and change the (Name) property of the command button to **cmdGo**.

11. Resize the Go button so it is approximately half as wide and twice as tall as the Exit button.

12. Click the **Start Debugging** button on the Standard toolbar to run the program (the Exit button will have the focus).

13. Press the **Tab** key to switch the focus between the command buttons.

14. Click **Close** to end the program.

15. Select and delete the **Go** button from the form.

16. Move the **Exit** button to the center of the form.

17. Click on the form and position the pointer on the lower-right corner. Resize the form so the Exit button appears in the lower-right corner.

18. Save the changes, then exit Visual Studio 2005.

CRITICAL *Thinking*

1. Start Visual Studio 2005 and create a new project named **Activity2-1**. This activity will involve experimenting with Command Buttons so that you can try them out in a number of ways.

2. Give the form a title and a descriptive (Name) property.

3. Add an Install button and a Cancel button to the form, giving each a new Text value and a descriptive name property.

4. Move and resize each object so the form looks similar to Figure 2-12.

FIGURE 2-12
A form with an Install button and a Cancel button

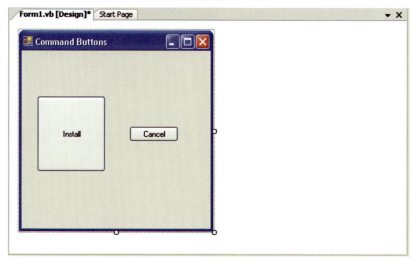

5. Save the project, then exit Visual Studio 2005.

EVENTS AND CODE

OBJECTIVES

Upon completion of this lesson, you should be able to:

- Describe events and how events are key to Windows programs.
- Access the Code window.
- Add code to a command button.
- Add a picture to a form.
- Set picture properties.
- Use code to set properties.
- Set the Cancel and Default command button properties.
- Create a stand-alone Windows program.

Estimated Time: 2 hours

VOCABULARY

Case-sensitive

Event

Event-driven

Event procedure

Method

Subroutine

Events

Windows is an event-driven environment. In an *event-driven* system, the computer is constantly waiting for the user to take some action with the mouse, keyboard, or other device. That action triggers an *event*, and the software in the computer attempts to find something to do with that event.

Each object has a set of events that are supported by the object. When you create an object, such as a command button, it is up to you to write the code that will handle the events. That code can be written in Visual Basic 2005.

You only have to write code for the events that you want to use in your program. For example, a command button supports events called Click, MouseDown, and MouseUp. The Click event occurs when the user clicks a command button. To be more specific, the MouseDown event occurs when the user presses the mouse button and holds it down over the command button. The MouseUp event occurs when the user releases the mouse button. Normally, you only need to write code for the Click event. The added control provided by MouseDown and MouseUp usually is not needed.

The code you write to handle a specific event is called an *event procedure*. You will write event procedures for events that you want to handle. For events you wish to ignore, you don't have to write anything.

In Lesson 2, you created two command buttons on a form and then ran the program. Recall that you clicked the command buttons, but nothing happened. When you clicked the Exit button that you created, a Click event was generated. Because your mouse pointer was over the Exit button, that command button was given the Click event to process. However, since you had not written any code for the command button, it did not know how to process the Click event, and the event was ignored.

In this lesson, you will add code for handling the Click event to the command buttons you created in the previous lesson. As you progress through the lessons in this book, you will learn about additional events and how to write code for those events.

Accessing the Code Window

The first step in adding code to an object is to access the Code window. To add code to a command button, open the form that contains the command button and double-click the command button. The Code window will appear.

STEP-BY-STEP 3.1

1. Start Visual Studio 2005. Open **MyVBProgram.sln** from the data files for this lesson.

2. If necessary, use the **View** menu to open the Solution Explorer and Properties windows.

3. If the form is not already on your screen, double-click **frmMyForm** in the Solution Explorer. The form appears on the left of the screen.

4. Double-click the **Exit** button. The Code window appears. Your screen should appear similar to Figure 3-1. Leave the project open for the next Step-by-Step.

FIGURE 3-1
The Code window allows you to enter code for an object or control

Notice that the Code window already has some code written in it. A *subroutine* (a section of code to perform a specific task) has been set up for you. The name of the subroutine (cmdExit_Click) indicates that the routine is to handle the Click event of the cmdExit button. The code for the Exit button will be added at the location where the cursor is blinking.

Adding Code to a Command Button

To add code to the Code window, you simply enter the code from the keyboard much like you would use a word processor. You can insert and delete text, and use cut, copy, and paste.

The Code window, however, has special features that automatically format your code and help you enter code more easily and more accurately. For example, using a technology called IntelliSense, it will anticipate what you are about to key and complete your statements for you. When you enter the name of an object, IntelliSense will show you a list of all the methods and properties that are available for that object. When you enter the name of a subroutine or a function, IntelliSense will show you what information you need to give it to use it correctly.

> **Did You Know?**
>
> The Code window does not automatically wrap text like a word processor. Each line of code should be complete on one line. Press **Enter** at the end of each line of code. Press the **Backspace** key to delete blank lines. You can resize the Code window to make seeing your code easier.

Visual Basic is not *case-sensitive*, meaning capitalization of key words and other elements of the code is not critical. Keying a command in all caps, all lowercase, or a combination of case has no effect on the functionality. However, to keep things neat and consistent, the Code window editor will automatically standardize the case of much of your code.

Let's begin by adding code for the Exit button. We will add the Visual Basic 2005 command to end a program—the End statement. By default, the IDE starts your new line of code indented by a tab stop. It is common practice to use indention to improve the readability of programming code. The usefulness of indenting code will become more apparent in later lessons when the code is more complex.

S TEP-BY-STEP 3.2

1. Key **end** and press **Enter**. Notice that Visual Studio 2005 capitalizes the word end and changes the color to blue. Your Code window should appear similar to Figure 3-2.

Note

The color in which the key words in the Code window appear may vary.

FIGURE 3-2
Visual Studio 2005 automatically formats key words

Indicates code changed and saved recently

Indicates code changed and not yet saved

Subroutine name

Code added

2. Press **Backspace** three times to remove the blank line below the code you just keyed.

3. Press the **frmMyForm.vb [Design]*** tab above the code window. The Code window moves behind the form window, and the form becomes active. (If the [Design] tab is not visible, select the **Designer** option from the **View** menu to display the design window.)

Hot Tip

A green line on the margin of the code window indicates recent code changes that were saved the last time the file was saved. A yellow line shows code that has not been saved.

4. Click the **Start Debugging** button from the Standard toolbar to run the program.

5. Click the **Exit** button. The event procedure you wrote is activated, and the program ends. Leave the project open for the next Step-by-Step.

Adding a Picture to a Form

Visual Studio 2005 allows you to easily add graphics to your programs. One of the easiest ways to add a picture to a form is to use the PictureBox tool (located toward the bottom of the Toolbox). The PictureBox tool creates an object called a PictureBox control. A PictureBox control provides a framework for displaying a picture on a form.

Like the Button tool, the PictureBox tool can be double-clicked to place an object of a default size on the form. You can also click the PictureBox tool once and then drag to draw a PictureBox control. The PictureBox control can be moved and resized like other controls.

STEP-BY-STEP 3.3

1. Double-click **PictureBox** on the Toolbox. A PictureBox control appears in the upper-left corner of the form.

2. Position the mouse pointer in the center of the PictureBox control and drag it a small distance from the upper-left corner. Drag the lower-right corner of the PictureBox control to resize it. Your form should look similar to Figure 3-3.

FIGURE 3-3
The PictureBox control allows graphics to be shown in a program

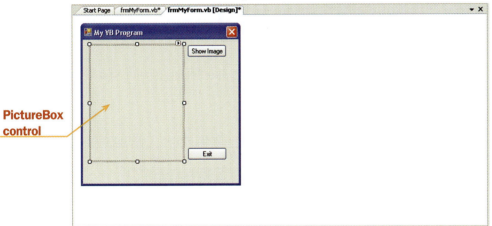

PictureBox control

STEP-BY-STEP 3.3 Continued

3. While the PictureBox control is selected (surrounded by sizing handles), click the **Image** property in the Properties window. A button with three tiny dots, called an ellipsis, appears in the Image property field, as shown in Figure 3-4. The ellipsis, in this case, indicates that you can browse your hard drive for a file that will serve as the source of the image, if necessary.

FIGURE 3-4
The ellipsis shown indicates that you can browse for a value

4. Click the ellipsis at the end of the Image property field. The Select Resource dialog box appears, as shown in Figure 3-5.

FIGURE 3-5
The Select Resource dialog box allows you to select either a new file or one that is already in the project's resource file

5. Select the **Local resource** option button and click the **Import** button. The Open dialog box appears, as shown in Figure 3-6.

STEP-BY-STEP 3.3 Continued

FIGURE 3-6
The Open dialog box allows you to select a picture that will be the source of the image

6. From the *Look in* box, select the drive and folder where your data files for this exercise are located. A list of picture files appears in the Open dialog box.

7. Select **Memphis** from the list of picture files and click **Open**. A picture of the Mississippi River appears within the Select Resource dialog box, as shown in Figure 3-7.

FIGURE 3-7
The selected picture appears in the Select Resource dialog box

8. Click the **OK** button. The picture of the Mississippi River appears in the PictureBox control.

9. Save the changes and leave the project open for the next Step-by-Step.

Setting Image Properties

Like other objects, image controls have an extensive set of properties that can be changed. For our purposes, there are three properties that are of particular interest: the (Name) property, the SizeMode property, and the Visible property.

The (Name) Property

Naming a PictureBox control is as important as naming other objects. The name you give the PictureBox control will be the name you use when you refer to the control in your Visual Basic code. The *pic* prefix is often used when naming PictureBox controls.

STEP-BY-STEP 3.4

1. If necessary, click on the PictureBox control to select it.

2. Scroll up in the Properties list and click the **(Name)** property. Remember, the Name property appears in parentheses at the top of the Properties list.

3. Change the name of the PictureBox control to **picMyImage** and press **Enter**.

4. Save the changes and leave the project open for the next Step-by-Step.

The SizeMode Property

When you selected the picture for the PictureBox control, the picture did not completely fill the available space. Often, however, you will want to have the picture expand or shrink to fill the available space. In other cases, you may want the available space to expand or shrink to fit the picture being loaded. The SizeMode property allows you to specify what should happen when the picture and the space available do not match.

The SizeMode property has several possible values. The Normal setting has the picture fill up all available space without changing the size of the picture or the PictureBox. In some cases, this will leave empty space around the picture. In other cases, the picture may be too large for the PictureBox, and not all of the picture will be visible. The Center setting also does not change the size of the picture or the PictureBox. In this case, the picture will be positioned in the center of the available space.

The StretchImage and AutoSize options will change the size of the picture or the PictureBox to make the picture fit. The StretchImage option will cause the picture to expand or shrink to fit the space available. This may cause some distortion in the picture. The AutoSize option will cause the PictureBox to expand or shrink to hold the picture completely. This can cause the PictureBox to expand beyond the size of the form.

STEP-BY-STEP 3.5

1. If necessary, click on the PictureBox control to select it. Resize the PictureBox control so it appears similar to Figure 3-8. Notice that the PictureBox control resizes, but the image itself remains the original size. The image does not resize because the SizeMode property is set to Normal.

FIGURE 3-8
PictureBox control resized while the SizeMode property is set to Normal

2. In the Properties window, change the SizeMode property to **StretchImage**. The image stretches to fit inside the PictureBox control, as shown in Figure 3-9.

FIGURE 3-9
Changing the SizeMode property to StretchImage causes the picture to resize to fit the control

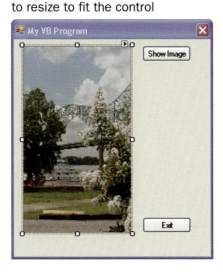

3. Click **Start Debugging** on the Standard toolbar to run the program. Notice the image appears in the window.

STEP-BY-STEP 3.5 Continued

4. Click **Exit** to end the program.

5. Save the changes and leave the project open for the next Step-by-Step.

The Visible Property

The Visible property gives you control over when a picture is visible to the user. Setting the Visible property to False makes the image invisible to the user. As you will see when you write the code for the Show Image button, the Visible property can be changed using code.

> **Note**
>
> In the Snake Game you played in Lesson 1, the large words "Snake Game" that appear when you first run the program are actually in a PictureBox control. The program uses the Visible property to make the words disappear when the game is started.

STEP-BY-STEP 3.6

1. Click on the PictureBox to select the PictureBox control, if necessary.

2. Change the Visible property of picMyImage to **False**.

3. Click **Start Debugging** on the Standard toolbar. The program begins, but because the Visible property of the PictureBox control is set to False, the picture does not appear on the form. Your screen should appear similar to Figure 3-10.

FIGURE 3-10
The Visible property allows the image to be hidden

4. Click **Exit** to end the program.

5. Save the changes and leave the project open for the next Step-by-Step.

Use Code to Set Properties

One of the most common tasks for Visual Basic code is setting properties of objects, such as controls and forms. While it is true that the properties of an object can be set when the object is created, you often will want to manipulate those properties while the program runs.

Visual Studio 2005 allows you to change a property by specifying the name of the control, the property, and the value you want to give the property. Figure 3-11 shows a line of code that changes a PictureBox control's Visible property to True.

FIGURE 3-11
Properties can be changed using code

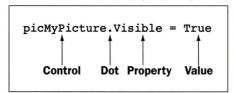

The period (usually referred to as a dot) separates the object from the property. The item to the right of the dot is called a **_method_**. The term _method_ is common to object-oriented programming languages. In Figure 3-11, the word _Visible_ is actually a method for changing the Visible property. There are other methods used in Visual Basic programming that do not relate to a property.

The PictureBox control object knows how to set its own Visible property, and it provides the Visible method for doing so. When you write the Visual Basic code, you are sending a message to the picMyPicture object, telling it to change its Visible property using the Visible method.

S TEP-BY-STEP 3.7

1. Double-click the **Show Image** button. The Code window appears on the screen.

2. Key **picMyImage.Visible = True**, as shown in Figure 3-12 (ignore the drop-down boxes that appear as you key).

FIGURE 3-12
The code in the Show Image button asks the PictureBox control to set its Visible property to True

New line of code entered

3. Close the Code window.

4. Click **Start Debugging** on the Standard toolbar. The program becomes active on the screen. Notice that the picture is not visible.

5. Click **Show Image** on the form. The image appears on the screen. Your screen should appear similar to Figure 3-13.

FIGURE 3-13
The image appears on the screen after the Show Image button is clicked

STEP-BY-STEP 3.7 Continued

6. Click **Exit**.

7. Save the changes and leave the project open for the next Step-by-Step.

Adding Access Keys to Command Buttons

You have probably noticed in most windows that include command buttons, that there is a letter that is underlined. If you press the Alt key and key that letter, the command button will respond as if it had been clicked. The same sort of underlined letter and action can be found in many menu items as well. This Access Key is declared in the Text property in Visual Basic programs.

An access key allows a user to activate a command without using a mouse. This is useful for people who are touch typists and others who find that using the mouse slows them down with some applications. With an access key, it does not matter where the mouse is pointing.

When setting the Text property (either in the Properties window, in the Menu Designer, or in code), enter an ampersand (&) prior to the letter you want to be underlined as the access key. For example, keying E&xit as the Text property of a command button will result in a menu item that appears as E<u>x</u>it.

STEP-BY-STEP 3.8

1. Click the **Show Image** button, if necessary, and set the Text property to **&Show Image**. Notice the *S* in *Show* is now underlined.

2. Click the **Exit** button and set the Text property to **E&xit**. Notice the *x* in *Exit* becomes underlined.

3. Click **Start Debugging** on the Standard toolbar to run the program.

4. Press the **Alt** and **S** keys. The Show Image button is activated, and the image appears.

5. Press the **Alt** and **X** keys. The Exit button is activated, and the program ends.

6. Save the changes and leave the project open for the next Step-by-Step.

Setting the AcceptButton and CancelButton Form Properties

You probably have noticed in most windows that include command buttons, that there is a command button that will be selected when you press the Enter key and a command button that will be selected when you press the Esc key. Often, the Enter key will select the OK button, and the Esc key will select the Cancel button.

There are two form properties involved in adding this functionality to your programs: the AcceptButton property and the CancelButton property. The AcceptButton property names the command button to be used when the user presses the Enter key and no other object that responds to it has focus. The CancelButton property holds the name of the command button on the form that will be activated when the user presses the Esc key.

Only one command button on a form can be named as the AcceptButton. The same is true for the CancelButton property.

STEP-BY-STEP 3.9

1. Click the form to access the form's properties and locate the AcceptButton property. Select the property and click the drop-down box. A list of command buttons will be displayed.

2. Select **cmdShow**.

3. Find and select the **CancelButton** property. Click the drop-down box. A list of command buttons will be displayed.

4. Select **cmdExit**.

5. Click **Start Debugging** on the Standard toolbar to run the program.

6. Press **Enter**. The Show Image button is activated, and the image appears.

7. Press **Esc**. The Exit button is activated, and the program ends.

8. Save the changes and close the project.

SUMMARY

In this lesson, you learned:

- Windows is an event-driven environment. In an event-driven system, the user triggers events that control the work.

- To control what happens when an event occurs, you must write event procedures for each event that you want to handle.

- To access the Code window, double-click an object, such as a command button.

- The code you write in Visual Basic is written in sections called subroutines.

- Adding code is much like working in a word processor. The basic text-editing features are available. In addition, Visual Studio 2005 has IntelliSense features to help format your program code.

- The End statement ends a program.

- The PictureBox tool allows you to add a PictureBox control to a form.

- Using the (Name) property, you can give a PictureBox control a name. That name will be used when you refer to the control in code.

■ Setting the SizeMode property to StretchImage causes a picture to resize to fit the dimensions of the PictureBox control. Setting the SizeMode property to AutoSize causes a PictureBox control to resize to fit the picture loaded into it.

■ The Visible property controls whether an object is shown or hidden.

■ Setting properties in code is one of the most common uses for Visual Basic code. Setting properties in code allows you to change properties while a program runs.

■ A command button with an ampersand (&) in front of a letter in the Text property causes that letter to become an access key.

■ The command button named in the form's AcceptButton property will be activated when the user presses the Enter key. The command button named in the form's CancelButton property will be activated when the user presses the Esc key.

VOCABULARY *Review*

Define the following terms:

Case-sensitive	Event-driven	Method
Event	Event procedure	Subroutine

REVIEW *Questions*

TRUE / FALSE

Circle T if the statement is true or F if the statement is false.

T F **1.** Microsoft Windows is an event-driven environment.

T F **2.** An event can be triggered only by the mouse.

T F **3.** Double-clicking a command button control brings up the Code window.

T F **4.** In Visual Basic, exact capitalization of all the key words is critical.

T F **5.** A PictureBox control provides a framework for a picture.

T F **6.** Setting the SizeMode property to StretchImage allows a picture to resize to fit the image control.

T F **7.** When setting properties from code, every property of the object must be specified.

T F **8.** The ampersand (&) sign before a character in a text property indicates an access key.

T F **9.** Only one command button can have an access key.

T F **10.** The CancelButton property identifies a command button that responds to the Esc key.

WRITTEN QUESTIONS

Write a brief answer to each of the following questions.

1. What is the term for code that handles a specific event?

2. What is the term for the section of code that is set up for you when you access the Code window?

3. What is IntelliSense?

4. What does an ellipsis (…) at the edge of a Properties field indicate?

5. Why is it important to give a meaningful name to a PictureBox control?

6. What is the purpose of the Visible property?

7. When setting a property in code, what is the item that immediately follows the dot in the line of code, and what does it do?

8. Write a line of code that will cause the image held in a PictureBox control named picLogo to be hidden.

9. What is the name of the key that is pressed with a letter key to activate an access key?

10. Why would you want to create an access key for a command button?

PROJECTS

PROJECT 3-1

In this project, you will use the Top property of a PictureBox control to move a picture on the form while the program is running.

1. Start Visual Studio 2005, if necessary, and create a new project called **HighLow**.

2. Give the form the name **frmHighLow** and change the Text property to **High Low**.

3. Use the Properties window to set the Height property of the form to **400** and the Width property to **450**.

Note ☑

Height and Width properties are measured in pixels, just like the Top (or Location.X) and Left (or Location.Y) properties.

4. Add a Cancel button to the form with the text **Cancel**. Name it **cmdCancel**. Drag the command button to the lower-right corner of the form.

5. Write an event procedure that will cause the program to end when the Cancel button is clicked.

6. Start debugging the program to test it.

7. Add a PictureBox control to the form. Drag it to the upper-left corner of the form, if necessary.

8. Load the **TimesSquare** image (from the data files for this lesson) into the Image property of the PictureBox control and set the SizeMode property to **StretchImage**. Name the picture **picTimesSquare**.

9. Set the PictureBox control's Height property to **234** and the Width property to **156**.

10. Set the Location X property of the PictureBox control to **12**.

11. Set the Location Y property of the PictureBox control to **12**.

12. Add a command button with the text **High** to the form. Name it **cmdHigh** and drag it to the upper-right corner of the form.

13. Add a command button with the text **Low** to the form. Name it **cmdLow** and place it below the High button.

14. Add the following code to the High command button Click event procedure.

    ```
    picTimesSquare.Top = 10
    ```

15. Add the following code to the Low command button Click event procedure.

    ```
    picTimesSquare.Top = 110
    ```

16. Make the first instance of the letter **C** an access key for the Cancel button.

17. Save the project.

18. Start debugging the program and test the command buttons. (Remember to press the **Alt+C** key combination to test the Cancel button.)

19. Close the project.

PROJECT 3-2

A command button's Enabled property can be used to disable a command button so that it can no longer be clicked. This is commonly used to prevent a user from selecting an option that is not currently available. In this project, you will open the project you created in the lesson and disable the Show Image button after the image is visible.

1. Start Visual Studio 2005, if necessary, click the **Open Project** button on the start page or **Open** and then **Project** from the **File** menu, and open the **MyVBProgram** project you created in this lesson.

2. If necessary, open the form.

3. If necessary, set the form's CancelButton property to the name of the exit command button.

4. Double-click the **Show Image** button to access its event procedure.

5. Press the right arrow key to move to the end of the code that makes the image visible, then press the **Enter** key.

6. Add the following line of code.

   ```
   cmdShow.Enabled = False
   ```

7. Close the Code window.

8. Start debugging the program to see the Show Image button become disabled after it is clicked. (When you run the program the image is invisible, then when you click the Show Image button, the image appears and the button is disabled.)

9. Press **Esc** to end the program.

10. Save the project (using the same name) and leave it open for Project 3-3.

PROJECT 3-3

If necessary, open the **MyVBProgram** project again and make the modifications listed below. (If you did not complete the steps in Project 3-2, perform those steps before making the modifications that follow.)

1. Create a command button with the text **Hide Image**. Give the command button an appropriate name and position it below the Show Image button.

2. From the Properties window, set the Enabled property of the Hide Image button to **False**.

3. Add code to the Show Image button event procedure that will enable the Hide Image button after the Show Image button is disabled.

4. Write an event procedure for the Hide Image button that hides the image, disables the Hide Image button, and enables the Show Image button.

5. Start debugging your program and test all command buttons.

6. Save your changes and close the project.

CRITICAL*Thinking*

Write a program that contains a form with four buttons on it. Set the Visible property of three of the buttons to False so they are not displayed when the program starts. Add code to each button so that when the button is clicked, another button becomes visible, and the button that was clicked becomes invisible. Test your program to make sure that every button appears and disappears.

Your First Visual Basic Program

MATCHING

Match the correct term in Column 1 to its description in Column 2.

Column 1

_____ **1.** form

_____ **2.** properties

_____ **3.** event procedure

_____ **4.** project file

_____ **5.** focus

_____ **6.** toolbox

_____ **7.** case-sensitive

_____ **8.** controls

_____ **9.** IntelliSense

_____ **10.** Solutions Explorer Window

Column 2

A. objects that make up the user interface

B. capitalization of key words and other elements of the code is critical

C. the file that holds information about the files that make up a project

D. objects that become the windows and dialog boxes when the application is run

E. the window that allows you to see the forms that you want to work on

F. the technology used in Visual Studio 2005 that will anticipate what you are about to key and will complete your statements for you

G. the characteristics of an object

H. the code written to handle a specific event

I. the collection of tools that allows you to add objects to the forms you create in Visual Basic

J. The object that is currently active is said to have the _____.

WRITTEN QUESTIONS

Write a brief answer to each of the following questions.

1. What appears when a command button on a form is double-clicked?

2. What happens when you click the Close button on a running Visual Studio 2005 program?

3. What key activates the Cancel object of a form?

4. What are the two icons for arranging displays in the Properties window?

5. What are two examples of command buttons found in other Windows programs?

6. What property controls whether an object is shown or hidden?

7. What key moves the focus from one control to another?

8. What icon on the IDE compiles and runs a program?

9. What contains the collection of tools that allows you to add objects to the forms you create in Visual Basic?

10. What property allows you to specify the text that appears in the title bar of a form?

PROJECTS

PROJECT 1-1

Write the name of the screen components from Figure U1-1 here.

A. _____

B. _____

C. _____

D. _____

E. _____

F. _____

FIGURE U1-1
Screen components

PROJECT 1-2

Start Visual Studio 2005 and create a new project using the name of your choice. Position the mouse pointer on each of the toolbar icons shown in Figure U1-2 and write the name of the tool in the spaces provided. Be sure the form is selected in the Solution Explorer.

A. _____

B. _____

C. _____

D. _____

E. _____

F. _____

FIGURE U1-2
Toolbar icons

SIMULATION

JOB 1-1

In this job, you will use the Left property of an image control to move an image on the form while the program is running.

1. If necessary, start Visual Studio and create a new project. Name the project **LeftRight**.

2. Use the Properties window to give the form the name **frmLeftRight** and the title text **LeftRight**.

3. Use the Properties window to set the **Height** property of the form to **250**, then press **Enter**.

4. Use the Properties window to set the **Width** property of the form to **400**, then press **Enter**.

5. Add an Exit button (with an appropriate caption and name) to the lower-right corner of the form. Add code to make the program end when the button is clicked.

6. Add the **TimesSquare** image from the Unit 1 Review data files to the form with the name **picTimesSquare** and set the SizeMode property to **StretchImage**.

7. Set both the Height and Width properties of the PictureBox control to **100**.

8. Set the Location.X property of the PictureBox control to **20**.

9. Set the Location.Y property of the PictureBox control to **20**.

10. Add a **Left** button to the lower-left corner of the form and give it an appropriate caption and name.

11. Add a **Right** button between the Left and Exit buttons and give it an appropriate caption and name.

12. Add code to the Left button that will position the image close to the left side of the form. (*Hint:* Use the method **picTimesSquare.Left.**)

13. Add code to the Right button that will position the image close to the right edge of the form.

14. Make the Exit button the button that will be activated when the Esc key is pressed.

15. Save and start debugging the program and test all of the buttons.

16. End the program and exit Visual Studio 2005.

> **Note**
>
> If the Left and Right buttons did not place the image correctly when you ran the program, double-click the command buttons, change the coordinates in the Code window, then run the program again.

CALCULATIONS AND DATA

Unit 2

Estimated Time for Unit 2: 8 hours

MATHEMATICAL OPERATORS

Performing Calculations in Visual Basic

It is no secret that computers are well suited for math. In fact, most of the tasks a computer performs can be reduced to some mathematical function. Like other programming languages, Visual Basic allows you to use mathematical equations in your programs. In this lesson, you will learn how to perform the basic mathematical functions using the mathematical operators.

Operators are symbols that perform specific operations in Visual Basic statements. As you will learn in later lessons, there are operators that perform functions that are not mathematical. But for now, we will only be concerned with performing basic math operations using the common operators.

Since you began learning basic math, you have been using operators, such as + and –, to add and subtract values. To make statements as easy to read as possible, the Visual Basic operator symbols are similar or identical to the symbols you are accustomed to using. Table 4-1 shows the mathematical operators you will use in this lesson.

TABLE 4-1
Common mathematical operators

OPERATOR	DESCRIPTION
=	Assignment
+	Addition or unary plus
–	Subtraction or unary minus
*	Multiplication
/	Division
\	Integer division
Mod	Modulus

Multiplication and division are represented by symbols that are slightly different from those used in standard mathematics. An asterisk (*) represents multiplication, and a forward slash (/) represents division. These symbols are used for multiplication and division in most programming languages because they are available on a standard computer keyboard.

> **Note**
>
> There may be a couple of operators in Table 4-1 that are new to you. Don't worry—in this lesson you will learn all about them and put each of them to work in a program.

Creating Label Controls

The *Label control* is used to place text on a form. Sometimes a label is used to identify a text box or to add a title or message to a form. The Text property of a label specifies what caption will appear on the label. The text that appears on the label cannot be changed directly by the user. Labels can also be used to provide output by writing code for the desired calculation. The result of the calculation is then assigned to the Text property of the label, and the result also appears on the label on the form.

In the following Step-by-Step, you will open a Windows Application project and create some labels.

> **Note**
>
> The text on a label control, command button, or other object that cannot be changed by the user at run time is often referred to as a caption. The Text property is used to refer to the caption's value to keep property names and operations consistent across objects.

STEP-BY-STEP 4.1

1. Start Visual Studio and open a new Windows Application project. Save the project in a location indicated by your instructor and call the project **Addition**.

STEP-BY-STEP 4.1 Continued

2. In the Properties window, give the new form the name **frmAddition** and the caption **Addition**.

> **Hot Tip**
>
> Remember that you change the caption by changing the Text property.

3. Double-click the **Label** tool, which is found in the Toolbox. A label appears on the form. The text for the label is **Label1**.

4. Select the value in the **Text** property in the Properties window.

5. Key your name as the caption for the label and press **Enter**. Notice that the caption changes on the label as you press **Enter**.

> **Hot Tip**
>
> Remember that another way to place controls, such as labels, on a form is to click the tool once, then drag to draw the control. You can then move, resize, or delete the control as needed.

6. Select the **(Name)** property value, key **lblMyName**, and press **Enter**.

7. Position the mouse pointer in the center of the label and drag it slightly away from the corner of the form.

8. Save the project and leave Visual Studio open for the next Step-by-Step.

Using the Addition and Assignment Operators

The addition operator (+) and *assignment operator* (=) perform just as you would expect. For example, in the statement below, the values 16 and 8 are added, and the result is placed in the caption of the label named lblAnswer. The assignment operator changes the value of the item on the left of the assignment operator to the value to the right of the assignment operator. After the statement is executed, the label will display the result of the addition (24).

```
lblAnswer.Text = 16 + 8
```

The statement above is not very realistic, however. In most cases, rather than writing code that adds two hard-coded values, you will be adding values that may be entered by a user or other values that may change each time the program is run. The term *hard-coded* refers to information that is entered directly into the source code and cannot change while the program runs. Values that are keyed directly into source code are also called *literals*.

STEP-BY-STEP 4.2

1. Click the **Label** tool in the Toolbox to select it.

2. Draw a label in the center of the form that is about half the size of the label created in the previous Step-by-Step.

3. Change the caption of the new label to the number zero (**0**) and press **Enter**.

4. Change the name of the new label to **lblAnswer**.

5. Click the **Button** tool and create a command button near the bottom-center of the form. Name the button **cmdCalculate** and change the button's caption to **Calculate**.

6. Double-click the **Calculate** button, and add the following code in the Click event procedure.

```
lblAnswer.Text = 16 + 8
```

7. Close the Code window. Click **Start Debugging** on the Standard toolbar to run the program. The Answer label in the center of the form currently has a caption of 0.

8. Click **Calculate**. The caption for the Answer label changes to 24, the result of adding 16 and 8, as shown in Figure 4-1. Your screen should show your name in the upper-left corner of the form.

FIGURE 4-1
The Text property of the label was changed by the code in the Calculate button

9. Click **Close** on the title bar to end the program.

10. Save and close the project, but leave Visual Studio open for the next Step-by-Step.

Using Text Boxes and the Val Function

Text boxes are the fields placed on dialog boxes and in other windows that allow the user to enter a value. You have seen and used text boxes in the previous lessons. In this lesson, you will learn how to extract the value from a text box and use it in a mathematical operation. Figure 4-2 shows an example of a text box (the *File name* text box). The Text property of a text box specifies what text will appear alongside the text box.

FIGURE 4-2
Text boxes are fields that receive input from the user

A text box

How Text Differs from Numeric Data

Text boxes accept data from the user. This data comes in the form of text. In a computer, text—which can include letters, symbols, and numbers—is treated differently from strictly numeric information. For example, if the user enters 234 in a text box, the computer treats that entry as three characters—a 2, a 3, and a 4. It does not automatically treat the entry as two hundred and thirty-four. Therefore, numbers in a text box must be converted to a true numeric value before they can be used in a calculation.

When a computer stores text, it uses a numeric value to represent each allowable character. For example, to your computer, the character "A" is represented by the value 65. The system of codes that the computer uses to represent characters is called the ASCII code. For now, it is important that you understand that the characters entered in text boxes need to be converted from text (including numeric text) to a numeric value before mathematical operations can be performed.

Using the Val Function

The action necessary to convert the numeric text characters in a text box to numeric values is done by the Val function. The *Val function* takes numbers that are in a text format and returns a numeric value that can be used in calculations. The Val function stops reading the string at the first character it does not recognize as part of a number. Symbols and characters that are often considered parts of numeric values, such as dollar signs and commas, are not recognized.

The statement below is an example of how the Val function is used. The items in parentheses are the text boxes.

```
lblTotal.Text = Val(txtPrice.Text) + Val(txtSalesTax.Text)
```

The statement above includes two Val functions. Notice that the text box names (txtPrice and txtSalesTax) in each Val function begin with the *txt* prefix. This makes it clear that the controls are text boxes. (Remember that controls are the objects you insert from the Toolbox.) The *Text* following the period in each Val function accesses the values entered by the user in the text boxes.

The *Text* following the period (for the label to the left of the assignment operator) indicates that the answer of the calculation will be assigned to the Text property of the label. The statement is instructing the computer to take the value in the txtPrice text box, add the value in the txtSalesTax text box to it, and assign the sum of the values to the Text property of the label named lblTotal.

You will practice using the `Val` function in the next Step-by-Step.

Splitting Code Statements among Lines

When you begin writing code that includes calculations, the lines of code often become long. Visual Basic provides a way to split a line of code among two or more lines. Within a line of code, you can key an underscore (_), known as the *line-continuation character*. The line-continuation character tells the compiler to skip to the next line and treat the text there as if it were a part of the same line. In the following Step-by-Step, you will use the line-continuation character to break a long line of code into two lines.

> **Important**
>
> Always key a space before the line-continuation character to avoid errors.

STEP-BY-STEP 4.3

1. Choose **Open, Project/Solution** from the **File** menu.

2. Open the **ProfitLoss** project from the **Step04-03** folder in the data files for this lesson.

3. If the form is not displayed, double-click the form **frmProfitLoss** in the Solution Explorer window. Your screen should appear similar to Figure 4-3.

FIGURE 4-3
The Profit & Loss form appears on your screen

STEP-BY-STEP 4.3 Continued

4. Double-click the **Calculate** button. The Code window appears.

5. Verify that your cursor is on the blank line below the `cmdCalculate_Click` line. Add the following code to total the expenses.

```
'Calculate Total Expenses
lblTotalExp.Text = Val(txtRent.Text) + Val(txtPayroll.Text) + _
Val(txtUtil.Text) + Val(txtSupp.Text) + Val(txtOther.Text)
```

This code will add the values in the Rent, Payroll, Utilities, Supplies, and Other text boxes and will assign the sum of the values to the Text property of the label named lblTotalExp. The Code window should appear similar to Figure 4-4.

Computer Concepts

The apostrophe (') at the beginning of the code for step 5 allows you to enter text into the code that the compiler will ignore. Everything from the apostrophe to the end of the line will be ignored. These notes in the code are called comments. You will learn more about comments in the next lesson.

FIGURE 4-4
The underscore character allows a line of code to be broken into multiple lines

New code added with line continuation

6. Close the Code window and click **Start Debugging** on the Standard toolbar to run the program.

Hot Tip

When you use parentheses in code, count to be sure that you have an equal number of left (and right) parentheses.

STEP-BY-STEP 4.3 Continued

7. Key the following data into the corresponding text boxes on the form.

Rent	**350**
Payroll	**600**
Utilities	**200**
Supplies	**100**
Other	**50**

8. Click **Calculate**. The expenses are totaled, and the results are stored in the Total Expenses field, as shown in Figure 4-5.

FIGURE 4-5
The Calculate button totals the data on the form

9. Click **Exit**. The Profit & Loss program closes.

10. Save the changes and leave the project open for the next Step-by-Step.

Using the Subtraction Operator

The subtraction operator subtracts the value to the right of the operator from the value to the left of the operator. In other words, it works just the way you learned in elementary school.

In the next Step-by-Step, notice that profit is calculated by subtracting the value in a label from the value in a text box. You extract the value from a label using the Text property.

STEP-BY-STEP 4.4

1. Double-click the **Calculate** button to open the Code window, if necessary.

2. Click at the end of the second line of code that you entered in the previous exercise, and press **Enter** to create a blank line.

STEP-BY-STEP 4.4 Continued

3. Add the following code to calculate the profit.

```
'Calculate Profit
lblProfit.Text = Val(txtRev.Text) - Val(lblTotalExp.Text)
```

This code will subtract the value in the label named lblTotalExp from the value in the text box named txtRev and will assign the result to the Text property of the label named lblProfit. Your screen should appear similar to Figure 4-6.

FIGURE 4-6
The subtraction operator subtracts one value from another

4. Close the Code window and start debugging the program.

5. Key the following data into the corresponding text boxes on the form.

Revenue	**1200**
Rent	**350**
Payroll	**600**
Utilities	**200**
Supplies	**100**
Other	**50**

Did You Know?

In the code for the profit calculation, the `Val` function is not necessary to extract the value from `lblTotalExp.Text`. Because earlier code set the caption to a numeric value, we could assume that the caption is still a numeric value. However, using the `Val` function in cases like these is good practice.

STEP-BY-STEP 4.4 Continued

6. Click **Calculate**. Both the Profit field and the Total Expenses field store the results of the calculation, as shown in Figure 4-7.

FIGURE 4-7
The Calculate button calculates the total expenses and the profit

7. Click **Exit** to close the program.

8. Save the changes and leave the project open for the next Step-by-Step.

Using Unary Minus

You can use the subtraction operator as *unary minus* to perform negation, which means making a positive value negative or making a negative value positive. For example, the statement below takes the value in the label named lblAnswer and changes the sign of the value. If lblAnswer is holding a negative number, the unary minus will make it positive. If the value in the label is already positive, the unary minus will make it negative.

```
lblNegatedAnswer.Text = -Val(lblAnswer.Text)
```

The addition operator can be used as a unary plus. The unary plus is rarely used, however, because it has little practical value. Values in Visual Basic are assumed to be positive unless they are specifically assigned as negative.

STEP-BY-STEP 4.5

1. Double-click the **Calculate** button to open the Code window, if necessary.

2. Add the following code beneath the code that calculates the profit.

```
'Calculate Loss
lblLoss.Text = -Val(lblProfit.Text)
```

STEP-BY-STEP 4.5 Continued

This code will convert the value in the label named lblProfit to its opposite value (a positive value if it is negative and a negative value if it is positive) and assign the result to the Text property of the label named lblLoss.

3. Close the Code window and start debugging the program.

4. Key the following data into the corresponding text boxes on the form.

Revenue	**1200**
Rent	**350**
Payroll	**600**
Utilities	**200**
Supplies	**100**
Other	**50**

5. Click **Calculate**. The loss is now calculated as well as the total expenses and profit, as shown in Figure 4-8.

FIGURE 4-8
The negated profit represents the loss

6. Click **Exit**.

7. Save the changes and leave the project open for the next Step-by-Step.

Using Fix

There are times when you are interested in only whole numbers after a calculation is performed. Most programming languages include a function that drops the fractional part of a number. In other words, the function removes everything to the right of the decimal point. This process is called *truncation*. In Visual Basic, the *Fix function* returns the truncated whole number.

In the program you have been creating in this lesson, you need to calculate the percentage of the total expenses, which are allocated to each of the expense categories. For example, in the case of the Rent expense, the amount spent on rent must be divided by the total expenses and then multiplied by 100 to obtain a percentage. Using the multiplication and division operators, that calculation can be performed with the following code.

```
Val(txtRent.Text) / Val(lblTotalExp.Text) * 100
```

The result of this calculation will commonly have a fractional part. If we are only interested in the whole-number percentage, the Fix function can be used to truncate the result.

```
Fix(Val(txtRent.Text) / Val(lblTotalExp.Text) * 100)
```

By placing the entire expression in parentheses, the Fix function is applied to the result of the entire expression.

S TEP-BY-STEP 4.6

1. Double-click the **Calculate** button to open the Code window, if necessary.

2. Add the following code beneath the code that calculates the loss.

```
'Calculate Expense Percentages
lblRentPerc.Text = Fix(Val(txtRent.Text) / _
      Val(lblTotalExp.Text) * 100)
lblPayrollPerc.Text = Fix(Val(txtPayroll.Text) / _
      Val(lblTotalExp.Text) * 100)
lblUtilPerc.Text = Fix(Val(txtUtil.Text) / _
      Val(lblTotalExp.Text) * 100)
lblSuppPerc.Text = Fix(Val(txtSupp.Text) / _
      Val(lblTotalExp.Text) * 100)
lblOtherPerc.Text = Fix(Val(txtOther.Text) / _
      Val(lblTotalExp.Text) * 100)
```

3. Close the Code window and start debugging the program.

4. Key the following data into the corresponding text boxes on the form.

Revenue	**1500**
Rent	**350**
Payroll	**700**
Utilities	**250**
Supplies	**100**
Other	**60**

5. Click **Calculate**. Each of the percentages is calculated as well as the total expenses, profit, and loss, as shown in Figure 4-9.

STEP-BY-STEP 4.6 Continued

FIGURE 4-9
The program calculates the percentage of the total that each
expense represents

6. Click **Exit**.

7. Save the changes to the project and then close the project. Leave Visual Studio open for the next Step-by-Step.

Performing Integer Division and Using the Modulus Operator

In computer programming, there are times when you want to work exclusively with whole numbers, called *integers*. When performing division, like percentages, the results are often fractional even when you begin with whole numbers. For example, 5 and 3 are both integers, but when you divide 5 by 3, the result is fractional (1.666667).

For cases in which you want to work strictly with integers, Visual Basic provides two special operations: integer division and modulus. *Integer division* returns only the whole number portion of the division of integers. *Modulus* returns the remainder of integer division.

Performing Integer Division

Integer division is performed using the backward slash (\), often called simply a backslash. (As opposed to the forward slash (/) usually used for division.) This operation returns a whole number. For example, 5 \ 3 returns 1 as the result.

> **Did You Know?**
>
> Using the Fix function—which returns the integer part of a number with regular division—gives the same result as doing integer division. The Fix function is most often used to truncate the results of a more complicated expression than a single division. In those cases, you usually want to retain the fractional parts of all operations until the end to maximize the accuracy of the result. Integer division is usually used for less complicated expressions.

STEP-BY-STEP 4.7

1. Choose **Open, Project/Solution** from the **File** menu. Open the **Division** project from the **step04-07** folder in the data files for this lesson.

2. If necessary, open the form **frmDivision**. Your screen should appear similar to Figure 4-10.

FIGURE 4-10
The Division form appears on your screen

3. Double-click the **Calculate** button to open the Code window.

4. Add the following code to calculate the quotient. Be sure to use the backslash (\) for integer division when keying the code.

```
'Calculate Quotient
lblQuotient.Text = Val(txtDividend.Text) \ Val(txtDivisor.Text)
```

5. Close the Code window and start debugging the program.

6. Enter **6** in the field outside the division bar (the divisor) and **10** inside the division bar (the dividend).

7. Click **Calculate**. The quotient is calculated, and the results are displayed to the left of the r, as shown in Figure 4-11.

STEP-BY-STEP 4.7 Continued

FIGURE 4-11
The Calculate button calculates the quotient as an integer

Integer quotient

8. Click **Exit**. The program closes.

9. Save the changes and leave the project open for the next Step-by-Step.

Using the Modulus Operator

The modulus operator (Mod) returns the remainder of integer division. For example, 5 Mod 3 returns the result 2 because 5 divided by 3 is 1 remainder 2.

> **Computer Concepts**
>
> Unlike other operators, Mod is not a single character. Nevertheless, Mod functions as an operator.

STEP-BY-STEP 4.8

1. Double-click the **Calculate** button, if necessary, to open the Code window.

2. Add the following code (after the code you entered in the previous exercise) to calculate the remainder.

```
'Calculate Remainder
lblRemainder.Text = Val(txtDividend.Text) Mod Val(txtDivisor.Text)
```

3. Close the Code window.

4. Change the form's AcceptButton property to refer to the Calculate button.

5. Change the form's CancelButton property to refer to the Exit button.

6. Start debugging the program. Enter **5** in the field outside the division bar (the divisor) and **27** inside the division bar (the dividend).

STEP-BY-STEP 4.8 Continued

7. Press **Enter** to activate the Calculate button. The quotient and remainder are calculated, and the results are displayed above the division bar, as shown in Figure 4-12.

FIGURE 4-12
The Calculate button calculates the quotient and the remainder

8. Press **Esc** to activate the **Exit** button. The program closes.

9. Save your changes and exit Visual Studio.

SUMMARY

In this lesson, you learned:

- Visual Basic allows you to use mathematical equations in your programs.

- Operators are symbols that perform specific operations in Visual Basic statements.
  - The addition operator (+) adds values.
  - The assignment operator (=) assigns the result of the expression on the right of the operator to the item to the left of the operator.
  - The subtraction operator (–) subtracts the value to the right of the operator from the value to the left of the operator. The subtraction operator can be used to perform negation. When used in this way, the subtraction operator is called the unary minus.

- Values keyed directly into Visual Basic code are called hard-coded values or literals.

- Text boxes are the fields placed on dialog boxes and in other windows that allow the user to enter a value.

- The numbers in a text box are considered to be text characters. To use the numbers as actual values in a calculation, the val function must be used to convert the numeric text to a numeric value.

- When a line of code is long, you can split the code into two lines in the Code window by keying an underscore at the end of the line and continuing the statement on the next line. The underscore is called the line-continuation character.

- Placing an apostrophe in code allows you to enter text (called a comment) into the code. Everything from the apostrophe to the end of the line will be ignored.

- Multiplication is represented by an asterisk (*). Division is represented by a forward slash (/).

- The Fix function removes the fractional portion of a number. The Fix function performs an operation called truncation.

- Integer division is represented by a backward slash (\). Integer division returns only the whole number portion of the division of integers. The modulus operator (Mod) returns the remainder of integer division.

VOCABULARY *Review*

Define the following terms:

Assignment operator	Label control	Text boxes
Fix function	Line-continuation character	Truncation
Hard-coded	Literals	Unary minus
Integer	Modulus	val function
Integer division	Operator	

REVIEW *Questions*

TRUE / FALSE

Circle T if the statement is true or F if the statement is false.

T   F   **1.** Operators are symbols that perform specific operations in Visual Basic statements.

T   F   **2.** Values entered directly into Visual Basic code are called hard-coded or literals.

T   F   **3.** Text boxes are fields on a form that allow the user to enter a value.

T   F   **4.** Text boxes store numeric values entered by the user in a numeric format.

T   F   **5.** The subtraction operator and the unary minus operator are two different characters.

T   F   **6.** The addition operator cannot be used as a unary plus.

T   F   **7.** The backslash character is used for integer division.

T   F   **8.** The result of integer division is the remainder of the division.

T   F   **9.** The val function truncates the fractional part of a number.

T   F   **10.** In Visual Basic, an expression cannot take up more than one line.

WRITTEN QUESTIONS

Write a brief answer to each of the following questions.

1. What are the seven mathematical operators covered in this lesson?

2. What are the differences between the forward slash and the backslash?

3. How would you find the remainder of integer division?

4. How do you continue a statement on a new line without getting an error?

5. How are comments created?

6. What is the purpose of the Fix function?

7. What prefix commonly begins text box names?

8. What must you do in order to use the information that is stored in the Text property of a text box in numeric calculations?

9. Write the code for a command button that will calculate the result of multiplying values in two text boxes, num1 and num2, and will display the result in a label called lblResult.

10. The following code appears in the cmd_Click subroutine of a command button. What will happen when the button is clicked?

```
lblResult.Text = 12 \ 7
```

PROJECTS

PROJECT 4-1

Your local high school is having a bake sale to raise money for a local charity. You have been asked to write a program that will calculate the total sales and show the percentages of each item sold during the bake sale. The program's user interface should look similar to Figure 4-13. The form and each item on the form should be given a caption (use Figure 4-13 as your guide). Use the following names for the form and the items on the form: **frmBakeSale, lblSalesPercent, lblCookies, lblCakes, lblPies, lblMuffins, txtCookies, txtCakes, txtPies, txtMuffins, lblCookiesPerc, lblCakesPerc, lblPiesPerc, lblMuffinsPerc, lblTotalSalesLabel, lblTotalSales, cmdExit,** and **cmdCalculate.** For the four percent labels and the total sales label, set the AutoSize property to False, delete the text in the Text property, use the BackColor property and the Custom tab to change the labels to a white background, and change the BorderStyle property to Fixed3D. You will need to align and resize items on the form by either dragging them or using the Top, Left, Height, and Width properties.

FIGURE 4-13
Create a program with a user interface similar to the one shown here

1. Start Visual Studio and open a new Windows Application project.

2. Save your project as **BakeSale**.

3. Create the form shown in Figure 4-13, using the guidelines given above.

4. Add code so the Exit button will end the program.

5. Add code so the amounts in the four text boxes will be added and the result assigned to the Text property of the label named **lblTotalSales**.

6. Add code to the Calculate button so that the percent of total sales will be calculated for Cookies, Cakes, Pies, and Muffins. (*Hint*: Use the Fix function.)

7. Close the Code window, start debugging the program, enter appropriate values, click **Calculate** to test the output labels, then end the program.

8. Save the changes to your program and close the project. Leave Visual Studio open for the next Project.

PROJECT 4-2

A local jewelry company has asked you to write a program that will calculate sales commission for their employees. The business gives their employees 4% of their total sales. Create a form similar to that shown in Figure 4-14.

FIGURE 4-14
Create a program with a form similar to the one shown in this figure

1. Create a new project and save it as **SalesCommission**.

2. Create the labels for **Employee** and **Total Sales** with appropriate names and captions.

3. Use the TextBox tool to create the text boxes to the right of Employee and Total Sales and give them appropriate names. Align them with the associated labels to the left.

4. Create the label for **Commission Earned** and name it **lblCommissionLabel** (don't forget the caption). Create a label to the right of Commission Earned with the name **lblCommission** (delete the text in the Text property box).

5. Create the Calculate and Exit command buttons with appropriate names and captions.

6. Add code to make the Exit button end the program.

7. Add code to calculate 4% of the amount entered in the Total Sales text box and assign the result to the caption of the label named **lblCommission**.

8. Close the Code window, start debugging the program, and enter appropriate values. Click **Calculate** to test the Commission Earned box, then click **Exit**.

9. Save your project. Leave Visual Studio open for the next project.

PROJECT 4-3

A common problem for many people is calculating the amount to tip a waiter or waitress at a restaurant. Write a program to calculate the amount of a tip based on the amount of the restaurant bill. Allow the user to select a 10% tip, a 15% tip, or a 20% tip. Do not worry about rounding the tip off to whole pennies. We will discuss formatting output in Lesson 7.

1. Create a new project and save it as **RestaurantBuddy**.

2. Create the labels for **Restaurant Bill** and **Tip** with appropriate names and captions.

3. Add a TextBox for the user to enter the amount of the bill and give it a name like **txtBill**.

4. Add a label box to display the tip value and give it a name like **lblTip**.

5. Add three command buttons labeled **10% Tip**, **15% Tip**, and **20% Tip**.

6. Add code to each of the three tip command buttons to calculate the appropriate tip value from the amount in the *txtBill* textbox and display the result in *lblTip*.

7. Create the **Exit** command button with an appropriate name and caption.

8. Add code to make the Exit button end the program.

9. Close the Code window, start debugging the program, and enter a value in the *Bill* text box. Click the three **Tip** command buttons to test the results, then click **Exit**.

10. Save your project and exit Visual Studio.

CRITICAL*Thinking*

Write a program to calculate the number of buses needed to transport a specified number of people to summer camp. Policy states that you can only order as many buses as you can completely fill. The remaining campers will ride in vans and cars. The program should prompt the user to input the number of people needing transportation and the number of people that can fit on a single bus. The program should calculate the number of buses that must be ordered and the number of people who will need to ride in vans and cars. (*Hint:* Use integer division and the modulus operator to calculate the outputs.) Save the project as **Buses**.

DATA TYPES AND VARIABLES

OBJECTIVES

Upon completion of this lesson, you should be able to:

- Describe the purpose of data types and variables.
- Use the AutoSize property.
- Declare and use variables.
- Describe the scope of variables.
- Describe the Object data type.

Estimated Time: 2 hours

VOCABULARY

AutoSize property

Declaring

Form-level variable

Global variable

Local variable

Object data type

Scope

Variable

Data Types

Computers are all about data. Practically all useful programs have some function in collecting, processing, storing, and delivering data. There are many kinds of data. You might first think of numbers when you hear the word data. Of course, data can be in the form of text, dates, sounds, and pictures.

All data in a computer is actually stored numerically. As you learned in an earlier lesson, even text is stored as numbers. When you program, however, it is often important to know what type of data you are working with and to specify the data types.

> **Note**
>
> You already have some experience with data types. The Val function converts one type of data (text) to another (a numeric value).

Visual Basic supports a certain set of data types. There are data types for whole numbers, floating-point numbers (decimals), text, dates, and more. Table 5-1 shows the fifteen most common Visual Basic data types.

TABLE 5-1
Data types

DATA TYPE	RANGE
Integer Data Types	
Byte	0 to 255 (unsigned)
SByte	-128 to 127
Short	-32,768 to 32,767
Integer	-2,147,483,648 to 2,147,483,647
Long	-9,223,372,036,854,775,808 to 9,223,372,036,854,775,807
UInteger	0 through 4,294,967,295 (unsigned)
ULong	0 through 18,446,744,073,709,551,615 (1.8...E+19) (unsigned)
UShort	0 through 65,535 (unsigned)
Decimal Types	
Single	-3.402823E+38 to 3.402823E+38
Double	-1.79769313486232E+308 to 1.79769313486232E+308
Decimal	-922,337,203,685,477.5808 to 922,337,203,685,477.5807
Other Types	
String	0 to approximately 2 billion Unicode characters
Date	12:00:00 midnight, January 1, 0001 to 11:59:59 P.M., December 31, 9999
Boolean	True or False
Object	Varies

The integer data types are used when you are working with whole numbers (numbers without a decimal point). There are four signed-integer data types and four unsigned-integer data types. The most common integer data type is the one named Integer. But if the values you intend to store might be outside of the range of an Integer, use the Long data type instead. The Byte, SByte, Short, and UShort data types are used when space is very limited and it is clear that only small numbers that will fit in these types will be used. The unsigned data types are used when you know you will only need positive numbers.

The decimal data types are Single, Double, and Decimal. The Single data type can store data with up to seven digits of precision. If you need more precision than that, use the Double data type. For dollar amounts, use the Decimal data type.

The other types of data are for storing text (string data type), dates, and True or False values (Boolean data type). The Object data type can hold any other type of data. You will learn more about these data types in later lessons.

You can choose to store data in memory locations called *variables*. Variables are a common feature of programming languages. They can be used to store and manipulate all kinds of data. For example, you can have a variable of the Short data type that can store numbers from -32,768 to 32,767. Variables get their name from the fact that the value can vary as the program runs.

Using the AutoSize Property

The *AutoSize property* will adjust the size of a control to fit its contents. In the case of a label, the AutoSize property will shrink or grow the label to fit the text.

To learn about AutoSize and how variables can be used in a program, we are going to create a program that calculates your age in months.

STEP-BY-STEP 5.1

1. Start Visual Studio 2005 and create a new Windows Application project called **MonthConverter**.

2. Add five label controls to the form. Position them as shown in Figure 5-1.

FIGURE 5-1
Position for five labels on the form

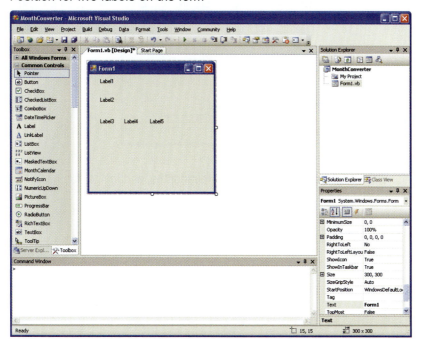

STEP-BY-STEP 5.1 Continued

3. Set the Name properties of the label controls to **lblAgeYears**, **lblMonths**, **lblYou**, **lblOutputMonths**, and **lblAgeMonths**.

4. Set the Name property of the form to **frmMonths** and the text to **Month Converter**.

5. Save the form file as **frmMonthConverter**.

6. Select all of the labels by positioning the pointer in the lower-right corner of the form and dragging up to the upper-left corner of the form.

7. From the Properties window, change the AutoSize property to **True**. The AutoSize of each of the selected labels is changed. If the AutoSize property is already set to True, set it to **False** to verify that all five are changed. Then set the AutoSize property back to **True**.

8. Set the texts of the five labels to **Age in years:**, **Months since last birthday:**, **You are**, **X**, and **months old.**, as shown in Figure 5-2. The size of each label changes as you key the text values.

9. Create two text boxes and one command button. Position and size the controls on the form, as shown in Figure 5-2.

10. Set the name of the command button to **cmdMonths** and set the text to **Calculate age in months**. You may have to change the AutoSize property to **True** for the whole message to be displayed.

11. Change the names of the two text boxes to **txtYears** and **txtMonths**. Your screen should appear similar to Figure 5-2.

FIGURE 5-2
Change captions; create text boxes and a command button

12. Change the Visible properties of lblYou, lblOutputMonths, and lblAgeMonths to **False**. The output will not be visible when the program first runs.

13. Save the changes and leave the form open for the next Step-by-Step.

Declaring Variables

The first steps to using a variable in your programs are to let the compiler know that you want to set up a memory location as a variable. You have to tell the compiler what you want to call the variable, and what data type you want the variable to have. This process is called *declaring* a variable. To declare a variable, use the Dim statement as shown here.

```
Dim VariableName As DataType
```

For example, the following statement declares a variable named intAnswer with the Integer data type.

```
Dim intAnswer As Integer
```

> **Hot Tip**
>
> Notice in the Dim statement example that the variable name is preceded by the int prefix. It is common to use naming prefixes with variables, as with controls.

Rules for Naming Variables

When naming variables, keep the following rules in mind.

1. Variable names must begin with an alphabetic character (a letter).

2. Following the first character, letters, numbers, and the underscore (_) are allowed.

3. Variable names cannot include any spaces. Some programmers use the underscore in places where they might want a space.

4. Variable names can be up to 255 characters long.

In the same way that a prefix can be used to identify a control's type, prefixes should be used to identify the data type of a variable. Table 5-2 shows the commonly used variable-naming prefixes.

TABLE 5-2
Data type prefixes

PREFIX	DATA TYPE	EXAMPLE
byt	Byte	bytCount
srt	Short	srtIndex
int	Integer	intPeople
lng	Long	lngInches
sng	Single	sngWeight
dbl	Double	dblMass
dec	Decimal	decSalary
str	String	strName
dte	Date	dteAnniversary
bln	Boolean	blnSold
obj	Object	objValue

In the next Step-by-Step exercise, you will declare a variable in a command button's Click event procedure. Later in this lesson, you will learn that where you declare a variable affects the usage of the variable.

STEP-BY-STEP 5.2

1. Double-click the **Calculate age in months** button. The Code window opens.

2. Key **Dim intMonths As Integer** at the top of the event procedure and press **Enter** twice. The intMonths variable will be used to store the user's age in months once that value is calculated. Leave the Code window open for the next Step-by-Step.

Using Variables

Variables can be used in the same way you have been using labels and text boxes. Use the assignment operator to assign a value to a variable. For example, the code below assigns the value in the txtMonths text box to an Integer variable named intMonths.

```
intMonths = Val(txtMonths.Text)
```

You can also assign hard-coded values to a variable. For example, the code below assigns a value to a variable of type Double.

```
dblMass = 3.4568973
```

You can use the mathematical operators to perform calculations with numeric variables, as shown in the following example.

```
sngTotalWeight = sngProductWeight + sngPackagingWeight
```

To output the value in a variable, you can assign the value in a variable to a label, as shown in the following example.

```
lblTotalWeight.Text = sngTotalWeight
```

Because variables have a specific data type, you do not have to use the Val function on a variable unless the variable is holding text (a string variable). Numeric variables cannot hold data that does not match the data type. Therefore, you can safely assume that the value in a numeric variable (such as sngTotalWeight) is a number.

STEP-BY-STEP 5.3

1. Below the variable declaration, add the following code to calculate the number of months.
```
'Calculate Months
intMonths = (Val(txtYears.Text) * 12) + Val(txtMonths.Text)
```

STEP-BY-STEP 5.3 Continued

2. Add the following code to display the results. Your screen should appear similar to Figure 5-3.

```
'Display Number of Months Old
lblOutputMonths.Text = intMonths
lblYou.Visible = True
lblOutputMonths.Visible = True
lblAgeMonths.Visible = True
```

FIGURE 5-3
The intMonths variable holds the results of the calculation

3. Close the Code window and start debugging the program.

4. Enter **5** in the *Age in years* text box and enter **4** in the *Months since last birthday* text box.

5. Click **Calculate age in months**. The three labels become visible and display the results, as shown in Figure 5-4.

FIGURE 5-4
The Calculate age in months command button calculates the results and displays them on the form

6. Click **Close** on the Month Converter program's title bar. The program closes.

7. Save the changes to the project. Leave the project open for the next Step-by-Step.

Scope

The term *scope* refers to the reach of a variable. In other words, a variable's scope indicates which procedures can use the variable. Where you declare a variable determines the scope of a variable.

Three Levels of Scope

The scope of a variable in Visual Basic can be local, form-level, or global.

A *local variable* is declared within an event procedure, like the intMonths variable you declared in this lesson. The variable is only accessible to the code within that event procedure. In fact, the variable does not even exist outside of that procedure. The memory space is reserved for a local variable at the time the variable is declared in the event procedure. When the procedure ends, the variable is no longer kept in memory. The procedure starts with the Sub or Function statement and ends with an End Sub or End Function statement. A variable declared inside the procedure can only be used until the End statement is executed.

A *form-level variable* is declared in the Declarations section of a form's Code window. You will learn how to access the Declarations section in the next section of this lesson. A form-level variable is accessible to all procedures in the form and remains in memory until the program ends.

A *global variable* is declared in a code module's Declarations section. Global variables are primarily used in programs that involve multiple forms in which data must be exchanged between the forms. You will not work with global variables in this textbook.

As a general rule, you should declare variables as locally as possible. For example, if a variable is needed only inside a particular event procedure, the variable should be declared locally. The more global a variable is, the more likely it is that programming errors will occur. When a variable is declared locally, it is easier to trace all of the code that might affect the variable. A global or form-level variable could be affected by code in many procedures. Therefore, if the variable is not needed outside of the local event procedure, declare the variable locally. If a variable is needed throughout a form, declare it at the form level. Use global variables only if the variable is required throughout all of the forms of a program.

The Declarations Section

You just learned that you can make a variable accessible to an entire form by declaring the variable in the Declarations section of a form's Code window. To access the Declarations section, select (Declarations) from the Method Name list that appears at the top of the Code window, as shown in Figure 5-5.

FIGURE 5-5

Access the Declarations section of the Code window by selecting (Declarations) from the Method Name list

In Lesson 7, we are going to extend the month converter project to calculate the user's age in dog years, cow years, and mouse years. In order to calculate the dog years, cow years, and mouse years, we need the intMonths variable to be a form-level variable. As a form-level variable, we will be able to access intMonths from other event procedures on the form.

In the following Step-by-Step exercise, you will move the `intMonths` variable declaration to the Declarations section to give it a form-level scope.

STEP-BY-STEP 5.4

1. Double-click the **Calculate age in months** button. The Code window opens.

2. Select **(Declarations)** from the Method Name list at the top of the Code window (currently showing *Click*). The Code window should appear similar to Figure 5-6.

FIGURE 5-6
The Declarations section is where you declare variables that need to be accessible to the whole form

Declarations section

3. Following the statement *Public Class frmMonths*, key **Dim intMonths As Integer** and press **Enter**.

4. Delete the `intMonths` declaration statement and the blank line below it from the Click event procedure.

5. Close the Code window.

6. Start debugging the program and test it with values (such as those shown in Figure 5-4) to verify that the program still works.

7. Click **Close** on the Month Converter program. Close the project and Visual Studio 2005.

Using the Object Data Type

The Object Type

The *Object data type* is very flexible. It can store many different types of data. It can store a number or text. An Object is similar to a cell in a spreadsheet that is set to a general format. When entering data in a spreadsheet, you do not have to declare a data type for each cell. If you key text in a spreadsheet cell, it will hold text. If you key an integer, it will hold an integer. If you key a dollar amount, it will hold that, too. Object variables can be declared by specifying the Object type or by declaring a variable and not assigning a type. Both of the lines that follow declare variables of Object type.

```
Dim objSampleData as Object
Dim objSpecialInfo
```

The Object type is not very efficient and should not be used unless you really need that flexibility. Whenever possible, you should select a specific data type for your variables.

SUMMARY

In this lesson, you learned:

- Data can be in the form of numbers, text, dates, pictures, and even sound.

- Visual Basic supports a set of data types. There are data types for whole numbers, floating-point numbers (decimals), text, dates, and more.

- You can choose to store data in memory locations called variables.

- The AutoSize property will adjust the size of a control to fit its contents.

- The first step to using a variable is to declare it using the Dim statement.

- When naming variables, keep the naming rules in mind. It is also a good idea to use naming prefixes to identify the data type of the variable.

- You can assign values to variables using the assignment operator. You can also use the other mathematical operators with numeric variables.

- A variable's scope indicates the procedures that have access to the variable. A variable's scope can be local, form-level, or global.

- The Declarations section of a form's Code window allows you to declare form-level variables.

- The Object data type can hold many different kinds of data, but is less efficient than specific data types.

VOCABULARY *Review*

Define the following terms:

AutoSize property	Global variable	Scope
Declaring	Local variable	Variable
Form-level variable	Object data type	

REVIEW *Questions*

TRUE / FALSE

Circle T if the statement is true or F if the statement is false.

T   F   **1.** The AutoSize property will adjust the value of a number so that it will be in the range of a Visual Basic data type.

T   F   **2.** All data in a computer is stored numerically.

T   F   **3.** A variable name can begin with any alphanumeric character.

T   F   **4.** In order to do calculations with variables, you must first convert them to hard-coded values.

T   F   **5.** The position in which you declare a variable affects the usage of the variable.

T   F   **6.** Variable scope refers to the range of the values a data type can hold.

T   F   **7.** You can assign the value of a numeric variable to a label or text box without using the `Val` function.

T   F   **8.** When naming variables, you should use prefixes that identify the type of the variable.

T   F   **9.** By declaring a variable in the Declarations section of a form's Code window, you can make the variable accessible to an entire program.

T   F   **10.** Using the Object data type is much more efficient than using any of the other Visual Basic data types.

WRITTEN QUESTIONS

Write a brief answer to each of the following questions.

1. Name four common integer data types.

2. What are the three common decimal data types?

3. What is the `Dim` statement used for?

4. How would you write Visual Basic code to declare an Integer variable called intNumber?

5. What are three of the commonly used prefixes for naming variables?

6. Which operator assigns a value to a variable named Speed?

7. What are the three levels of variable scope? Give a brief description of each.

8. What type of data can be stored in an Object variable?

9. What data type is given by default to variables whose type is not specified?

10. What data type should be used for monetary amounts?

PROJECTS

PROJECT 5-1

1. Start Visual Basic and create a new project.

2. Create the form shown in Figure 5-7.

FIGURE 5-7
Example of form for Project 5-1

3. Code the Calculate button to perform the following:
   a. Declare five variables of type Double to store miles per hour, kilometers per hour, feet per second, meters per second, and knots.
   b. Copy the text from the text box in the variable you created to store miles per hour.
   c. Calculate kilometers per hour, feet per second, meters per second, and knots and store the results in the appropriate variables. Use the conversion formulas below.
      1 mile per hour = 1.609344 kilometers per hour
      1 mile per hour = 1.4666667 feet per second

1 mile per hour = 0.44704 meters per second
1 mile per hour = 0.8689762 knots

d. Set the Text properties of the invisible labels to the corresponding variable.

4. Code the Exit button to end the program.

5. Start debugging the program and verify that it works.

PROJECT 5-2

A railroad company has asked you to write a program to calculate the number of cars on a train and the total weight of the train when the cars are empty. The user interface of the program has already been created and saved as **Train Template**. The owner has given you the data in Table 5-3 to use in each calculation.

TABLE 5-3
Data for Project 5-2

TYPE OF CAR	WEIGHT OF CAR
Box Car	65000
Caboose	48000
Refrigerated Car	59400
Tank Car	45200
Hopper Car	51300

1. Start Visual Studio 2005 and open **Train Template** from the data files for this lesson.

2. Create two variables in the Declarations section that store the number of cars and the total weight of the train:
   a. Double-click any of the car command buttons and select (**Declarations**) from the Method Name list box at the right. Then, under the line that reads Inherits System.Windows.Forms.Form, add the code indicated in steps 2b and 2c.
   b. Key **Dim intTotalWeight As Long** and press **Enter**. (This variable will increment the text for the lblWeight label each time you click a car command button when you run the program.)
   c. Key **Dim intCounter As Integer** and press **Enter**. (This variable will increment the text for the lblNumber label each time you click a car command button when you run the program.)
   d. Close the Code window.

3. Add code (and comments) to each command button that adds the weight of the car named on the command button to the total weight of the train. Also add code to each button that adds 1 to the number of cars on the train. Display the results on the screen:
   a. Double-click the **Box Car** button.
   b. Key '**Add weight of car to total weight of train** and press **Enter**.
   c. Key **intTotalWeight = intTotalWeight + 65000**, then press **Enter** twice.
   d. Key '**Count total number of cars** and press **Enter**.
   e. Key **intCounter = intCounter + 1** and press **Enter** twice.
   f. Key '**Display results** and press **Enter**.

g. Key **lblNumber.Text = intCounter** and press **Enter**.

h. Key **lblWeight.Text = intTotalWeight** and press **Enter**.

i. Close the Code window, then repeat steps a-h for each of the car's command buttons, using the appropriate weight from the chart. (*Hint:* You can copy the code from one car's event procedure to another, and then change the weight.)

4. Add code to the Exit button to end the program.

5. Start debugging the program and test it by clicking car command buttons at random. Each time you click a command button, the number of cars should increment by 1, and the total weight should increase by the weight of the car whose command button you clicked.

6. End the program, but leave the project open if you will be completing the Critical Thinking Activity.

PROJECT 5-3

You have a lot of change in your pockets, and you want to know how much money you have in dollars and cents. Write a computer program that accepts the number of pennies, nickels, dimes, and quarters in your pocket and calculates the total value in dollars and cents.

1. Start Visual Studio 2005, if necessary, and create a new project named **ChangeValue**.

2. Add text boxes for the user to enter amounts for pennies, nickles, dimes, and quarters. Give all text boxes names that are easy to use and remember, such as **txtPennies**, **txtNickels**, **txtDimes**, and **txtQuarters**.

3. Add labels to identify each text box.

4. Add a command button to calculate the value of the money entered and a label box to display the result. Be sure to give the label box an easy-to-remember name.

5. Write code for the command button that calculates the value of the change in the text boxes. There are several ways that this can be done. The integer values in the text boxes can be used to calculate the number of pennies and then divide the number of pennies by 100 to convert to dollars using code like the sample below.

```
Dim Total As Decimal
Total = Val(txtPennies.Text)
Total = Total + Val(txtNickels.Text) * 5
Total = Total + Val(txtDimes.Text) * 10
Total = Total + Val(txtQuarters.Text) * 25
Total = Total / 100
lblTotal.Text = Total
```

6. Start debugging the program and test it by entering amounts into each of the text boxes, then clicking the command button and checking the reuslts. Your results may look something like Figure 5-8.

FIGURE 5-8
Example of form for Project 5-3

7. End the program, but leave Visual Studio 2005 open for the Critical Thinking activity.

CRITICAL*Thinking*

The railroad company has asked you to modify the program you created in Project 5-2. The railroad would like the program to calculate the total length of the train as well as the total weight. Use the values in Table 5-4 for the length of each car. Under the total weight label on the form, add a label for the total length, and then add code for the length of each car. (*Hint*: Do not forget to add a line of code in the Declarations section.)

TABLE 5-4
Data for Activity 5-1

TYPE OF CAR	LENGTH OF CAR IN FEET
Box Car	55
Caboose	36
Refrigerated Car	39
Tank Car	35
Hopper Car	46

EXPONENTIATION, ORDER OF OPERATIONS, AND ERROR HANDLING

Exponentiation

In Lesson 4, you learned about the basic mathematical operators. There is one more operator in the set of math operators: exponentiation. *Exponentiation* is the process of raising a number to a power.

The symbol that represents exponentiation is the caret (^). Exponentiation raises the number to the left of the caret to the power that appears to the right of the caret. For example, to raise 2 to the 16th power, the Visual Basic code would appear as follows:

```
2^16
```

Order of Operations

From your math classes, you may recall the rules that govern the order in which operations are performed. These rules are called the *order of operations*. Visual Basic uses the same set of rules for its calculations.

Ask yourself, what is the result of the calculation that follows?

x = 1 + 2 * 3

If your answer was 9, you did not follow the order of operations rules. The order of operations states that multiplication is performed before addition, so the calculation is performed as shown in Figure 6-1, resulting in the correct answer, which is 7.

FIGURE 6-1
The order of operations requires multiplication to be performed before addition

$$X = 1 + 2 * 3$$
$$X = 1 + 6$$
$$X = 7$$

The basic order of operations is as follows:

1. Exponentiation

2. Unary plus and minus

3. Multiplication, division, integer division, Modulus

4. Addition and subtraction

Operations are performed from left to right. For example, if a formula includes three addition operators and two multiplication operators, the multiplication operators are applied from left to right, then the addition operators are applied from left to right.

Visual Basic allows you to use parentheses to override the order of operations. If you intend for 1 + 2 * 3 to result in 9, then you can use parentheses to force the addition to be performed first, as shown in Figure 6-2.

Note

Operations within parentheses are performed first. But within the parentheses, the order of operations still applies. You can, however, place parentheses inside of parentheses.

FIGURE 6-2
Parentheses can be used to override the order of operations

$$X = (1 + 2) * 3$$
$$X = 3 * 3$$
$$X = 9$$

STEP-BY-STEP 6.1

In this exercise, you will work on the Interest project. This project will calculate the amount of money you will have in a savings account in the future, if a specified amount of money is put into a savings account today.

1. Start Visual Studio 2005.

2. Open the **Interest** project from the **step06-01** folder in the data files for this lesson.

3. If necessary, double-click the form icon for **frmInterest** on the Solutions Explorer window. Your screen should appear similar to Figure 6-3.

FIGURE 6-3
The Interest Calculation form appears on your screen

4. Double-click the **Calculate** button to open the Code window.

5. Add the following code to calculate the total in the account at the end of the savings period, and to output the number of years entered by the user.

Note ✅

A Short is an integer type that has a maximum value of 32767 and a minimum value of –32768. There will be more information about Shorts in the next lesson.

STEP-BY-STEP 6.1 Continued

```
'Calculate future value
Dim myYears As Short
myYears = Val(txtYears.Text)

'Extract values from the txtDeposit and txtInterest boxes and calculate
'the total interest
lblTotal.Text = Fix(Val(txtDeposit.Text) * _
    (1 + (Val(txtInterest.Text) / 100)) ^ myYears)

'Repeat the number of years saved in the output
lblYearsSaved.Text = myYears
```

Your screen should appear similar to Figure 6-4.

FIGURE 6-4
The formula that calculates the future value of the saved money uses exponentiation

6. Close the Code window. Start debugging the program.

7. Enter the following data into the form.

Amount Deposited	**1500**
Interest Rate in %	**8**
Number of Years Saved	**15**

Hot Tip

When calculating the future value, the Val function is used to extract the numeric values from the text boxes. The multiplication, addition, division, and exponentiation operators are used to perform the required calculation. The Fix function truncates the result to round it down to the nearest whole number. The truncated result is assigned to the Text property of the label named lblTotal.

STEP-BY-STEP 6.1 Continued

8. Click **Calculate**. The data is calculated and displayed on the form as shown in Figure 6-5.

FIGURE 6-5
The Calculate button calculates the data and displays it on the form

9. Click **Exit**. The program closes.

10. Save the changes to the project and leave it open for the next Step-by-Step.

Using the Visible Property to Enhance Output

You have used the Visible property to make an image appear and disappear. There are many more uses for the Visible property. Another useful application of the Visible property is preventing labels from appearing until you are ready for the user to see the label.

For example, in the Interest project, the user enters an amount of money deposited, the interest rate, and the number of years the money will be in the account. The program may have a cleaner appearance if the line that displays the output is not visible until the output has been calculated.

By initially setting the Visible property of the output labels to False, the output will remain invisible until you make the labels visible in the code.

STEP-BY-STEP 6.2

1. Click the lower-left label with the Text value *Amount in savings after*.

2. Change the Visible property to **False**.

3. Click the lower-right label with the Text value *years is $*.

4. Change the Visible property to **False**.

STEP-BY-STEP 6.2 Continued

5. Start debugging the program to see that the labels do not appear, as shown in Figure 6-6.

FIGURE 6-6
The Visible property is used to hide the output labels

6. Click **Exit**.

7. Save the changes to the project and leave it open for the next Step-by-Step.

The code to make the labels visible can be placed in the Calculate button's Click event procedure.

STEP-BY-STEP 6.3

1. Double-click the **Calculate** button. The Code window appears.

2. Add the following code at the bottom of the procedure to set the Visible property of the two hidden labels to **True** when the Calculate button is clicked.

```
'Make output visible
lblLabel1.Visible = True
lblLabel2.Visible = True
```

3. Close the Code window and start debugging the program.

4. Enter the following values in the input fields.

Amount Deposited	**2500**
Interest Rate in %	**7.5**
Number of Years Saved	**10**

STEP-BY-STEP 6.3 Continued

5. Click **Calculate**. The output labels appear, as shown in Figure 6-7.

FIGURE 6-7
The Calculate button sets the bottom two labels' Visible properties
to True

6. Click **Exit**.

7. Save the changes to the project and leave it open for the next Step-by-Step.

Using Comments

In the previous lessons, and in the Interest project you have been working on, you used the apostrophe to create *comments* in your code. Whenever you want to add a note or comment to a program, you can key an apostrophe, followed by any text you want to add to the line. The compiler will ignore everything from the apostrophe to the end of that line.

Comments can appear on their own lines, like the comments you entered in the previous Step-by-Steps. Comments can also be added to the end of a line of code. For example, the code that follows has a comment attached to the end of the statement.

```
lblAnswer.Visible = False 'Hide lblAnswer
```

When writing a program, you may think that you will always remember what you did and why. Most programmers, however, eventually forget. But more importantly, others may need to make changes in a program you wrote. They probably will be unaware of what you did when you wrote the program. That is why comments are important.

> **Important**
>
> Remember, the compiler will ignore everything on the line that follows the apostrophe. Therefore, you can add a comment to the right of a code statement, but code added to the right of a comment will not execute.

You can use comments to:

- explain the purpose of a program

- keep notes regarding changes to the source code

- store the names of programmers for future reference

- explain the parts of your program

- temporarily remove lines from the program during testing

Comments added to programs are often called *internal documentation*.

Handling Run-Time Errors

The programs you have written up to this point have assumed that the user will always enter valid data and that nothing will go wrong with the calculations. In the real world, however, users will enter all kinds of unexpected data, or fail to enter required data. These error conditions are sometimes called *exceptions*. The term exception comes from the idea that normally things will go smoothly, with the exception of certain instances.

Exceptions are also called *run-time errors*. A run-time error is any error that occurs when the program is running. Run-time errors are not detectable at the time the program is compiled because the error is caused by conditions that do not exist until the program is running. A common run-time error is division by zero. Division by zero is not a legal mathematical operation. So if conditions are such that division by zero occurs while a program is running, a run-time error or exception occurs.

Another common exception is an overflow error. An overflow occurs when an attempt is made to put a number that is too large into a variable. Two examples are trying to copy a number higher than 32,767 into a Short or larger than 255 into a Byte.

Hot Tip

Comments can help you debug programs (find and correct errors). If you are unsure whether a line of code should be removed from a program, add an apostrophe to the left of the code, rather than deleting the code. The line will be ignored the next time you run the program. If you change your mind about removing the line of code, just remove the apostrophe. This is called "commenting out" a line because you are taking the line out of the lines that are to be executed by making it a comment.

Note

The behavior of division by zero in Visual Basic is a little different from that in some environments. When using integer division, a division by zero will throw an exception, as you would expect. In floating-point division, however, an exception does not occur when division by zero takes place. The result may be positive infinity, negative infinity, or NaN, which means "not a number."

When a run-time error occurs, the system throws an exception. This means that a signal is sent to the program that needs to be handled or caught. If the program does not catch the exception, the system will stop the program's execution.

Let's take a look at an example of what happens when an error occurs in a Visual Basic program. The Interest project should still be open on your screen.

S TEP-BY-STEP 6.4

1. Start debugging the **Interest** program.

2. Enter **999999** for Amount Deposited and for the Number of Years Saved and enter **99** for Interest Rate.

3. Click **Calculate**. The program is stopped, and you are returned to the IDE. Your screen should appear similar to Figure 6-8. The highlighted line is where the error occurred. The variable myYears cannot hold a number greater than 32,767, so an overflow error has been thrown. A message box tells you what error has occurred, provides some suggestions for where to look, and points to the highlighted line.

FIGURE 6-8
The program is stopped and information about the error is displayed

4. From the **Debug** menu select the **Stop Debugging** option. The program ends.

5. Save the changes to the project and leave the project open for the next Step-by-Step.

Trapping Run-Time Errors with the Try/Catch Structure

When an error or exception does occur, you would rather your program handle the situation gracefully, rather than halt with some standard error message.

Visual Basic allows you to write code that will be executed when a run-time error occurs. To specify the code that will execute when an error occurs, you must turn on error trapping. *Error trapping* is the process of interrupting the normal chain of events that occurs when an error is encountered and replacing that chain of events with your own code.

To turn on error trapping, place a `Try` statement above the code that may generate a run-time error. The `Try` statement identifies a statement or a group of statements that may generate an error at run-time. Enter the `Catch` statement after the code that could generate an exception. The `Catch` statement indicates the start of code that will execute if any of the lines in the `Try` section generates an exception. The `End Try` statement ends the code that is part of the `Catch` statement. The general format of the `Try/Catch` structure is a `Try` statement that starts the block of code to be tried, a `Catch` statement that starts the block of code that runs if a problem develops, and an `End Try` statement that ends the code block for the `Catch`. The code looks something like the following.

```
Try
'   Some code that may have an error
Catch
'   Some code that executes if there is a problem
End Try
```

The code that will be executed if an error occurs is often called an ***error handler*** or ***error-handling routine***. If the code between the Try and Catch statements does not generate a run-time error, then the error-handling routine will not be executed.

STEP-BY-STEP 6.5

1. Double-click the **Calculate** button to open the Code window.

2. Add the `Try` statement above the code that saves the year value in myYears.

3. Add the following code after the line that saves the year value in myYears.

```
Catch
'   Set myYears to the largest possible value
myYears = 32767
End Try
```

Your screen should appear similar to Figure 6-9.

> **Note**
>
> The Error Handler changes the value of myYears to 32767. This avoids having the overflow error stop your program, but may affect other parts of a program. Care must be taken to use the right solution to potential errors.

STEP-BY-STEP 6.2 Continued

FIGURE 6-9

The `Try/Catch` structure causes the execution to take additional steps to handle exceptional conditions

Try statement

Catch statement

End Try statement

4. Close the Code window and start debugging the program.

5. Enter **99** for Interest Rate and **999999** for the other two values.

6. Click **Calculate**. Notice that this time the progam is not stopped, and you do not return to the IDE. When the program trys to copy a value that will not fit into the variable, the program executes the code in the Catch procedure. The code in the catch prodecure assigns a value that will work with the rest of the code in the subroutine.

7. Click **Exit**.

8. Save the changes to the project and leave it open for the next Step-by-Step.

Using MsgBox

One of the easiest ways to display a message of your own, such as an error message, is to use the `MsgBox` function. The `MsgBox` function causes a dialog box to pop up, displaying a message that you specify. This function is easy to use and gives your programs a more professional look and feel.

The `MsgBox` function provides a convenient way to display an error message when you trap an error with the `Try/Catch` structure. You can add the code for the `MsgBox` function after the `Catch` statement to cause a dialog box to appear, explaining the error to the user.

An example of the `MsgBox` function appears below. In the parentheses that follow the `MsgBox` keyword, you can place a custom message that you want to appear in the dialog box. The message must appear in quotation marks.

```
MsgBox("Illegal entry. Please try again.")
```

STEP-BY-STEP 6.6

1. Double-click the **Calculate** button to open the Code window.

2. Add the following code just below the `Catch` statement to display a message box when an error occurs.

```
MsgBox ("The number of years must be less than 32,767. Try again.")
```

3. Close the Code window and start debugging the program.

4. Enter **99** for Interest Rate and **999999** for the other two values.

5. Click **Calculate**. A message box appears explaining that incorrect values were entered, as shown in Figure 6-10.

FIGURE 6-10
A message box appears when an error occurs

6. Click **OK** to close the message box.

7. Click **Exit**.

8. Save the changes to the project and leave it open for the next Step-by-Step.

Using Exit Sub to Exit a Subroutine

In our Interest program, the Try/Catch structure traps the error so that the program does not crash and, instead, gives an error message. The program also gives a result that may or may not be what the user is seeking. This is because the program is still using numbers higher than it is designed to handle. When saving money for 32,767 years, the program is showing infinity as the total amount saved.

You can use the `Exit Sub` statement to prevent this from occurring. The `Exit Sub` statement forces the event procedure to end, regardless of whether there is more code in the procedure. By placing the `Exit Sub` statement inside the error handler and after the message box is displayed, no calculations will take place. The procedure will end when the flow of execution reaches the `Exit Sub` statement. The `Exit Sub` statement can be used in more than one place in the subroutine. This allows the programmer to exit the subroutine for different reasons.

Figure 6-11 shows the revised event procedure code, with error handling and the `Exit Sub` statements in place.

FIGURE 6-11
The `Exit Sub` statement ensures proper program flow

```
Private Sub cmdCalculate_Click(ByVal sender As System.Object, _
    ByVal e As System.EventArgs) Handles cmdCalculate.Click
    'Calculate future value
    Dim myYears As Short
    Try
        myYears = Val(txtYears.Text)
    Catch
        MsgBox("The number of years must be less than 32,767. Try again.")
        Exit Sub
    End Try

    'Extract values from the txtDeposit and txtInterest boxes and calculate
    'the total interest
    lblTotal.Text = Fix(Val(txtDeposit.Text) * _
        (1 + (Val(txtInterest.Text) / 100)) ^ myYears)

    'Repeat the number of years saved in the output
    lblYearsSaved.Text = myYears

    'Make output visible
    lblLabel1.Visible = True
    lblLabel2.Visible = True
End Sub
```

Exit Sub statement → (points to `Exit Sub`)

S TEP-BY-STEP 6.7

1. Double-click the **Calculate** button to open the Code window.

2. Modify the code in the `cmdCalculate_Click` event procedure to match the code shown in Figure 6-11. (Note that the line that sets myYears to 32767 has been deleted.) After the message box is closed, the subroutine will exit, and no calculation will be performed.

3. Close the Code window.

4. Start debugging the program, enter **99** for the Interest Rate and **999999** for the other two values, and click **Calculate** to generate the error.

5. Click **OK** to close the dialog box. Notice that the answer label boxes are not made visible.

6. Enter **2500**, **7.5**, and **10** in the input fields and calculate again. When no error occurs, the message box is not displayed, and the answer labels are made visible.

7. End the program.

8. Save the changes to the project and exit Visual Studio 2005.

SUMMARY

In this lesson, you learned:

- The exponential operator (^) raises a number to a power.

- Order of operations are the rules that dictate the order in which math operators are applied in a formula.

- Parentheses can be used to override the order of operations.

- The Visible property can be used to hide a label until you are ready for the user to see it.

- The apostrophe is used to add comments to Visual Basic code. Comments allow you to keep track of changes in code and to explain the purpose of code. Comments are often called internal documentation.

- Errors that occur while a program is running are called run-time errors or exceptions. Visual Basic allows you to trap errors, using `Try/Catch`, and execute special code that you specify to handle the error.

- The `MsgBox` function pops up a dialog box, delivering a message to the user.

- When you detect errors that cannot be handled completely, you should send the user a message and use an `Exit Sub` statement to end the event procedure before the error can cause additional problems.

VOCABULARY *Review*

Define the following terms:

Comment	Exceptions	Order of operations
Error handler	Exponentiation	Run-time error
Error trapping	Internal documentation	

REVIEW *Questions*

TRUE / FALSE

Circle T if the statement is true or F if the statement is false.

T   F   **1.** Exponentiation is the process of raising a number to a power.

T   F   **2.** Addition and subtraction are evaluated before multiplication and division.

T   F   **3.** Exponentiation will be evaluated first since it appears first in the order of operations.

T   F   **4.** Parentheses in expressions can appear within another set of parentheses.

T   F   **5.** You cannot override the order of operations in Visual Basic.

T   F   **6.** The Visible property can be used on labels as well as images.

T   F   **7.** Visual Basic code will be executed if it appears to the right of comment statements.

T   F   **8.** A program will not compile if it contains a run-time error.

T   F   **9.** The `Exit Sub` statement can appear more than once in a subroutine.

T   F   **10.** You can use the `MsgBox` function to display custom error messages.

WRITTEN QUESTIONS

Write a brief answer to each of the following questions.

1. Which symbol is used for the exponentiation operator?

2. Why is it important that programmers be aware of the order of operations?

3. Why might parentheses be used in an expression?

4. What symbol indicates a comment?

5. What is internal documentation?

6. What statement structure is used to trap exceptions?

7. Why would an object be made invisible?

8. What is an error-handling routine?

9. What happens when an Exit Sub statement is executed?

10. What is another name for run-time errors?

PROJECTS

PROJECT 6-1

Calculate the following expressions.

Expression	Result
1. 2 * 3 + 1	
2. 1 + 2 * 3	
3. 4 / 2 + 6 * 2	
4. 4 / (2 + 6) * 2	
5. 4 * 4 + 2 − 1	
6. 7 + 2 * 3 − 2	

7. $1 + 2 * 3 - 9 / 3$ _____

8. $12 / 3 + 1 + 12 * 2 - 5$ _____

9. $(5 + 7) / 3 + 7 * 2 - 5$ _____

10. $5 + 8 / 2 - 16 / 2 + 3 * 6$ _____

PROJECT 6-2

Write a program that prompts the users for two values, as shown in Figure 6-12. The program should use the exponential operator to calculate the result of raising the first number to the second.

FIGURE 6-12
A form for users to enter two values to raise one number to a power

1. Start Visual Studio 2005 and open a new project. Save the project as **Exponent.**

2. Use the TextBox tool to insert two text boxes with one slightly above and to the right of the other one, as shown in Figure 6-12. The lower text box should be named **txtBase**, and the upper text box should be named **txtExponent**. Change the Text property for both text boxes to **0.**

3. Use the Label tool to add the label for the equal sign. It should be named **lblEqual**, and the caption should be the = sign. Change the Font Size property to **14 point.**

4. Use the Label tool to add a blank label to the right of the equal sign. It should be named **lblResult,** and the caption should be deleted. The font should also be **14** point.

5. Add a **Calculate** button.

6. Give your form an appropriate title for the Title bar.

7. Add code to the **Calculate** button so that the Text value of the label named lblResult will contain the answer of the number entered for txtBase raised to the number entered for txtExponent.

8. Close the Code window, start debugging the program, enter a value for the base (the lower text box) and a value for the exponent (the upper text box), and click **Calculate.**

9. End the program.

10. Save your program and close the project. Leave Visual Studio 2005 open for the next Project.

PROJECT 6-3

1. Open the **Division** project you worked with in the Lesson 4 Step-by-Steps. (If you do not have this completed project, ask your instructor for the required solution files from that lesson.)

2. Add code to the **Calculate** button for `Try/Catch` error handling to handle divide by zero or other errors in division. Be sure to include comments for your code.

3. Add code for a message of your choice.

4. Start debugging the program with no values, and then click **OK** to dismiss the error message.

5. Test the program again with valid entries.

6. Test the program again, attempting to divide by zero.

7. End the program.

8. Save your program and close the project. Leave Visual Studio 2005 open for the next Project.

PROJECT 6-4

1. Open the **Buses** project created in the Critical Thinking Activity in Lesson 4. (If you do not have this completed project, ask your instructor for the required solution files from that lesson.)

2. Change the Visible property of the four labels used to display results (number of buses and campers for vans) to **False** so that they won't display when you first run the program.

3. Modify the code for the **Calculate** button so that the four labels whose Visible property you changed to False will be displayed when you run the program with valid entries to calculate. Use `Try/Catch` so that the labels are only made visible if no errors occur during calculation. Display a message box if an error occurs.

4. Run the program to verify that it works. (The four display labels should be invisible until you enter numbers in the top two text boxes and click **Calculate**.)

5. Save the changes to the project.

6. Exit Visual Studio 2005.

CRITICAL *Thinking*

The National Weather Service at your local airport measures rainfall by taking readings from three rain gauges at different locations on the airport property. These three readings are averaged to determine the official rainfall total. Write a program that will accept the rainfall amounts from three rain gauges and output an average of the three readings. Save the project as **RainAverage**.

STRINGS AND DECIMAL TYPES

OBJECTIVES

Upon completion of this lesson, you should be able to:

- Declare string variables.
- Assign text to string variables.
- Concatenate strings.
- Use decimal data types.
- Use the Format function.
- Use the Enable property.
- Use the `SelectionStart` and `SelectionLength` properties.

Estimated Time: 2 hours

VOCABULARY

Alphanumeric

Concatenation

Decimal data type

Double data type

Enabled property

`SelectionLength` property

`SelectionStart` property

Single data type

String

String literal

Declaring String Variables

Text is often called *alphanumeric* data because it can include letters or numbers. Text can also include other characters, such as periods, commas, or other symbols.

In previous lessons, you learned that Visual Basic has a special `String` data type for working with text. The term *string* is used because text is a series of characters that have been *strung* together. When you declare a string using a statement like the one below, the resulting variable can hold a string of any practical length. The length of the string can also change as the program runs. The memory space required for the string is allocated as needed.

```
Dim strFirstName As String
```

Did You Know?

Visual Basic does provide a way to create strings of fixed length. You will not use fixed-length strings in this book. However, information about fixed-length strings can be found in the Visual Basic online help.

Assigning Text to String Variables

When assigning text to a string variable, you must place the text in quotation marks, as shown in the code below.

```
strFirstName = "Kaley"
```

Hard-coded text, like the name *Kaley* in the example above, is called a ***string literal***. You can also assign the text from a text box to a string variable, as shown in the following example.

```
strFirstName = txtFirstName.Text
```

Often, you will assign the text from one string variable to another, as shown here.

```
strFirstName = strMyName
```

Actually, any expression that results in a string value can be assigned to a string variable. You will see other examples later.

Like a numeric variable, a string variable can hold only one string. Each time you assign a string to a string variable, the existing data in the variable is replaced.

S TEP-BY-STEP 7.1

1. Start Visual Studio 2005.

2. Open **StringCopy** from the **step07-01** folder in the data files for this lesson and, if necessary, open the **frmCopy** form. Your screen should appear similar to Figure 7-1.

FIGURE 7-1
This program will provide you with some practice declaring and using strings

STEP-BY-STEP 7.1 Continued

3. Double-click the **Copy Text** button. The code window opens.

4. Select **(Declarations)** from the Method Name list box (currently showing *Click*), then add the following code under the `Public Class frmCopy` statement.

```
Dim strText As String
```

5. Select **cmdCopy** from the Class Name list box. If necessary, move the cursor just above the **End Sub** statement and press the **Tab** key.

6. Add the following code to copy the text in the first text box to a string variable, and then copy the variable to the second text box.

```
'Copy txtText1 to txtText2
strText = txtText1.Text
txtText2.Text = strText
```

7. Select **cmdReset** from the Class Name list box. Then select **Click** from the Method Name list box. A new section of code for the Reset Text Box 1 button appears in the code window, as shown in Figure 7-2.

FIGURE 7-2
The Method Name list box generates the beginning code for an existing control

8. Add the following code to clear the text in the first text box and reset the strText variable.

```
'Reset the string variable and txtText1
strText = " "
txtText1.Text = strText
```

9. Start Debugging the program.

10. Key **Visual Basic** in the first text box.

11. Click **Copy Text**. The words *Visual Basic* are copied to the second text box.

12. Click **Reset Text Box 1**. The first text is cleared.

13. Click **Copy Text** again. The contents of the `strText` variable (now blank) are copied to the second text box.

14. End the program and save the changes to the project.

15. Choose **Close Project** from the **File** menu. The project closes. Leave Visual Studio 2005 open for the next Step-by-Step.

Concatenation

In the previous section you learned that each time you assign text to a string, the text already in the string is replaced. There are times, however, when you would like to add text to the existing string. In other words, you would like to "string" on more characters. Visual Basic allows you to do just that, using an operation called *concatenation*.

Concatenation appends one string to the end of another. The ampersand (&) is used for concatenation. For example, the following code concatenates two string literals, resulting in a compound word, *bookkeeper*.

```
strCompoundWord = "book" & "keeper"
```

You can concatenate more than two strings in one expression. In addition, the strings can come from other variables or can be string literals. In the example below, the first, middle, and last names are concatenated. String literals (in this case, a pair of quotation marks with a blank space between them) are used to place a blank space between the names.

```
strFullName = strFirstName & " " & strMiddleName & " " & strLastName
```

The first, middle, and last names could just as easily come from text boxes.

```
strFullName = txtFirstName.Text & " " & txtMiddleName.Text & " " &
  txtLastName.Text
```

STEP-BY-STEP 7.2

1. Open **FullName** from the **step07-02** folder in the data files for this lesson and, if necessary, open the **frmName** form. Your screen should appear similar to Figure 7-3.

FIGURE 7-3
This program will use concatenation to create a string of your full name

2. Double-click the **OK** button.

3. Select **(Declarations)** from the Method Name list box (currently showing *Click*), then add the following code under the line that says Public Class frmName.

```
Dim strFirstName As String
Dim strMiddleName As String

Dim strLastName As String
Dim strFullName As String
```

4. Select **cmdOk** from the Class Name list box. If necessary, select **Click** from the Method Name list box to move the cursor to the **cmdOk_Click** subroutine.

5. Add the following code to cmdOk_Click to set the variables equal to their corresponding text box.

```
'Initialize Variables
strFirstName = txtFirstName.Text
strMiddleName = txtMiddleName.Text
strLastName = txtLastName.Text
```

6. Press **Enter** twice, then add the following code to concatenate the FirstName, MiddleName, and LastName variables into the FullName variable.

```
strFullName = strFirstName & " " & strMiddleName & " " & strLastName
```

7. Press **Enter** twice, then add the following code to display the string on the form.

```
lblFullName.Text = strFullName
lblFullName.Visible = True
```

STEP-BY-STEP 7.2 Continued

8. Start debugging the program.

9. Key your first, middle, and last names into the appropriate text boxes.

10. Click **OK**. Your name appears at the bottom of the form, as shown in Figure 7-4.

FIGURE 7-4
The concatenated string appears at the bottom of the form

11. End the program and save the changes to the project.

12. Choose **Close Project** from the **File** menu. The project closes. Leave Visual Studio 2005 open for the next Step-by-Step.

You can also use concatenation when creating the text for a label. In Step-by-Step 7.3, you will use concatenation to create a single label to provide the user with the necessary output. You will work with a program that is similar to the program you created earlier, which calculated the number of months you have lived. By the end of this lesson, this program will convert your age into dog years. First, however, the following exercise will use concatenation to output your age in months.

S TEP-BY-STEP 7.3

1. Open the **DogYears** program from the **step07-03** folder in the data files for this lesson.

2. If necessary, open the form **frmDogYears**. Your screen should appear similar to Figure 7-5.

FIGURE 7-5
This program will convert your age into dog years

3. Double-click the **Calculate age in months** button. The code window appears.

4. Add blank lines below the `intMonths` code (above the `EndSub` statement), and then add the following code to create a string that will display the results.

```
'Display Number of Months Old
lblOutputMonths.Text = "You are " & intMonths & " months old."
lblOutputMonths.Visible = True
```

5. Close the code window and start debugging the program.

6. Key **634** in the *Age in years:* text box.

STEP-BY-STEP 7.3 Continued

7. Click **Calculate age in months**. The answer is displayed above the button. Your screen should appear similar to Figure 7-6.

FIGURE 7-6
The label shows the concatenated string

8. End the program and save your changes. Leave the project open for the next Step-by-Step.

Using Decimal Types

The programs you have worked with up to this point have involved integer values. However, as you learned in Lesson 5, there are three data types for handling decimal data, also known as floating-point numbers.

The Single and Double data types are used for general decimal values. The *Single data type* is used for decimal values that have less than 38 digits. The *Double data type* is used for decimal values with more than 38 digits.

When you are working with dollars and cents, the *Decimal data type* is ideal. It is specially designed to be precise with calculations involving money.

> **Hot Tip**
>
> The Double data type uses more memory than the Single type. Therefore, you should use the Single data type, except in cases in which the extra capacity of the Double data type is needed.

STEP-BY-STEP 7.4

1. Double-click the **Calculate age in months** button.

2. Add the following code to the end of cmdMonths (just above End Sub) to make the instructions for the program visible after the *Calculate age in months* button is clicked. (The instructions are the line that reads *Click the Dog button to estimate your age in dog years.*)

```
'Display Instructions
lblInstructions.Visible = True
```

STEP-BY-STEP 7.4 Continued

3. Select the **cmdDog** object from the Class Name drop-down box. Select the **Click** event from the Method Name drop-down box. A new event procedure is created in the code window.

4. At the beginning of the `cmdDog` event procedure, key **Dim strYears as String**, press **Enter**, key **Dim sngYears As Single**, and press **Enter** to declare `strYears` and `sngYears` as String and Single variable data types.

5. Add the following code to calculate the number of dog years and set it equal to the variable `sngYears`. Remember that the `sng` (Single) variable allows for your answer to contain a value with up to 38 decimal places.

```
'Calculate Dog Years
sngYears = (7 * intMonths) / 12
```

6. Press **Enter**, and then add the following code so that the instructions will be hidden after the Dog button has been clicked when you start debugging the program.

```
'Hide Instructions
lblInstructions.Visible = False
```

7. Save the changes to your project and leave the code window open for the next Step-by-Step.

Using the Format Function

When you provide the result of a calculation as output, it is important for the data to appear in a format that is attractive and useful to the user. The Format function allows you to apply custom formatting to a number before displaying the value. The Format function can be used to format decimal values, phone numbers, and more.

You specify the format you want by using special symbols. For example, the following code formats the value 1234.56 to appear as $1,234.56.

```
strAmount = Format(1234.56, "$#,###.00")
```

Did You Know?

The Format function can also be used to apply formatting to strings, dates, and times. The Visual Basic online help has additional information about how to format these data types.

The Format function can take a little getting used to. The first step is to learn the most common symbols used to apply formatting to numbers. Table 7-1 shows the symbols you will use when formatting numeric values. All of these are used in the code above except the % sign.

TABLE 7-1
Formatting symbols

SYMBOL	DESCRIPTION
0	Causes a digit to appear in the space. If the data has no value for that digit, a zero appears.
#	Similar to the 0 symbol. The difference is that nothing appears in the space if the number being formatted does not require that digit to be used.
.	Used to specify where you want the decimal point to appear in the format.
,	By placing commas in the format in the usual places, commas will appear in the output.
%	Causes a number to be multiplied by 100 and a percent sign to be placed at the end of the number.

You can use the symbols in Table 7-1 to create formats for your values. Table 7-2 illustrates the results of applying different formats to the same number.

TABLE 7-2
Sample formats

CODE	RESULT
Format(12345.67, "000000.000")	012345.670
Format(12345.67, "######.000")	12345.670
Format(12345.67, "######.###")	12345.67
Format(12345.67, "###,###.##")	12,345.67
Format(12345.67, "$###,###.##")	$12,345.67
Format(0.89, "##%")	89%

S TEP-BY-STEP 7.5

1. Add the following code to the end of the cmdDog Click event procedure to display the results and format the lblOutputAnimalYears label to display up to three digits followed by one required decimal place.

```
'Display Results
strYears = Format(sngYears, "###.0")
lblOutputAnimalYears.Text = "In dog years, you are " & _
    strYears & " years old."
lblOutputAnimalYears.Visible = True
```

STEP-BY-STEP 7.5 Continued

2. Start debugging the program.

3. Enter **15** in the *Age in years* text box and enter **4** in the *Months since last birthday:* text box.

4. Click **Calculate age in months**. Your age in months appears, and the instructions for the Dog button appear.

5. Click **Dog**. The Visible property of lblOutputAnimalYears is set to True, the instructions disappear, and the results are displayed, as shown in Figure 7-7.

FIGURE 7-7
The Dog button displays the results on the form

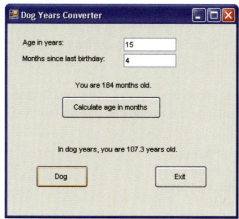

6. End the program.

7. Save the changes to your project and leave the project open for the next Step-by-Step.

Using the Enabled Property

You have used the Visible property to make command buttons and other controls appear and disappear from a form. The *Enabled property* performs a similar function. Using the Enabled property, you can make a control, such as a command button, take on a grayed appearance, making it inactive but still visible. Objects that are inactive can be seen by the user, but will not respond to user actions.

By default, objects are enabled. To disable an object, set the Enabled property to False using a statement like the one that follows.

```
cmdCalculate.Enabled = False
```

S TEP-BY-STEP 7.6

1. Open the **frmDogYears** form, if necessary. Click the **Dog** button and change its **Enabled** property to **False**.

2. Double-click the **txtYears** text box. The code window appears, showing an event procedure for the `TextChanged` event.

3. Add the following code to disable the Dog button when the data in the text box is changed, hide the existing results on the form, and enable the *Calculate age in months* button.

```
'Enable Human Months Button
cmdMonths.Enabled = True
'Disable Dog Command Button
cmdDog.Enabled = False
lblOutputAnimalYears.Visible = False
```

4. Select **txtMonths** from the Class Name list box at the top of the code window. Select **TextChanged** from the Method Name list box.

5. Add the following code just above the `End Sub` statement to disable the Dog button when the data in the text box is changed, hide the existing results on the form, and enable the *Calculate age in months* button.

```
'Enable Human Months Button
cmdMonths.Enabled = True
'Disable Dog Command Button
cmdDog.Enabled = False
lblOutputAnimalYears.Visible = False
```

6. Select **cmdMonths** from the Class Name list box. Select **Click** from the Method Name list box, if necessary.

7. Add the following code to enable the Dog button when the human months are calculated.

```
'Enable Dog Command Button
cmdDog.Enabled = True
```

8. Close the code window and start debugging the program. Notice that the Dog button is disabled when the program starts.

9. Enter **21** in the *Age in years:* text box and enter **1** in the *Months since last birthday* text box.

10. Click **Calculate age in months**. The Dog button becomes enabled, and the instructions appear as well as the age in months.

11. Click **Dog**. The results for the number of dog years are displayed on the form.

> ### Hot Tip
>
> You can use the slider bar at the right of the code window to move directly up or down to any existing subroutine in the form.

STEP-BY-STEP 7.6 Continued

12. Change the *Age in years:* text box to **30**. The Dog button becomes disabled, and the previous results for the number of dog years disappear, as shown in Figure 7-8.

FIGURE 7-8
The Dog button becomes disabled when new data is entered

13. Click **Calculate age in months** to recalculate the number of human months. The Dog button becomes enabled.

14. Click **Dog**. The recalculated results for the number of dog years appear on the form.

15. End the program.

16. Save the changes and leave the project open for the next Step-by-Step.

Using the SelectionStart and SelectionLength Properties

In the dialog boxes of various programs you have used, you may have noticed that when you tab to a text box it sometimes gets focus; that is, the text in the box is automatically highlighted. The advantage of this feature is that replacing the value in the text box with new characters requires only that you begin keying. This only happens when the text in the box was entered at design time and not modified at run-time. It is often desirable to have this functionality every time you tab to a box and give it focus. You can add this functionality to your programs using the `SelectionStart` and `SelectionLength` properties.

The ***SelectionStart property*** specifies the location where the insertion point will be inserted when the text box gets the focus. The ***SelectionLength property*** specifies how many characters should be selected to the right of the cursor. So to select the text in the text box, `SelectionStart` is set to zero to place the cursor at the far left of the text box. Then `SelectionLength` is set to the length of the text in the text box.

Hot Tip

By using different `SelectionStart` and `SelectionLength` values, you can cause any individual or group of characters in the text box to be highlighted.

Because the length of the text in the text box will vary, we will use a new function. The *Len* function determines the length of the text in the text box. The following shows the code required to select the text in a text box named `txtFirstName`.

```
txtFirstName.SelectionStart = 0
txtFirstName.SelectionLength = Len(txtFirstName.Text)
```

The first line of the code above positions the cursor before the first character in the `txtFirstName` text box. The second line of code uses the Len function to determine the length of the text in the text box. The value returned by the Len function is the number of characters currently in the text box. Setting the `SelectionLength` property to the length of the text in the text box causes all of the characters in the text box to be highlighted, as if you selected them with the mouse.

S TEP-BY-STEP 7.7

1. Double-click the **txtYears** text box.

2. Select **Enter** from the Method Name list box. An event procedure for the `Enter` event is added to the code window.

3. Add the following code to highlight the text in the `txtYears` text box when it receives the focus.

```
'Select Text
txtYears.SelectionStart = 0
txtYears.SelectionLength = Len(txtYears.Text)
```

Your screen should appear similar to Figure 7-9.

FIGURE 7-9
The code will automatically select the text in the `txtYears` text box when the user tabs to the text box

STEP-BY-STEP 7.7 Continued

4. Select **txtMonths** from the Class Name list box and select **Enter** from the Method Name list box.

5. Add the following code to highlight the text in the `txtMonths` text box when it receives the focus.

```
'Select Text
txtMonths.SelectionStart = 0
txtMonths.SelectionLength = Len(txtMonths.Text)
```

6. Close the code window and start debugging the program.

7. Enter **49** in the *Age in years* text box and enter **7** in the *Months since last birthday:* text box.

8. Click **Calculate age in months**.

9. Click **Dog**. The results are displayed on the form.

10. Tab to the *Age in years:* text box. Notice that the number *49* becomes highlighted, as shown in Figure 7-10.

FIGURE 7-10
The contents in the Age in years text box become highlighted when you tab to the text box

11. Change the number to **24** and click **Calculate age in months**.

12. Click **Dog**. The results are again displayed on the form.

13. End the program. Save the changes to the project and exit Visual Studio 2005.

SUMMARY

In this lesson, you learned:

- Strings hold text or alphanumeric data.

- Visual Basic has a data type for strings.

- Text assigned to a string variable must be placed in quotation marks.

- You can use the assignment operator to assign text from a text box to a string variable or from a string variable to another string variable.

- Concatenation is the process of appending one string to the end of another.

- The ampersand (&) is the symbol used for concatenation.

- The Single, Double, and Decimal data types hold decimal data.

- The Decimal data type is specially designed for handling dollars and cents.

- The Format function uses a string of symbols to format decimal values, phone numbers, and more.

- The Enabled property is used to make a control inactive or active.

- The `SelectionStart` and `SelectionLength` properties and the Len function can be used together to highlight the text in a text box.

VOCABULARY *Review*

Define the following terms:

Alphanumeric	Enabled property	Single data type
Concatenation	`SelectionLength` property	String
Decimal data type	`SelectionStart` property	String literal
Double data type		

REVIEW *Questions*

TRUE / FALSE

Circle T if the statement is true or F if the statement is false.

T   F   **1.** Visual Basic contains a built-in data type for working with strings.

T   F   **2.** The length of a string cannot change as a program runs.

T   F   **3.** The assignment operator can be used to assign text to a string.

T   F   **4.** You cannot assign text from one string variable to another.

T F   **5.** Concatenation appends one string to the end of another.

T F   **6.** You can concatenate more than two strings in one expression.

T F   **7.** The Single data type uses less memory than the Double data type.

T F   **8.** The `Format` function cannot be used on strings.

T F   **9.** The `Enabled` property behaves the same as the `Visible` property.

T F **10.** The `SelectionLength` property alone can be used to select the text in a text box.

WRITTEN QUESTIONS

Write a brief answer to each of the following questions.

1. What term describes a series of characters that have been strung together?

2. What is the difference between a string variable and a string literal?

3. What characters must a string literal be enclosed in?

4. Which operator is used for concatenation?

5. What are the differences between the Single and Double data types?

6. Which floating-point data type allows you to do calculations with money?

7. What is the `Format` function used for?

8. What is the purpose of the # symbol when used with the `Format` function?

9. What property allows you to disable a control, making it inactive but still visible?

10. Which two properties allow you to select text in a text box?

PROJECTS

PROJECT 7-1

1. Start Visual Studio 2005 and open **Interest Calculation** from the **proj07-01** folder in the data files for this lesson. (The program is similar to the Interest program you worked with in Lessons 5 and 6.)

2. Add code for the three text boxes so that the text will be highlighted when the text box is selected.

3. Close the code window, and then double-click the **Calculate** button.

4. Create a String variable named **strOutput** and a Single variable named **sngTotal**.

5. Under the *Calculate future value* comment, delete *lblOutput.Text* and replace it with **sngTotal**.

6. Add the following code to store the output in the strOutput variable and display it on the form.

```
'Make output visible
strOutput = "Amount in savings after " & txtYears.Text & _
      " years is $" & Format(sngTotal, "#,###.00")
lblOutput.Text = strOutput
lblOutput.Visible = True
```

7. Start debugging the program.

8. Enter data into the text boxes to verify that everything works correctly (you can use interest rates that are not whole numbers).

9. Save the changes to your project, close the solution, and leave Visual Studio 2005 open for the next Project.

PROJECT 7-2

Your school library has asked you to create a program that will calculate late fees students owe on overdue books. Your school charges $.05 per week for each book that is late.

1. Open **Library** from the **proj07-02** folder in the data files for this lesson.

2. Add code to each text box that will highlight the text when the text box is selected.

3. Double-click the **Calculate Late Fee** button.

4. Create a String variable named **strFullName** and a Single variable named **sngFine**.

5. Add the following code to set `strFullName` equal to the `txtFirst` and `txtLast` text boxes.

```
'Combine first and last name
strFullName = txtFirst.Text & " " & txtLast.Text
```

6. Add the following code to calculate the late fee.

```
'Calculate late fee
sngFine = Val(txtBooks.Text) * Val(txtWeeks.Text) * 0.05
```

7. Add the following code to display the results.

```
'Display Results
lblOutput.Text = strFullName & " owes " & Format(sngFine, "$###.00")
lblOutput.Visible = True
```

8. Close the code window and start debugging the program.

9. Enter data into the text boxes to verify that the program works.

10. Change the data to verify that the text in the text boxes gets selected when you tab into the text boxes.

11. Save your changes, close the solution, and leave Visual Studio 2005 open.

PROJECT 7-3

1. Open **TransportationNeeds** from the **proj07-03** folder in the data files for this lesson.

2. Set the `Enabled` property of the Calculate button to **False**.

3. Add code to the `txtPeople` and `txtPeoplePerBus` TextChanged event procedure that will enable the Calculate button.

4. Add code to each text box that will highlight the text when the text box is selected.

5. Add code to the Calculate button that will disable the command button when it is clicked.

6. Start debugging the program and verify that it works.

7. Save your changes, close the solution, and leave Visual Studio 2005 open for the Critical Thinking activity.

CRITICAL *Thinking*

Modify the **Dog Years** program you worked with in this lesson to include two new command buttons that convert human months to cow years and mouse years. (You may have to widen the form and reposition the controls. Don't forget to disable the new buttons.) Change the text for the instructions so it applies to all three animals. The result of all calculations should be displayed in the label `lblOutputAnimalYears`. Use the following formulas to calculate the cow and mouse years. Your solution may look something like Figure 7-11.

Cow years   = (5 * # of human months) / 12

Mouse years = (25 * # of human months) / 12

FIGURE 7-11
A possible form for calculating dog, cow, and mouse years

(*Hint:* Move the `strYears` and `sngYears` variables to the Declarations section. You can then copy and paste from one section of code to another and change code as needed. Don't forget the code to enable and disable the buttons in the appropriate places.)

CALCULATIONS AND DATA

REVIEW *Questions*

MATCHING

Match the correct term in Column 1 to its description in Column 2.

Column 1

Column 2

_____ 1. alphanumeric

A. declared within an event procedure and accessible only within that procedure

_____ 2. scope

B. the process of removing everything to the right of the decimal point

_____ 3. object

C. memory locations where temporary data is stored

_____ 4. truncation

D. the process of interrupting the normal chain of events that occurs when an error is encountered, and replacing that chain of events with your own code

_____ 5. concatenation

E. text that can include letters or numbers

_____ 6. comments

F. the rules related to the order in which operations are performed in mathematical calculations

_____ 7. local variable

G. the reach of a variable

_____ 8. order of operations

H. appending one string to the end of another

_____ 9. variables

I. a data type that can hold data of any type

_____ 10. error handling

J. notes in the code that will be ignored by the compiler

WRITTEN QUESTIONS

Write a brief answer to each of the following questions.

1. What property sets the location of the cursor when a text box is clicked or tabbed into?

2. What are symbols that perform specific operations in Visual Basic statements?

3. What are values entered directly into Visual Basic code?

4. What function converts data in a text box to a number?

5. What are fields on a form that allow the user to enter a value?

6. What function can display custom error messages?

7. What code can force an event procedure to end regardless of whether or not there is more code?

8. What property can inactivate a command button?

9. What is evaluated first in the order of operations?

10. What kind of error occurs when a program is running?

SIMULATIONS

JOB 2-1

Evaluate the expressions shown in Table U2-1.

TABLE U2-1
Expressions to be evaluated

EXPRESSION	RESULT
3 * 2 + 4	
3 + 3 * 2 − 1	
2 + 6 / 3 + 1 * 6 − 7	
(2 + 6) / (3 + 1) * 6 − 7	
(2 + 6) / (3 + 1) * (6 − 7)	

JOB 2-2

1. Start Visual Basic and open **Stock** from the **job02-02** folder in the data files for this unit review.

2. Add code to each of the four text boxes so that the text will be highlighted when the text box is tabbed into.

3. Create two form-level variables, strOutput and sngChange. strOutput should be declared as a String data type, and sngChange should be declared as a Single data type.

4. Select **cmdGainLoss** from the Class Name list box and **Click** from the Method Name list box.

5. Add the following code to create five local variables.

```
'Declare variables
Dim sngGainLoss As Single
Dim strGainLoss As String
Dim strChange As String
Dim strTotal As String
Dim sngTotal As Single
```

6. Add the following code to calculate the change per share.

```
'Calculate change per share
sngChange = Val(txtClose.Text) - Val(txtOpen.Text)
```

7. Add the following code to calculate the gain or loss.

```
'Calculate gain or loss
sngGainLoss = sngChange * Val(txtShares.Text)
```

8. Add the following code to calculate the total value of the stock.

```
'Calculate total worth
sngTotal = Val(txtClose.Text) * Val(txtShares.Text)
```

9. Add the following code to format each variable and set strOutput equal to the output.

```
'Copy data to output variable
strChange = Format(sngChange, "$##.00")
strGainLoss = Format(sngGainLoss, "$#,###,###.00")
strTotal = Format(sngTotal, "$###,###,###.00")
strOutput = "The total value of your " & txtName.Text & _
   " stock is " & strTotal & ". The " & txtName.Text & _
   " stock's change in price per share is " & strChange & _
   " for a total change of " & strGainLoss & "."
```

10. Add the following code to display the output and enable the Change button.

```
'Display output
MsgBox (strOutput)
cmdChange.Enabled = True
cmdGainLoss.Enabled = False
```

11. Select **cmdChange** from the Class Name list box and **Click** from the Method Name list box.

12. Add the following code to create a string variable and single variable to store the percent change.

```
'Declare variables
Dim sngPercentChange As Single
Dim strPercentChange As String
```

13. Add the following code to calculate the percent change.

```
'Calculate percent change
sngPercentChange = (100 * (sngChange / Val(txtOpen.Text)))
```

14. Add the following code to display the percent change.

```
'Display Output
strPercentChange = Format(sngPercentChange, "####.0")
strOutput = "The percent change was " & strPercentChange & "%."
MsgBox (strOutput)
```

15. Add the following code to clear the strOutput string and enable the GainLoss button.

```
'Clear strOutput and enable GainLoss button
strOutput = " "
cmdGainLoss.Enabled = True
cmdChange.Enabled = False
```

16. Start debugging the program and verify that it gives the correct answers. The input data may look something like Figure U2-1. The result of clicking the Gain/Loss button with this sample data should look like Figure U2-2. The result of clicking the Percent Change button should look like Figure U2-3.

FIGURE U2-1
Sample test data in the program form

FIGURE U2-2
The gain value is displayed for the sample test data

FIGURE U2-3
The percent gain is displayed for the sample test data

17. Save the changes to the project, and then close the solution.

JOB 2-3

Write code for the following scenarios.

1. Simple interest is calculated based on the formula below.
   Interest = Principal * Annual Interest Rate * Period in Years

   Assuming you have a program that includes text boxes named **txtPrincipal, txtInterest,** and **txtYears,** write code in the space below to declare a variable of type Decimal named **decInterestEarned.** Also write code to calculate simple interest based on the information and formula provided.

2. The amount of electrical current that flows through a resistor is calculated using the following formula.
   Current in amps = Voltage / Resistance in ohms

   Assuming you have a program that includes text boxes named **txtVoltage** and **txtOhms,** write code in the space below to declare a variable of type Single named **sngAmps.** Also write code to calculate the current in amps based on the information and formula provided.

3. Assume you have a program that includes a text box named **txtMinutes.** The program prompts the user to enter the length of a movie in minutes. In the space below, write code that will declare a variable of type Single named **sngHours.** Also write code to calculate the length of the movie in hours.

JOB 2-4

Select one of the three scenarios in Job 2-3 and create a complete program based on the calculation performed in the scenario. Your program should include all of the following that are applicable.

1. A form with appropriately named and captioned labels and text boxes (include a label for the output).

2. Code with appropriate comments.

3. Meaningful variable names (including form-level variables, if applicable) that use the appropriate naming prefixes.

4. The `Val` function for extracting values from text boxes.

5. Hiding of the output with the Visible property until appropriate to display, or use of the `MsgBox` function to display output.

6. Use of `SelectionStart` and `SelectionLength` for text boxes.

7. Use of the `Format` function to properly format output.

DECISION MAKING

Unit 3

Lesson 8   2 hrs.
If Statements

Lesson 9   2 hrs.
**Nested If Statements
and Radio Buttons**

🕐 **Estimated Time for Unit 3: 4 hours**

IF STATEMENTS

The Building Blocks of Decision Making

When you make a decision, your brain goes through a process of comparisons. For example, when you shop for clothes, you compare the price with prices you have previously seen or paid. You compare the quality to other clothes you have seen or owned. You probably compare the clothes to what other people are wearing or what is in style. You might even compare the purchase of clothes to other possible uses for your available money.

Although your brain's method of decision making is much more complex than what a computer is capable of, decision making in computers is also based on comparing data.

Programs are limited without the ability to make decisions. Although some programs, like the ones you have been writing up to this point, progress through a fairly straightforward path, most programs require some decision making along the way. When two or more possible paths of execution are available, the program must have a means to make a decision.

Suppose you have a dialog box that asks the user the weight of a package that he or she wants to ship (see Figure 8-1). You cannot control what keys the user will press. What you can do, however, is verify that what the user enters is valid. When the user clicks the OK button, you want to ensure that the value entered by the user is not less than zero (a package cannot weigh less than zero pounds), and that they have actually entered a value.

FIGURE 8-1
A program that prompts the user for a value

Decision making in a computer is generally done in terms of a comparison that returns a True or False response. In the example shown in Figure 8-1, the program asks "is the value entered by the user less than zero?" If the answer is Yes or True, the program can stop the operation and prompt the user again.

Using the Conditional Operators

The first step to making a decision in a program is to make a comparison. Comparisons are made using the *conditional operators*. They are similar to the symbols you have used in mathematics when working with equations and inequalities. The conditional operators are shown in Table 8-1.

TABLE 8-1
Conditional operators

OPERATOR	DESCRIPTION
=	Equal to
>	Greater than
<	Less than
>=	Greater than or equal to
<=	Less than or equal to
<>	Not equal to

The conditional operators are used to compare two values. The result of the comparison is either True or False. Recall from Lesson 5 that Visual Basic has a Boolean data type that can hold the values True or False. A Boolean variable can be used to store the results of an expression that includes conditional operators. Following are some examples of conditional operators in use.

```
blnTooBig = (Val(txtHeight.Text) > 72)
```

If the value keyed in the txtHeight text box is greater than 72, the variable `blnTooBig` is set to True.

```
lblOutput.Text = (intLength >= 100)
```

If the value in `intLength` is greater than or equal to 100, the Text property of the `lblOutput` label is set to True.

```
blnEqual = (sngA = sngB)
```

If the values in `sngA` and `sngB` are equal, the variable `blnEqual` is set to True.

> **Hot Tip**
>
> When the Text of a label is set to a Boolean result, the label is set to either the word *True* or the word *False*.

STEP-BY-STEP 8.1

1. Start Visual Studio 2005 and open **Compare** from the **step08-01** folder in the data files for this lesson. If necessary, open the form in the Solution Explorer.

2. Double-click the **Compare** button and add the following code to compare the values of each text box.
   ```
   lblOutput.Text = (Val(txtLeft.Text) = Val(txtRight.Text))
   ```

3. Close the code window and start debugging the program.

4. Key **10** in both text boxes and click **Compare**. The word *True* appears as the label text, as shown in Figure 8-2.

FIGURE 8-2
The label Text is set to the result of the expression

5. Change the value in the text box to the right of the equal sign to **15**.

6. Click **Compare**. The word *False* appears as the label text.

7. End the program and save the changes to the project.

8. Close the project and leave Visual Studio 2005 open for the next Step-by-Step.

Using If Statements

In Visual Basic, the If statement is the most common way to make a decision. An *If statement* allows you to execute specified code when the result of a conditional expression is true. For example, an If statement can be used to present the user with a message box if the user enters a value that is out of the normal range of values.

Suppose you have a program that asks the user to enter the weight in pounds of a package that is to be shipped. The shipping method requires that you enter the weight to the nearest pound with a one pound minimum. You can use an If statement like the one below to ensure that the user does not enter zero or a negative number for the weight.

```
intPackageWeight = Val(txtWeight.Text)
If (intPackageWeight < 1) Then
     MsgBox("Package weight must be one or more pounds.")
End If
```

The code above converts the user's entry in the text box into an Integer variable. Remember that if the user has entered a real number with a fractional part, that part will be dropped. Then a conditional operator is used to test whether the value in the variable is less than one. The If statement is saying that if the result of the comparison is true, then present the message box. The End If statement marks the end of the If statement.

In many cases, there is more than one line of code between the If statement and the End If statement. All of the lines of code that appear between the If statement and End If statements are executed if the conditions specified in the If statement are true. Otherwise, the code between the If statement and the End If statement is skipped.

STEP-BY-STEP 8.2

1. Open the **Division** project you worked with in Lesson 6 and, if necessary, open the form. (If you do not have this project completed, you can open the **Division** project from the **step08-02** folder in the data files for this lesson.)

2. Double-click the **Calculate** button and add the following to the beginning of the code to display a warning message if the divisor equals 0.

```
'If divisor is 0 display message
If Val(txtDivisor.Text) = 0 Then
     MsgBox ("The divisor cannot be zero.")
End If
```

STEP-BY-STEP 8.2 Continued

3. Add code so the text in the two text boxes will be highlighted when you click in them. (*Hint:* Use the `SelectionStart` and `SelectionLength` properties.)

4. Close the code window and start debugging the program.

5. Enter **9** for the divisor and **17** for the dividend and click **Calculate**. The program displays the result (1 r 8).

6. Enter **0** for the divisor and **5** for the dividend and click **Calculate**. A message box appears warning you that the divisor cannot be zero, as shown in Figure 8-3.

FIGURE 8-3
The message box displayed is a result of the If statement

7. Click **OK** in the message box. A second error message appears based on the MsgBox code you added in Lesson 4.

8. Click **OK** to dismiss this message, then end the program.

9. Save the changes to the project and close it. Leave Visual Studio 2005 open for the next Step-by-Step.

Creating and Reading Flowcharts

Now that you have used an `If` statement, you can see that programs often do more than just execute a list of instructions without variation. Input from a user or other conditions may require that a program's execution take a turn in a new direction or skip certain code. As the flow of execution in a program becomes more complex, it is often helpful to see the possible paths that a program might take in a visual form.

For many years, programmers have been using *flowcharts* to plan and document program code. A flowchart uses symbols and shapes connected by lines to illustrate the steps of a program. Figure 8-4 shows a flowchart of the `If` statement discussed earlier.

FIGURE 8-4
A flowchart gives a visual representation of the flow of execution in a program

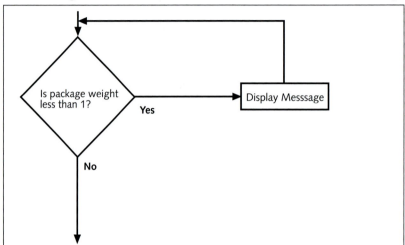

There are many symbols used to create flowcharts. For our purposes, we will be concerned only with the three most basic flowchart symbols, shown in Figure 8-5. The rectangle represents processing data or taking action. Use the diamond for making decisions, such as an If statement. Use the parallelogram to represent input and output.

> **Computer Concepts**
>
> Because Visual Basic is an event-driven environment, flowcharts are not generally used to chart an entire program. However, flowcharts can be very useful for organizing the flow of execution within an event procedure.

FIGURE 8-5
Each shape in a flowchart has a special meaning

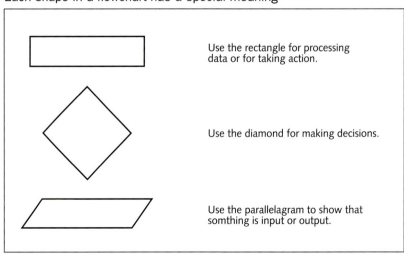

Using If...Else Statements

An If statement makes a decision to either perform some task or to do nothing. An If statement is called a one-way selection structure. A **one-way selection structure** is a program structure in which the decision is to go "one way" or just bypass the code in the If statement. But as you know from the everyday decisions you make, sometimes the decision involves more than Yes or No. Decisions are often a matter of choosing between two or more alternatives.

The If...Else statement allows you to choose between two paths. In an If...Else statement, one block of code is executed if the result of an expression is true, and another block is executed if the result is false.

The code below displays one of two messages. If the value being tested is less than zero, a message is displayed announcing that the value is negative. If the value is not less than zero, a message is displayed saying that the value is either zero or positive.

```
If (intValue < 0) Then
     MsgBox("The value is negative.")
Else
     MsgBox("The value is zero or positive.")
End If
```

An If...Else statement is called a two-way selection structure. A **two-way selection structure** is a program structure in which one block of code is executed if the specified conditions are true, or another block of code is executed if the specified conditions are false. The flowchart in Figure 8-6 charts the code just shown.

FIGURE 8-6
An If...Else statement is a two-way selection structure

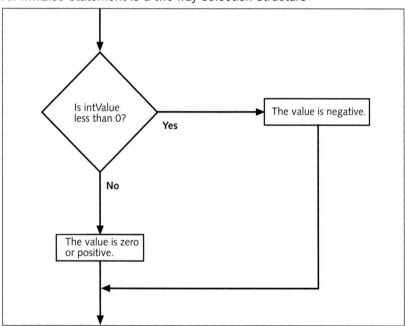

STEP-BY-STEP 8.3

1. Open **Numbers** from the **step08-03** folder in the data files for this lesson and, if necessary, open the form.

2. Double-click the **OK** button and add the following code to display the positive message if the number is greater than or equal to 0.

```
'Determine if number is positive or negative
If Val(txtNumber.Text) >= 0 Then
   lblResult.Text = "The number is positive."
```

3. Add the following code to display the negative message if the number is not greater than or equal to 0.

```
Else
   lblResult.Text = "The number is negative."
End If
```

4. Close the code window and start debugging the program.

5. Key **38** in the text box and click **OK**. The output below the text box indicates that the number is positive, as shown in Figure 8-7.

FIGURE 8-7
The If...Else statement determined that the number is positive

6. Key **–7** in the text box and click **OK**. The output indicates that the number is negative.

7. End the program and save the changes to the project.

8. Close the project and leave Visual Studio 2005 open for the next Step-by-Step.

Using Check Boxes

Check boxes are an important part of the Windows interface. *Check boxes* allow the program to ask the user a Yes or No question or to turn an option on or off. For example, Figure 8-8 shows the Options dialog box from Visual Basic. The dialog box includes many commands that are selected by clicking check boxes. The commands with a check in the box are on, and the commands without a check in the box are off.

FIGURE 8-8
A check box allows the user to visually turn commands on and off

Checked Property

Each check box has a Checked property that is set to True if the box is checked and False if the box is not checked. The label that appears beside the check box is part of the check box control; therefore, you do not have to create a label control next to the check box. The check box has a Text property that specifies its label.

STEP-BY-STEP 8.4

1. Open **Coaster** from the **step08-04** folder in the data files and, if necessary, open the form.

2. Double-click the **CheckBox** tool on the toolbar. A check box control is added to the form.

3. Move the check box control below the **Height in inches** label.

4. Create another check box control.

STEP-BY-STEP 8.4 Continued

5. Resize and position the two check box controls so your screen appears similar to Figure 8-9.

6. Change the (Name) property of the first check box control to **chkBack**.

7. Change the Text property of chkBack to **Back Trouble**. If necessary, resize the control so that the entire message is displayed on one line.

8. Change the (Name) property of the second check box control to **chkHeart**.

9. Change the Text property of chkHeart to **Heart Trouble**. If necessary, resize the control so that the entire message is displayed on one line.

10. Save the changes to the project and leave the project open for the next Step-by-Step.

Setting the Default Checked Property

Check boxes can be set to be either checked or unchecked by default, as shown in Figure 8-10. To have a check box checked by default, set the Checked property to True. To have it unchecked by default, set the Checked property to False.

FIGURE 8-10
Check boxes can default to a checked or unchecked state

STEP-BY-STEP 8.5

1. Start debugging the program. Notice that each check box is empty.

2. End the program.

3. Click the **Heart Trouble** check box control to select it, if necessary.

4. Change the Checked property from **False** to **True**. Notice that a check mark appears in the check box on the form.

5. Start debugging the program. The Heart Trouble check box is checked by default.

6. End the program.

7. Change the Checked property of the Heart Trouble check box back to False. Leave the project open for the next Step-by-Step.

> **Computer Concepts**
>
> In Visual Basic, the equal sign (=) is used for two operations. It is used to assign values and to compare values to determine if they are equal.

Setting the Checked Property with Code

The Checked property can be set and/or read from code. For example, the following code assigns True to a check box, causing it to appear checked.

```
chkHeart.Checked = True
```

Similar code can be used to test whether the check box is checked.

```
If (chkHeart.Checked = True) Then
     MsgBox("The check box is checked")
End If
```

STEP-BY-STEP 8.6

1. Double-click the **OK** button and add the following code to declare a variable named blnOKtoRide and set it equal to True. The blnOKtoRide variable will be used to track whether the rider passes the three tests for riding the roller coaster. The program will assume the rider is able to ride unless one of the pieces of information entered by the user disqualifies the rider.

```
Dim blnOKtoRide As Boolean
blnOKtoRide = True
```

2. Add the following code to determine if the rider is less than 45 inches tall. If the rider is less than 45 inches, the blnOKtoRide variable is set equal to False.

```
'Check if rider is less than 45 inches tall
If Val(txtHeight.Text) < 45 Then
  blnOKtoRide = False
End If
```

3. Add the following to determine if the rider has back problems. If back problems are reported, the rider is not allowed to ride.

```
'Check for back problems
If chkBack.Checked = True Then
  blnOKtoRide = False
End If
```

4. Add the following code to determine if the rider has heart problems. If heart problems are reported, the rider is not allowed to ride.

```
'Check for heart problems
If chkHeart.Checked = True Then
  blnOKtoRide = False
End If
```

STEP-BY-STEP 8.6 Continued

5. Add the following code to display whether the potential roller coaster rider can ride, depending on the value of `blnOKtoRide`. After all the code is entered, your screen should appear similar to Figure 8-11.

```
'Display results
If blnOKtoRide = True Then
  lblResult.Text = "OK to Ride."
Else
  lblResult.Text = "Can't Ride!"
End If
```

FIGURE 8-11
The code assumes the rider is allowed to ride unless one of the checks causes the Boolean variable `blnOKtoRide` to change to False

6. Close the code window and start debugging the program.

7. Key **30** in the text box and click **OK**. The label *Can't Ride!* appears on the form.

8. Key **46** in the text box, click the **Back Trouble** check box to add a check mark, and click **OK**. Again the label *Can't Ride!* appears on the form.

9. Remove the check mark from the **Back Trouble** check box, and click **OK**. The label *OK to Ride.* appears on the form.

10. Check the **Heart Trouble** check box and click **OK**. The rider is refused.

11. End the program and save the changes to the program. Leave the project open for the next Step-by-Step.

Using the Logical Operators

The logical operators are another important set of operators. *Logical operators* can be used to combine several comparisons into one statement. Table 8-2 shows the three most common logical operators. Logical operators are used with True and False values. For example, the Not operator reverses the value. In other words, True becomes False and False becomes True.

TABLE 8-2
Logical operators

OPERATOR	DESCRIPTION
Not	Reverses the value.
And	All expressions or values connected by the And operator must be True in order for the result to be True.
Or	Only one of the expressions or values connected by the Or operator must be True for the result to be True.

The And operator works as you might expect. The result of the And operator is True if both values connected by the And operator are True. For example, the code below sets the Boolean variable `blnInRange` to True if the variable `intA` is in the range of 0 to 100. It determines this by verifying that the value in `intA` is greater than or equal to 0 *and* less than or equal to 100.

```
blnInRange = (intA >= 0) And (intA <= 100)
```

The Or operator returns a True result if either of the values connected by the Or operator are True. For example, the code below sets the `blnSellStock` variable to True if the stock price moves higher than 92.5 per share or if the profits are less than one million.

```
blnSellStock = (sngStockPrice > 92.5) Or (curProfits < 1000000)
```

Order of Logical Operators

In the order of operations, logical operators are processed after the mathematical and conditional operators. Table 8-3 shows the order of operations, combining the mathematical, conditional, and logical operators. The table lists the operations from the first to the last. Items in parentheses are always evaluated first and will override the order shown in this table.

TABLE 8-3
Order of operations

ORDER	OPERATION
1	Exponentiation
2	Unary plus and unary minus
3	Multiplication, division, integer division, and Mod
4	Addition and subtraction
5	The conditional operators
6	Not
7	And
8	Or

STEP-BY-STEP 8.7

1. Double-click the **OK** button.

2. Delete the three segments of code that check for height and for back and heart problems.

3. Add the following code to replace the lines you just deleted to combine the three If statements into one.

```
'Check if rider is legal to ride
If (Val(txtHeight.Text) < 45) Or (chkBack.Checked = True) Or _
   (chkHeart.Checked = True) Then
        blnOKtoRide = False
End If
```

4. Start debugging the program.

5. Key **25** in the text box and click **OK**. The label *Can't Ride!* appears on the form.

6. Key **73** in the text box, click the **Heart Trouble** check box to add a check mark, and click **OK**. Again the label *Can't Ride!* appears on the form.

STEP-BY-STEP 8.7 Continued

7. Remove the check mark from the **Heart Trouble** check box, and click **OK**. The label *OK to Ride*. appears on the form.

8. Click the **Back Trouble** check box to add a check mark and click **OK**. The label *Can't Ride!* appears on the form.

9. End the program, save the changes to the project, and exit Visual Studio 2005.

SUMMARY

In this lesson, you learned:

■ Decisions are reached by making comparisons. Comparisons in a computer generally return either a True or False value.

■ The conditional operators compare two values and return either True or False, depending on whether the expression is True or False.

■ A Boolean variable can be used to store the results of an expression that includes conditional operators.

■ The If statement is the most common way to make a decision in a program. An If statement is a one-way selection structure. In an If statement, the code between the If and the End If is executed if the conditions in the If statement are met.

■ Flowcharts allow programmers to plan and document program code using symbols connected by lines.

■ An If...Else statement makes a decision between two paths. An If...Else statement is a two-way selection structure.

■ Check boxes allow your program to ask the user Yes or No questions or to turn an option on or off. The Checked property of a check box is set to True when the check box is checked and False when the box is not checked. A check box can be set to be checked or unchecked by default.

■ Logical operators can be used to combine several comparisons into one statement. Logical operators are used with True and False values. The Not operator reverses the value of a Boolean variable or expression. The And operator returns True if the values connected by the And operator are both True. The Or operator returns True if either value connected by the Or operator is True.

■ The logical operators are last in the order of operations. Of the logical operators, Not comes first, then And, then Or.

VOCABULARY *Review*

Define the following terms:

Boolean data type   Flowchart   One-way selection structure
Check boxes   If statement   Two-way selection structure
Conditional operator   Logical operators

REVIEW *Questions*

TRUE/FALSE

Circle T if the statement is true or F if the statement is false.

T   F   **1.** Decision making in computers is based on comparing data.

T   F   **2.** Boolean variables can be used to store the result of a comparison.

T   F   **3.** You cannot set the Text of a label to the result of a comparison.

T   F   **4.** Flowcharts are generally used to chart an entire Visual Basic program.

T   F   **5.** An If...Else statement is considered a one-way selection structure.

T   F   **6.** An End If statement does not need to be used in conjunction with the If...Else statement.

T   F   **7.** The check box control includes a label that can be set with the Text property.

T   F   **8.** Check boxes are always set to be unchecked by default.

T   F   **9.** The same operator is used for assignment and equal comparison in Visual Basic.

T   F   **10.** Logical operators can be used to combine several comparisons into one statement.

WRITTEN QUESTIONS

Write a brief answer to each of the following questions.

1. What type of operator is used to compare two values?

2. What is the result of a comparison in Visual Basic?

3. What operator is used to represent "Not equal to"?

4. What two types of statements are used to make decisions in a Visual Basic program?

5. What statement marks the end of an If statement?

6. Why are flowcharts important to programming?

7. What two possible values can be stored in the Checked property of a check box control?

8. What are the three logical operators?

9. Where do the logical operators fall in the order of operations?

10. What is the Not operator used for?

PROJECTS

PROJECT 8-1

1. Start Visual Studio 2005 and open the **Buses** program you worked with in the Lesson 4 Critical Thinking Activity. (If you do not have this program, ask your instructor to supply it.)

2. Open the form if necessary.

3. Add the following code to the Calculate button to display a warning message and exit the subroutine if the number of people equals 0.

```
'Check number of riders
If Val(txtNumCampers.Text) = 0 Then
    MsgBox ("The number of riders cannot be zero.")
    Exit Sub
End If
```

4. Close the code window and start debugging the program.

5. Enter a 0 (zero) for number of people and click **Calculate** to verify that the changes made to the program work correctly.

6. Click **OK** to dismiss the message, then end the program.

7. Save the changes to the project and close it. Leave Visual Studio 2005 open for the next Project.

PROJECT 8-2

Draw a flowchart of the roller coaster ride program created in this lesson.

PROJECT 8-3

1. Open the **Numbers** program you worked with in this lesson.

2. Change the Text of the form to **Even or Odd?**.

3. Change the instructions at the top of the form to explain that the program will determine if the number is even or odd.

4. Edit the code for the OK button so it looks like the following code.

```
'Determine if number is even or odd
If Val(txtNumber.Text Mod 2) = 0 Then
     lblResult.Text = "The number is even."
Else
     lblResult.Text = "The number is odd."
End If
```

5. Start debugging the program to verify that it can determine whether a number is even or odd, then end the program.

6. Save the changes to the project and close it. Leave Visual Studio 2005 open.

PROJECT 8-4

Your school is planning a trip for spring break. They have asked you to write a program that will calculate the total cost of the trip for each student. The basic price for the trip is $200.00. There are three additional options for the trip: rappelling, backpacking, and canoeing. Complete the steps below to finish the program.

1. Open **Trip** from the **proj08-04** folder in the data files for this lesson.

2. Add three check boxes and change their Texts so the form appears similar to Figure 8-12 (resize and reposition as necessary).

FIGURE 8-12
Add three check boxes as shown here

3. Change the (Name) property of the check boxes to `chkRappel`, `chkBackpack`, and `chkCanoe`.

4. Add the following code to the Calculate button to declare three variables and initialize decTotal to 200.

```
Dim decTotal As Decimal
Dim strTotal As String
Dim strOutput As String
decTotal = 200
```

5. Add the following code to add $30 to decTotal if the *rappelling* check box is checked.

```
'Check if Rappelling
If chkRappel.Checked = True Then
    decTotal = decTotal + 30
End If
```

6. Add the following code to add $45 to decTotal if the *backpacking* check box is checked.

```
'Check if Backpacking
If chkBackpack.Checked = True Then
    decTotal = decTotal + 45
End If
```

7. Add the following code to add $25 to decTotal if the *canoeing* check box is checked.

```
'Check if Canoeing
If chkCanoe.Checked = True Then
    decTotal = decTotal + 25
End If
```

8. Add the following code to display the results.

```
'Display Output
strTotal = Format(decTotal, "$###.00")
strOutput = "The total price of your trip will be " & strTotal & "."
lblOutput.Text = strOutput
```

9. Start debugging the program to verify that all three check boxes work correctly (you can check more than one check box at a time).

10. End the program, save the changes to the project, and exit Visual Studio 2005.

CRITICAL *Thinking*

Extend the **Coaster** program to do additional verification. The program should ask for the age of the rider. Regardless of height, if the rider is under 10 years old, the Child with Adult check box must be checked before the child can ride.

Make modifications to the user interface to match Figure 8-13 and add the required code to perform the checks. (*Hint:* Use *And* rather than *Or* in the code for the age requirement.)

FIGURE 8-13
Modify the Coaster form to include a new label, text box, and check box

NESTED IF STATEMENTS AND RADIO BUTTONS

OBJECTIVES

Upon completion of this lesson, you should be able to:

- Use Nested If statements.
- Use Radio buttons.
- Use the Form Load event.
- Use the Select Case statement.

Estimated Time: 2 hours

VOCABULARY

GroupBox control

Load event

Nested If statement

Option group

Radio buttons

Select Case statement

Using Nested If Statements

Decision-making is sometimes more complicated than selecting one of two paths. Once on a path, there are often more decisions to be made. For example, suppose a homeowner is deciding whether to paint her house this year or next year. If she decides to do the job this year, she will have to make additional decisions, such as color. She will not have to decide what color to purchase unless she makes the decision to go ahead and paint.

In programming, you regularly have decision-making similar to the example above. Recall that you can place multiple lines of code between an If statement and its End If statement. The lines of code within an If statement can be practically any kind of Visual Basic 2005 code, including more If statements.

When you place an If statement inside another If statement, the If statement inside is called a *nested If statement*. The following code reports the status of an automobile's fuel level to the driver. The first If statement checks to see if the fuel level is less than one-quarter of a tank. If more than one-quarter of a tank exists, the Else clause reports that the Fuel level is fine. If less than one-quarter of a tank exists, an additional If statement checks the distance to the next gas station. Based on the distance to the next possible fill-up, the driver is either alerted to get fuel now or warned that fuel will be needed soon.

```
If sngFuelLevel < 0.25 Then
     If sngDistanceToNextGas > 30 Then
          MsgBox("Get fuel now.")
     Else
          MsgBox("Will need fuel soon.")
     End If
Else
     MsgBox("Fuel level OK.")
End If
```

When using nested If statements, it is important that you properly indent the code to make it easy to read and to maintain. As you can see, the code above is a little confusing at first. Just imagine how confusing it would be if there were no indentation to group the statements logically. That is why it is important to make sure you follow the same indentation conventions that you see used here. This makes the code easier to understand and read.

Other than careful attention to indentation, there is no new or special syntax to learn in order to use nested If statements. However, you will get errors if you fail to include the End If for every If statement.

In the exercise that follows, you will use nested If statements to recommend a type of checking account to a new bank customer. Banks normally have two or more types of checking accounts that are tailored for customers with different amounts of money to keep in the accounts. Often, banks have low-cost accounts for people who plan to keep low balances, and free checking accounts for those who will maintain slightly higher balances. They may also have an account that pays the customer interest if the customer will maintain a certain minimum balance.

The code shown in Figure 9-1 (which you will implement in the following exercise) will recommend an account to the user. First, an If statement determines if the amount being deposited is less than $1000. If the deposit is less than $1000, further comparisons must be made. If the deposit is $1000 or greater, the Else clause recommends the interest-bearing account.

FIGURE 9-1
Nested If statements allow multilevel decisions

```
'Determine checking account
If curDeposit < 1000 Then
    If curDeposit < 100 Then
         lblOutput.Text = "Consider the EconoCheck account."
    Else
         lblOutput.Text = "Consider the FreeCheck account."
    End If
Else
    lblOutput.Text = "Consider an interest-bearing account."
End If
```

The nested If statement is only executed if the deposit is less than $1000. Its job is to choose between the two accounts that do not pay interest. If the deposit is less than $100, the EconoCheck account is recommended; otherwise (or else), the FreeCheck account is recommended.

S TEP-BY-STEP 9.1

1. Start Visual Studio 2005 and open **Check** from the **step09-01** folder in the data files for this lesson. If necessary, open **frmMain** from the **Solution Explorer**.

2. Double-click the **OK** button and add the following code to declare `curDeposit` as a Decimal variable.

   ```
   Dim curDeposit As Decimal
   ```

3. Add the following code to set `curDeposit` equal to the value in the text box.

   ```
   curDeposit = Val(txtDeposit.Text)
   ```

4. Add the code from Figure 9-1 into the event procedure. Your screen should appear similar to Figure 9-2.

   FIGURE 9-2
   Code for the Main form in the Check project

5. Close the Code window and start debugging the program.

6. Key **700** into the text box and click **OK**. The output "Consider the FreeCheck account." appears on the form.

7. Key **50** into the text box and click **OK**. The output "Consider the EconoCheck account." replaces the previous output.

8. Key **3500** into the text box and click **OK**. The output "Consider an interest-bearing account." appears on the form.

9. End the program and save the changes to the project.

10. Close the project, but leave Visual Studio 2005 open for the next Step-by-Step.

Using Radio Buttons

Radio buttons are similar to check boxes, with one important difference. Radio buttons always appear in groups, and only one button in the group can be selected at a time. For example, the dialog box in Figure 9-3 is a typical Page Setup dialog box. When printing to most printers, you have the option of printing across the narrow width of the page (portrait orientation) or across the wide width of the page (landscape orientation). You can only select one of the two options. Therefore, radio buttons are ideal for selecting the page orientation in the Page Setup dialog box. Radio buttons are often called option buttons because they allow a user to select from several options.

FIGURE 9-3
Only one radio button in a group can be selected

Using radio buttons in your programs is more complex than working with any of the other controls you have included in your programs up to this point. To use radio buttons successfully, three steps are involved.

1. Create a GroupBox control to group the radio buttons.

2. Create the radio buttons in the GroupBox.

3. Write code to use the radio buttons.

These three steps are discussed in the following sections.

Did You Know?

Radio buttons got their names from car radios. The buttons on a car radio that move the dial to a preset station are like radio buttons in a form—you can have only one station selected at a time.

Creating a GroupBox Control

A *GroupBox control* is a container for other controls. The controls that you place inside a GroupBox are treated as one unit. If you move the GroupBox, the controls in the GroupBox move with it. If you delete the GroupBox, the controls in the GroupBox are also deleted. Figure 9-4 shows an example of a GroupBox in a dialog box (the "Choose a planet" GroupBox).

FIGURE 9-4
GroupBoxes are used to group controls into one unit

It is important to create the GroupBox that will contain the radio buttons before you create the radio buttons themselves. When you draw the radio buttons, you will draw them in the GroupBox with which they are to be associated. Radio buttons in a GroupBox are sometimes referred to as an *option group*.

The two most important GroupBox properties are (Name) and Text. As in other controls, the (Name) property allows you to associate a name with the object in Visual Basic code. In a GroupBox, the Text property specifies the text that will appear at the top of the GroupBox.

In Step-by-Step 9.2 through Step-by-Step 9.8, you will create the program shown in Figure 9-4. The program will calculate your weight on other planets. You will select the planet for the calculation using radio buttons.

STEP-BY-STEP 9.2

1. Open **Planets** from the **step09-02** folder in the data files for this lesson and, if necessary, open **frmPlanets** from the **Solution Explorer**.

2. Double-click the **GroupBox** control from the toolbox. A GroupBox appears on the form.

STEP-BY-STEP 9.2 Continued

3. Resize and move the GroupBox so your screen appears similar to Figure 9-5.

FIGURE 9-5
Creating a GroupBox is the first step to creating radio buttons

4. Change the (Name) property of the GroupBox to **grpPlanets** and change the Text property to **Choose a planet**.

5. Save your changes and leave the project open for the next Step-by-Step.

Creating Radio Buttons in the GroupBox

Now that the GroupBox is created, the next step is to add radio buttons to the GroupBox.

STEP-BY-STEP 9.3

1. Click the **RadioButton** control from the toolbox.

2. Position the mouse pointer inside the GroupBox.

3. Drag to draw a radio button inside the GroupBox. The button should be about 1/4 inch tall and 1-1/2 inches wide (96 × 24 pixels).

4. Create three more identical radio buttons inside the GroupBox. Your screen should appear similar to Figure 9-6.

Important

When you create radio buttons, single-click the RadioButton tool from the toolbox and drag within the GroupBox to create the radio button. If you double-click the RadioButton tool, the radio button that is created will not be associated with the GroupBox, even if it appears to be in the GroupBox.

STEP-BY-STEP 9.3 Continued

FIGURE 9-6
Drawing radio buttons in a GroupBox will automatically associate
them with the GroupBox

5. Save your changes and leave the project open for the next Step-by-Step.

Setting Radio Button Name and Text Properties

Like other controls, radio buttons need to be named appropriately by using the Name property. The Text property of a radio button is similar to the Text property of a check box. The Text property specifies the message for the attached label.

STEP-BY-STEP 9.4

1. Select the first radio button.

2. Change the (Name) property to **optMars** and change the Text property to **Mars**.

3. Set the properties of the remaining radio buttons to the values shown in Table 9-1.

TABLE 9-1
Properties for radio buttons

(NAME)	TEXT
optJupiter	Jupiter
optSaturn	Saturn
optPluto	Pluto

4. Start debugging the program.

5. Click each of the radio buttons to see that they are operating correctly (that you are able to make only one selection at a time).

6. End the program and save your changes. Leave the project open for the next Step-by-Step.

Adding Code to the Radio Buttons

Coding radio buttons requires that you think in an event-driven way. Let us consider what happens when the user clicks a radio button. The click on the radio button generates a Click event. In addition, as you saw in the previous exercise, the clicked radio button is filled with the dot that indicates that it is selected. The Click event procedure provides the opportunity to specify what you want to happen if the option linked to a particular radio button is selected.

The process is not that simple, however. The user may click several radio buttons before finally settling on a choice. This means you must keep track of the most recently clicked radio button in the group and yet be prepared for another radio button to be clicked instead.

To run the correct event, use form-level variables as the scope to keep track of the option that has been selected. For example, in the program that will calculate your weight on other planets, the Click event of each radio button will set two variables. The first variable will store the name of the planet the user selected. The second variable will store the conversion factor necessary to calculate the user's weight on that particular planet. The code for the Mars radio button `CheckedChanged` event appears as follows.

```
Private Sub optMars_CheckedChanged(ByVal sender As System.Object,_
ByVal e As System.EventArgs) Handles optMars.Click
        sngPlanetWeight = 0.38
        strPlanetName = "Mars"
End Sub
```

Each of the radio buttons will have a `CheckedChanged` event procedure similar to the one shown above. So no matter how many radio buttons the user clicks, the variables will reflect the values of the most recently clicked radio button. Then, when the user clicks the Calculate button, the values set in the radio button's `CheckedChanged` event procedure will be used in the calculation.

S TEP-BY-STEP 9.5

1. Double-click the **Calculate** button to open the code editor window, and select **(Declarations)** from the Method Name list box.

2. Add the following code after the `Public Class frmPlanets` statement to create two form-level variables.

   ```
   Dim sngPlanetWeight As Single
   Dim strPlanetName As String
   ```

3. Select **optMars** from the Class Name list box and **CheckedChanged** from the Method Name list box, and add the following code to assign the appropriate values to the two form-level variables when the Mars radio button is clicked.

   ```
   sngPlanetWeight = 0.38
   strPlanetName = "Mars"
   ```

   Hot Tip

   Remember, the variables used in each of the radio button event procedures must be declared at the form level.

STEP-BY-STEP 9.5 Continued

4. Select **optJupiter** from the Class Name list box and **CheckedChanged** from the Method Name list box, and add the following code for the Jupiter `CheckedChanged` event procedure.

```
sngPlanetWeight = 2.64
strPlanetName = "Jupiter"
```

5. Select **optSaturn** from the Class Name list box and **CheckedChanged** from the Method Name list box, and add the following code for the Saturn `CheckedChanged` event procedure.

```
sngPlanetWeight = 1.15
strPlanetName = "Saturn"
```

6. Select **optPluto** from the Class Name list box and **CheckedChanged** from the Method Name list box, and add the following code to initialize the two form-level variables when the Pluto radio button is selected.

```
sngPlanetWeight = 0.04
strPlanetName = "Pluto"
```

Your screen should appear similar to Figure 9-7.

FIGURE 9-7
Each radio button must have a `CheckedChanged` event procedure

```
frmPlanets.vb   frmPlanets.vb [Design]                              ▼ ×
optPluto                        ▼    CheckedChanged                  ▼
Public Class frmPlanets
     Dim sngPlanetWeight As Single
     Dim strPlanetName As String

     Private Sub cmdExit_Click(ByVal sender As System.Object, By
          End
     End Sub

     Private Sub optMars_CheckedChanged(ByVal sender As System.
          sngPlanetWeight = 0.38
          strPlanetName = "Mars"
     End Sub

     Private Sub optJupiter_CheckedChanged(ByVal sender As Objec
          sngPlanetWeight = 2.64
          strPlanetName = "Jupiter"
     End Sub

     Private Sub optSaturn_CheckedChanged(ByVal sender As Object
          sngPlanetWeight = 1.15
          strPlanetName = "Saturn"
     End Sub

     Private Sub optPluto_CheckedChanged(ByVal sender As Object,
          sngPlanetWeight = 0.04
          strPlanetName = "Pluto"
     End Sub
End Class
```

7. Close the Code window and save your changes. Leave the project open for the next Step-by-Step.

Processing the Data

The final step is to calculate the result and create the output. To process the data properly, we will declare two variables in the Calculate command button's Click event procedure. We will use an integer to hold the result of the weight conversion and a string variable to hold the formatted result.

STEP-BY-STEP 9.6

1. Double-click the **Calculate** button and add the following code to declare the necessary local variables.

```
Dim intWeight As Integer
Dim strWeight As String
```

2. Add the following code to set `intWeight` equal to the value in the text box multiplied by the variable `sngPlanetWeight`.

```
'Calculate Weight
intWeight = Fix(sngPlanetWeight * Val(txtWeight.Text))
strWeight = Format(intWeight, "####")
```

3. Add a label box under the GroupBox and name it **lblOutput**. Clear the label box's Text property.

4. Add the following code to the Calculate button's click event procedure to display the results in the Text of the `lblOutput` label.

```
'Display Output
lblOutput.Text = "Your weight on " & strPlanetName _
            & " would be " & strWeight & " pounds."
```

5. Close the Code window and start debugging the program.

6. Enter **150** into the text box.

7. Click the **Jupiter** radio button and click **Calculate**. The answer appears on the form.

8. Click each of the other radio buttons and click **Calculate** to test them. The answer should change each time.

9. Save your changes and leave the project open for the next Step-by-Step.

Using a Form Load Event Procedure

Although our program works, there is still a problem. When the program runs, none of the radio buttons are marked as selected. So if the user fails to click any of the radio buttons and clicks the Calculate button, the program will give no weight and will have no planet name to display.

STEP-BY-STEP 9.7

1. Start debugging the program.

2. Enter **150** into the text box and click **Calculate**. The output displays "Your weight on would be pounds." with no weight or planet name because a radio button was not selected.

3. End the program and leave the project open for the next Step-by-Step.

To correct this, we need to have one of the radio buttons selected by default. Radio buttons have a property that allows you to simulate a user's click from code. By setting the Checked property of a radio button to True, the radio button is selected. In addition, the button's `CheckedChanged` event is triggered. Any code in the `CheckedChanged` event handler will automatically be executed. The following code, for example, will make the Mars radio button the default button.

```
optMars.Checked = True
```

But where can you place the code so that it is executed before the user has the opportunity to click the Calculate button? When a form is loaded and opened by the program, a special event called a *Load event* is triggered. Like other events, you can write an event procedure for the form's Load event.

STEP-BY-STEP 9.8

1. Double-click the form (but not the title bar or one of the controls) displayed on the screen. The Code window opens, displaying the form's Load event procedure.

2. Add the following code to set the Mars radio button as the default when the program is run.
```
optMars.Checked = True
```

3. Start debugging the program. Notice that the Mars radio button is already selected.

4. Enter **123** into the text box and click **Calculate**. The program calculates the weight on Mars.

5. End the program and save the changes to the project.

6. Close the project and leave Visual Basic 2005 open for the next Step-by-Step.

Using Select Case

If statements allow you to program one-way decisions, and `If…Else` statements allow you to program two-way decisions. By nesting `If` statements, you have seen that you can make decisions that branch in more than two paths. Visual Studio 2005, however, provides a statement especially for multi-way decisions: the `Select Case` statement.

In a *Select Case statement*, you specify a variable to test and then list a number of cases for which you want to test. For example, the following code uses a `Select Case` statement to recommend a type of vehicle that should be rented, based on the number of passengers.

```
'Select type of vehicle to rent
Select Case intPassengers
    Case 1 To 2
        lblOutput.Text = "You should rent a compact car."
    Case 3 To 4
        lblOutput.Text = "You should rent a full size car."
    Case 5 To 7
        lblOutput.Text = "You should rent a minivan."
    Case 8 To 15
        lblOutput.Text = "You should rent a 15-passenger van."
    Case Is > 15
        lblOutput.Text = "You should rent a bus."
    Case Else
        lblOutput.Text = "Incorrect data"
End Select
```

The first line in the `Select Case` statement specifies the piece of data that is involved in the decision; in this case, the number of passengers (`intPassengers`). The `Select Case` statement ends with an `End Select` statement. Between the `Select Case` and `End Select` statements are a series of `Case` statements. In this code, most of the `Case` statements specify a range of values. For example, if the value of `intPassengers` is 6, the third `Case` statement will apply because 6 is in the range of 5 to 7.

You can use conditional operators in a `Case` statement as well. Using a conditional operator requires that you include the `Is` keyword. The fifth `Case` statement is an example of the use of a conditional operator. If the value in `intPassengers` is greater than 15, the recommendation is to rent a bus.

Finally, as a default, the code under the `Case Else` statement will be applied if no other `Case` statement catches it first. In this case, the `Case Else` will be triggered if the value is zero or less.

S TEP-BY-STEP 9.9

1. Open **Transportation** from the **step09-09** folder in the data files for this lesson and, if necessary, open **frmMain** from the **Solution Explorer**.

2. Double-click the **OK** button and add the following code to declare an integer variable and set it equal to the value in the text box.

```
Dim intPassengers As Integer
intPassengers = Val(txtPassengers.Text)
```

STEP-BY-STEP 9.9 Continued

3. Add the following `Select Case` statement.

```
'Select type of vehicle to rent
Select Case intPassengers
    Case 1 To 2
        lblOutput.Text = "You should rent a compact car."
    Case 3 To 4
        lblOutput.Text = "You should rent a full size car."
    Case 5 To 7
        lblOutput.Text = "You should rent a minivan."
    Case 8 To 15
        lblOutput.Text = "You should rent a 15-passenger van."
    Case Is > 15
        lblOutput.Text = "You should rent a bus."
    Case Else
        lblOutput.Text = "Incorrect data"
End Select
```

4. Start debugging the program.

5. Key **14** as the number of passengers and click **OK**. The output shown in Figure 9-8 appears.

FIGURE 9-8
The `Select Case` statement selects the output to display

6. Enter other values and click **OK** to verify that each case works correctly.

7. Change the number of passengers to **0** and click **OK**. The output states that you entered incorrect data.

8. End the program and save the changes to the project, then exit Visual Studio 2005.

SUMMARY

In this lesson, you learned:

- `If` statements can be nested to make additional decisions within the code of the `If` statement.

- It is important to indent the code in a nested `If` statement to make the code readable.

- Each `If` statement within a nested `If` statement must end with the `End If` statement.

- Radio buttons appear in groups. Only one radio button in the group can be selected at a time.

- Radio buttons are sometimes called option buttons.

- The first step in creating a group of radio buttons is to create a GroupBox control to contain the radio buttons. The controls within a GroupBox are treated as one unit.

- The Text property of a GroupBox control specifies the text that appears at the top of the GroupBox.

- To associate a radio button with a GroupBox, you must click the RadioButton tool only once and draw the radio button in the GroupBox. If you double-click to create a radio button, it will not associate itself with the GroupBox.

- The Text property of a radio button specifies the text that appears on the label attached to the radio button.

- Coding radio buttons involves using form-level variables that carry values that reflect the selected radio button.

- A form's Load event procedure is executed each time a form is loaded and opened by the program.

- The `Select Case` statement allows you to make multi-way selections. The `Case` statements in a `Select Case` can test a range or use conditional operators.

- Conditional operators in a `Case` statement must include the `Is` keyword.

- As a default, the `Case Else` statement is applied if no other `Case` is true.

VOCABULARY *Review*

Define the following terms:

GroupBox control	Nested `If` statement	Radio buttons
Load event	Option group	Select Case statement

REVIEW *Questions*

TRUE / FALSE

Circle T if the statement is true or F if the statement is false.

T   F   **1.** It is possible to write nested `If` statements in Visual Studio 2005.

T   F   **2.** Only one radio button in a group can be selected.

T   F   **3.** The first radio button you place on a form automatically creates a GroupBox in which you can place other radio buttons.

T   F   **4.** The controls you place inside a GroupBox are treated as one unit.

T   F   **5.** Drawing radio buttons in a GroupBox will automatically associate them with that GroupBox.

T   F   **6.** The first radio button you add to a form will be selected by default when you run the program.

T   F   **7.** Double-clicking on a form will display the (`Declarations`) section of the code for that form.

T   F   **8.** To use a conditional operator in a `Select Case` statement, you must use the keyword `Is`.

T   F   **9.** The `Select Case` statement ends with an `End Select` statement.

T   F   **10.** Code in the `Case Else` section of a `Select Case` statement is executed if no other case matches.

WRITTEN QUESTIONS

Write a brief answer to each of the following questions.

1. Why is it important to properly indent your code when using multi-way selection structures?

2. What is the main difference between radio buttons and check boxes?

3. What is another name for radio buttons?

4. What three steps are involved in creating a group of radio buttons?

5. Which property specifies the text for the label attached to a radio button?

6. What scope should the variables you use to keep track of a user's selection have?

7. How do you change the default selection in a group of radio buttons?

8. What key word is used in a `Case` statement to check for a range of values?

9. What event procedure is triggered when a form is loaded?

10. Where in a `Select Case` statement is the data to be compared specified?

PROJECTS

PROJECT 9-1

1. Start Visual Studio 2005 and open **Final** from the **proj09-01** folder in the data files for this lesson.

2. Create a Boolean form-level variable named **blnExempt**.

3. In the OK `click` event procedure, set `blnExempt` equal to **False**.

4. Add the following code to determine if the student needs to take the final exam.

```
'Determine if final needs to be taken
If Val(txtAverage.Text) >= 90 Then
    If Val(txtAbsences.Text) <= 3 Then
        blnExempt = True
    End If
Else
    If Val(txtAverage.Text) >= 80 Then
        If Val(txtAbsences.Text) <= 1 Then
            blnExempt = True
        End If
    End If
End If
```

5. Add the following code to display the results.

```
'Display Results
If blnExempt = True Then
    lblResult.Text = "You DO NOT need to take the final exam."
Else
    lblResult.Text = "You DO need to take the final exam."
End If
lblResult.Visible = True
```

6. Debug the program using various scores and number of absences to verify that it works correctly.

7. Save the changes to the project and close the project. Leave Visual Studio 2005 open for the next Project.

PROJECT 9-2

1. Open **Animal Years** from the **proj09-02** folder in the data files for this lesson.

2. Add a GroupBox with three radio buttons to the form, as shown in Figure 9-9.

FIGURE 9-9
Add a GroupBox with three radio buttons

3. Use the information shown in Figure 9-9 to key the Text properties of the GroupBox and radio buttons. Name the GroupBox **grpAnimal** and name the radio buttons **optDog, optCow**, and **optMouse**.

4. Add the following code in the (Declarations) section to declare two new variables.

```
Dim strYears As String
Dim sngYears As Single
```

5. Add the following code into the CheckedChanged event procedure of the Dog radio button to calculate the number of Dog years.

```
'Calculate Dog Years
sngYears = (7 * intMonths) / 12
```

6. Add the following code into the CheckedChanged event procedure of the Cow radio button to calculate the number of Cow years.

```
'Calculate Cow Years
sngYears = (5 * intMonths) / 12
```

7. Add the following code into the CheckedChanged event procedure of the Mouse radio button to calculate the number of Mouse years.

```
'Calculate Mouse Years
sngYears = (25 * intMonths) / 12
```

8. Add the following code into the Click event procedure of the cmdCalculate button to display the results.

```
'Display Results
strYears = Format(sngYears, "###.0")
lblOutputAnimalYears.Text = "In animal years, you are " & _
        strYears & " years old."
lblOutputAnimalYears.Visible = True
```

9. Add the following code into the Click event procedure of the cmdMonths command button that will set the Dog radio button to **True**.

```
'Set Dog radio button as default
optDog.Checked= True
```

10. Debug the program and verify that everything works correctly.

11. Save the changes to the project and close the project. Leave Visual Studio 2005 open for the next Project.

PROJECT 9-3

Photocopy businesses charge different amounts depending on how many copies of a page are desired. Write a program that will determine the price per copy based on Table 9-2.

TABLE 9-2
Price per copy costs

NUMBER OF COPIES	PRICE PER COPY
1–200	0.10
201–500	0.08
501–1000	0.06
>1000	0.05

1. Open **Copies** from the **proj09-03** folder in the data files for this lesson.

2. Add the following code to the OK button to declare four different variables and set intNumber equal to the value in the text box.

```
Dim intNumber As Integer
Dim strNumber As String
Dim curTotal As Decimal
Dim strTotal As String
intNumber = Fix(Val(txtCopies.Text))
```

3. Add the `Select Case` statement as follows to determine the total cost.

```
'Determine total cost
Select Case intNumber
     Case 1 To 200
          curTotal = intNumber * 0.1
     Case 201 To 500
          curTotal = intNumber * 0.08
     Case 501 To 1000
          curTotal = intNumber * 0.06
     Case Is > 1000
          curTotal = intNumber * 0.05
     Case Else
          lblOutput.Text = "Incorrect data was entered."
End Select
```

4. Add the following code to display the results.

```
'Display results
If intNumber > 0 Then
     strNumber = intNumber
     strTotal = Format(curTotal, "$#,###.00")
     lblOutput.Text = "The total cost for " & strNumber & _
          " copies is " & strTotal & "."
End If
```

5. Debug the program and verify that everything works correctly with various numbers of copies, including entering a 0 (zero) to generate the incorrect data output.

6. End the program and save the changes to the project, then exit Visual Studio 2005.

CRITICAL *Thinking*

Modify the **Planets** program you created in this lesson so it calculates a person's weight on every planet in the solar system (except Earth). (Resize your form and GroupBox to include the new radio buttons.) Make Mercury the default radio button. Use the conversion factors shown in Table 9-3 for the new planets.

TABLE 9-3
Conversion factors

PLANET	MULTIPLY BY
Mercury	0.37
Neptune	1.12
Venus	0.88
Uranus	1.15

DECISION MAKING

MATCHING

Match the correct term in Column 1 to its description in Column 2.

Column 1	Column 2

  ____ **1.** conditional operators

      A. the event that is triggered when a form is loaded and opened

  ____ **2.** radio buttons

      B. an `If` statement inside another `If` statement

  ____ **3.** load event

      C. a program structure in which the decision is whether to go "one way" or just bypass the code in the `If` statement

  ____ **4.** two-way selection structure

      D. symbols used in making comparisons

  ____ **5.** GroupBox control

      E. radio buttons in a GroupBox

  ____ **6.** nested `If` statement

      F. a container for other controls

  ____ **7.** flowcharts

      G. allows you to execute specified code when the result of a conditional expression is True

  ____ **8.** option group

      H. a group of buttons that can only be selected one at a time

  ____ **9.** one-way selection structure

      I. used to plan and document program code

  ____ **10.** `If` statement

      J. a program structure in which one block of code is executed if the specified conditions are True, or another block of code is executed if the specified conditions are False

WRITTEN QUESTIONS

Write a brief answer to each of the following questions.

1. What type of result does a comparison return?

2. How can you set a check box to be checked by default?

3. How do you label a check box?

4. Why might you use a logical operator?

5. How do you associate an option button with a GroupBox?

6. How do you set the default selection for a group of option buttons?

7. Why might you write a nested If statement?

8. What statement ends the `Select Case` statement?

9. Which case in a `Select Case` statement is the default case?

10. How can you use a conditional operator in a `Case` statement?

PROJECTS

PROJECT 3-1

Write a statement that assigns the word **True** to the Caption property of the label named `lblEqual` if the value in `sngA` is equal to the value in `sngB`.

PROJECT 3-2

Write a statement that warns the user of a division-by-zero error if the value in `intDivisor` is equal to zero.

PROJECT 3-3

Write a statement that presents a message box that says **Value is too high** if `decPrice` is greater than $750 and a message box that says **Value is too low** if `curPrice` is less than $1.

SIMULATIONS

JOB 3-1

Payment plans are often set up as an amount to be paid each month, each year, or on a similar time interval. People often want to calculate their cost per quarter or per year based on their periodic payments. In this simulation, you will finish a program that takes a monthly car insurance payment and lets a user calculate the quarterly or annual payment. You will also allow the user to apply a good-driver discount.

1. Start Visual Studio 2005 and open **Insurance** from the **job03-01** folder in the data files for this lesson.

2. Add a GroupBox with three radio buttons to the form, as shown in Figure U3-1.

FIGURE U3-1
A form with three radio buttons

3. Create a check box under the GroupBox, as shown in Figure U3-1.

4. Use Figure U3-1 to key the Text properties of the GroupBox, radio buttons, and check box. Name the GroupBox **grpMethod**; name the option buttons **optMonth**, **optQuarter**, and **optAnnual**; and name the check box **chkGoodDriver**.

5. Add the following code after the code section generated by Windows Form Designer to declare two new variables.

```
Dim intMultiplier As Integer
Dim strPayment As String
```

6. Add the following code into the CheckedChanged event procedure of the Monthly option button.

```
intMultiplier = 1
strPayment = "monthly"
```

7. Add the following code into the CheckedChanged event procedure of the Quarterly option button.

```
intMultiplier = 3
strPayment = "quarterly"
```

8. Add the following code into the CheckedChanged event procedure of the Annually option button.

```
intMultiplier = 12
strPayment = "annual"
```

9. Add the following code into the Click event procedure of the **OK** command button to declare and initialize three variables, determine whether a discount applies, and display the output.

```
Dim strTotalPayment As String
Dim curTotalPayment As Decimal
Dim curMonthlyPayment As Decimal
curMonthlyPayment = Val(txtPayment.Text)
curTotalPayment = curMonthlyPayment * intMultiplier
'Discount?
If chkGoodDriver.Checked = True Then
    curTotalPayment = curTotalPayment * 0.95
End If
'Display Results
strTotalPayment = Format(curTotalPayment, "$#,###.00")
lblOutput.Text = "Your " & strPayment & " payment will be " _
        & strTotalPayment & "."
```

10. Add the following code into the Form Load event procedure to set the monthly option button as the default.

```
optMonth.Checked = True
```

11. Start debugging the program to verify that it works correctly.

12. Save the changes to the project and close it. Leave Visual Studio 2005 open for the next Job.

JOB 3-2

It is common for a computer to be connected to a device called an uninterruptible power supply (UPS). A UPS is a battery backup that immediately begins supplying power to the computer when a power outage or other power problem occurs. UPSs come in many sizes, which are measured in volt-amps. When you purchase a UPS, you must decide how large a unit is necessary for your system. For example, if you just need time to save your documents and shut down the computer in the event of an outage, you may only need 5 or 10 minutes of power to be provided by the UPS. Some computers, such as network servers, need much more time. In fact, you hope that the power will be restored to normal before the battery backup is exhausted.

In this Job, you will design a program that recommends a UPS to a user based on the number of minutes of backup time required. The program should prompt the user for a number of minutes and use the following select case statement to decide which model UPS to recommend.

```
Select Case intMinutes
    Case 1 To 9
        strModel = "Power 300"
    Case 10 To 15
        strModel = "Power 450"
    Case 16 To 30
        strModel = "Power 650"
    Case 31 To 40
        strModel = "Power 750"
    Case 41 To 60
        strModel = "Power 1000"
    Case Is > 60
        strModel = "See sales representative"
    Case Else
        strModel = "Invalid or incomplete data"
End Select
```

Create the program using your own user interface design and save the project as **UPS Configuration.**

LOOPS AND ARRAYS

Unit 4

Estimated Time for Unit 4: 6 hours

DO LOOPS

What Are Loops?

You have probably noticed that much of the work a computer does is repeated many times. For example, when a computer prints a personalized form letter for each person in a database, the same operation is repeated for each recipient. When a program repeats a group of statements a number of times, the repetition is accomplished using a *loop*. The code required to create a loop is sometimes called an *iteration structure*.

In Visual Studio 2005, there are three kinds of loops. In this lesson, you will learn about the two `Do` loops: the `Do While` and `Do Until` loop. You will learn about `For Next` loops in the next lesson. Both types of `Do` loops repeat a block of code statements a number of times. The *Do While loop* repeats the statements *while* a certain condition is True. The *Do Until loop* repeats the statements *until* a certain condition is True.

Using the Do Loops

Knowing which of the `Do` loops to use is just a matter of experience. Often, the same result can be achieved with either a `Do While` or a `Do Until`. It may come down to a decision of which loop is easier to understand in a specific case.

Both types of Do loops rely on a condition to be either True or False. A loop's condition is similar to the condition used in an If statement. The condition applies a test to determine either a True or False result. Consider the Do While loop in the code below.

```
intValue = 1
Do While intValue < 10
    intValue = intValue + 1
Loop
```

In this code, the variable intValue is assigned the value 1. The Do While loop will repeat the indented statement until intValue is no longer less than 10. The Loop keyword at the end of the code indicates the end of the block of code statements that are included in the loop.

Using Do While

A Do While loop is used when you want a block of code to repeat as long as a condition remains True. For example, suppose you want to write a program that calculates the number of times that a given number can be divided by two before the result of the division is less than 1. A Do While loop can be used in this case. The code below shows a Do While loop that will repeatedly divide a number in half as long as the result of the division is greater than or equal to 1.

```
Do While dblX >= 1
    dblX = dblX / 2
Loop
```

Suppose we want to write a program that counts the number of times the division must occur before the result is no longer greater than or equal to 1. The code below adds a counter to the loop to count the number of times the code in the loop is executed.

```
intCounter = 0
'Divide number
Do While dblX >= 1
    dblX = dblX / 2
    intCounter = intCounter + 1
Loop
```

S TEP-BY-STEP 10.1

1. Start Visual Studio 2005 and open **DoLoop** from the **step10-01** folder in the data files for this lesson. If necessary, open the form.

2. Double-click the **Count** button and add the following code to count the number of times a value can be divided by two before the result is less than one.

```
Dim dblX As Double
Dim intCounter As Integer
'Initialize variables
dblX = Val(txtStart.Text)
```

STEP-BY-STEP 10.1 Continued

```
intCounter = 0
'Divide number
Do While dblX >= 1
    dblX = dblX / 2
    intCounter = intCounter + 1
Loop
'Display Results
lblCounter.Text = intCounter
lblCounter.Visible = True
```

3. Close the Code window and start debugging the program.

4. Key **8** and click **Count**. The program shows that 8 must be divided by 2, four times to obtain a result less than 1, as shown in Figure 10-1.

FIGURE 10-1
The program reports the value of `intCounter`

5. End the program and save your changes. Leave the project open for the next Step-by-Step.

Using Do Until

A Do Until loop is used when you want a block of code to repeat until a condition is no longer true. For example, the program from the previous exercise could easily be rewritten to use a Do Until loop instead of a Do While. Consider the following code.

```
intCounter = 0
Do
    dblX = dblX / 2
    intCounter = intCounter + 1
Loop Until dblX < 1
```

In the code above, the loop uses reverse logic. Instead of repeating as long as the number being divided is greater than or equal to 1, the code repeats until the number being divided becomes less than 1.

S TEP-BY-STEP 10.2

1. Double-click the **Count** button and replace the loop between the comments *Divide number* and *Display Results* with the following code.

```
Do
    dblX = dblX / 2
    intCounter = intCounter + 1
Loop Until dblX < 1
```

Your screen should appear similar to Figure 10-2.

FIGURE 10-2
The Do While loop is replaced with a Do Until loop

```
Form1.vb [Design]   Form1.vb                                          ▾ ✕
⬧ frmDoLoop                              ∨   ▦(Declarations)              ∨
⊟ Public Class frmDoLoop                                                 ▴

⊟      Private Sub txtStart_GotFocus(ByVal sender As Object, ByVal e As Syste
            txtStart.SelectionStart = 0
            txtStart.SelectionLength = Len(txtStart.Text)
       End Sub

⊟      Private Sub cmdCount_Click(ByVal sender As System.Object, ByVal e As S
            Dim dblX As Double
            Dim intCounter As Integer
            'Initialize variables
            dblX = Val(txtStart.Text)
            intCounter = 0
            'Divide number
            Do
                dblX = dblX / 2
                intCounter = intCounter + 1
            Loop Until dblX < 1
            'Display Results
            lblCounter.Text = intCounter
            lblCounter.Visible = True
       End Sub
 End Class                                                               ▾
  ◂         ▥                                               ▸
```

2. Close the Code window and start debugging the program.

3. Key **156** and click **Count**. The number 156 can be divided eight times before the result is less than 1.

4. End the program. Save the project and leave it open for the next Step-by-Step.

Choosing Do While or Do Until

One of the primary differences between the two kinds of Do loops is where the condition is tested. A Do While loop tests the condition at the top of the loop. If the condition is False, the code inside the loop is never executed. The Do Until loop tests the condition at the bottom of the loop. Therefore, in a Do Until loop, the code in the loop is always executed at least once.

The difference between the Do While and Do Until loops is important. For example, the program in Step-by-Step 10.2 actually provides an inaccurate answer in some cases because of the behavior of the Do Until loop. In the following exercise, we will run the Do Until loop again and identify the problem.

STEP-BY-STEP 10.3

1. Start debugging the program.

2. Key **.75** and click **Count**. Notice that the program reports that the division occurred one time, as shown in Figure 10-3. Because the condition is tested at the end of the loop, the instructions in the loop are performed at least once, even though they did not need to be performed. Therefore, the program produced an incorrect result.

FIGURE 10-3
In this case, the Do Until loop did not generate the correct answer

3. End the program and close the project. Leave Visual Studio 2005 open for the next Step-by-Step.

The program that uses the Do Until can be fixed by adding an If statement that causes the loop to be skipped if the value in dblX is already less than 1, as shown.

```
intCounter = 0
If dblX >= 1 Then
    Do
        dblX = dblX / 2
        intCounter = intCounter + 1
    Loop Until dblX < 1
End If
```

Rather than add the If statement to the code, however, most programmers would probably choose to use the Do While loop. A Do Until loop should only be used if you are sure that you want the loop to always execute at least once. A Do While loop will not execute unless the test condition is true before it begins.

Using the InputBox Function

The InputBox function could be considered the opposite of the MsgBox function. Recall that the MsgBox function creates a window to display output. The InputBox function displays a window to ask the user for input. Figure 10-4 shows an example of an input box created with the InputBox function.

FIGURE 10-4
The InputBox function displays a window to prompt the user for information

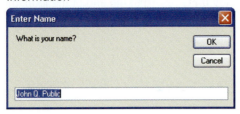

To use the InputBox function, you must supply two strings: the text that will prompt the user and the title for the window's title bar. Supplying a third string—the text that you want to appear in the text box by default—is optional. The InputBox function will return a string value. For example, the following code will create the input box shown in Figure 10-4.

```
strName = InputBox("What is your name?", "Enter Name", _
     "John Q. Public")
```

In the code above, strName is the string variable that will hold the text entered by the user. Inside the parentheses that follow the InputBox keyword, separated by commas, you supply the prompt that the user will see, the title bar text, and the optional default entry.

S TEP-BY-STEP 10.4

1. Open **QuestionBox** from the **step10-04** folder in the data files for this lesson and, if necessary, open the form.

2. Double-click the **Enter Name** button and add the following code to create an input box and display the text entered into it.

```
Dim strName As String
'Input name
strName = InputBox("What is your name?", "Enter Name", _
     "John Q. Public")
'Display name
lblName.Text = strName
```

3. Close the code window and start debugging the program.

STEP-BY-STEP 10.4 Continued

4. Click **Enter Name**. An input box appears on your screen, as shown in Figure 10-5.

FIGURE 10-5
The input box appears when the Enter Name button is clicked

5. Key your name and click **OK**. Your name appears on the form.

6. End the program, save your changes, and close the project. Leave Visual Studio 2005 open for the next Step-by-Step.

Using the InputBox Function within a Do Until Loop

The InputBox function can be used inside a Do Until loop to repeatedly ask the user for data until a specified condition is met. For example, suppose you want to prompt the user for a list of numbers to be averaged. You do not know how many numbers the user will enter. All you know is that when the user enters a zero (0), the program should stop accepting numbers and calculate the average. This can be accomplished by placing a call to the InputBox function inside a Do Until loop.

STEP-BY-STEP 10.5

1. Open **Numbers10** from the **step10-05** folder in the data files for this lesson and, if necessary, open the form.

2. Double-click the **Input Numbers** button and add the following code to declare and initialize the variables in the program.

```
Dim intNumber As Integer
Dim intAverage As Integer
Dim strAverage As String
Dim lngSum As Long
Dim strSum As String
Dim intCounter As Integer
Dim strCounter As String
Dim strDisplayTotal As String
Dim strDisplayAverage As String
Dim strDisplaySum As String
intCounter = 0
lngSum = 0
```

STEP-BY-STEP 10.5 Continued

3. Add the following code to input the numbers entered, perform the calculations, and display the results.

```
'Input Numbers
Do
    intNumber = Val(InputBox("Enter an Integer (0 to Quit):", _
        "Input Number"))
    If (intNumber > 0) Then
        lngSum = lngSum + intNumber
        intCounter = intCounter + 1
    End If
Loop Until (intNumber = 0)
intAverage = lngSum / intCounter
'Store Results
strAverage = Format(intAverage, "###")
strCounter = Format(intCounter, "#####")
strSum = Format(lngSum, "#####")
strDisplayTotal = "Numbers entered:   " & strCounter
strDisplaySum = "Sum of numbers:   " & strSum
strDisplayAverage = "Average of numbers:   " & strAverage
'Display Results
lblTotal.Text = strDisplayTotal
lblSum.Text = strDisplaySum
lblAverage.Text = strDisplayAverage
lblTotal.Visible = True
lblSum.Visible = True
lblAverage.Visible = True
```

4. Close the Code window and start debugging the program.

5. Click **Input Numbers**. An input box appears.

6. Key **10** and click **OK**. The input box reappears because a zero was not entered.

7. Key **20** and click **OK**.

8. Key **30** and click **OK**.

9. Key **0** and click **OK**. Because a zero was entered, the loop stops, and the program displays the results on the form, as shown in Figure 10-6.

FIGURE 10-6
Keying a zero stops the Do Until loop and displays the results

10. End the program, save your changes, and close the project. Leave Visual Studio 2005 open for the next Step-by-Step.

Potential Event Procedure Problems and Solutions

As you already know, when an event is triggered, an event procedure is executed to handle the event. The event procedures you have created up to this point have been relatively short. The computer executes the code in the event procedure so quickly that you may not notice that it takes any time at all. There are, however, some potential problems that could occur which we must consider and prevent, if possible.

In the following sections, we will first look at the potential problems and then look at a solution to these problems using the `Application.DoEvent` statement. This statement introduces another potential error; we will discuss this error and its solution.

Event Procedure Problems

When you begin using loops, an event procedure may occupy several seconds of the computer's time. This could be very noticeable to the user. There is also the potential that an endless loop may occur.

Long Event Procedures

Suppose you have written a program that includes a loop that processes thousands of instructions. While the program is busy executing the loop, the program is unresponsive to other events because it is busy handling the current event.

S TEP-BY-STEP 10.6

1. Open **LongLoop** from the **step10-06** folder in the data files for this lesson and, if necessary, open the form.

2. Double-click the **Go** button and add the following code to create a loop that will count to 500 million.

```
Dim lngCounter As Long
lngCounter = 1
Do While lngCounter < 500000000
    lngCounter = lngCounter + 1
Loop
lblStatus.Text = "Loop Ended"
```

> **Hot Tip**
>
> Depending on the speed of your computer, you may want to adjust the value in the `Do While` loop's condition expression to more or less than 500 million.

3. Close the Code window and start debugging the program.

4. Click **Go**. Notice that the program is unresponsive for a few seconds before the "Loop Ended" message appears.

5. Click **Clear Label**. The label becomes blank.

6. Click **Go**. Again the program becomes unresponsive.

7. End the program and save your changes. Leave the project open for the next Step-by-Step.

Endless Loops

In an *endless loop*, the condition that is supposed to stop the loop from repeating never becomes True. This is usually a programming error. Inside every loop there should be code that causes a change that will eventually lead to the end of the looping. If no such code exists inside the loop, the loop may repeat endlessly.

S TEP-BY-STEP 10.7

1. Double-click the **Go** button.

2. Change the code inside the loop from *lngCounter = lngCounter + 1* to **lngCounter = lngCounter + 0**.

   Your screen should appear similar to Figure 10-7.

   This will create an endless loop because the counter will never reach 500 million.

3. Close the Code window and start debugging the program.

4. Click **Go**. Notice that the computer seems to freeze.

5. Allow a short time to confirm that the computer is not responding, and then click on the **Break All** button of the IDE. The Code window opens and highlights the code where the program stopped.

FIGURE 10-7
Changing the code in the loop, as shown, will produce an endless loop

6. Click **Stop Debugging** to end the program.

7. Change the code in the loop back to **lngCounter = lngCounter + 1**.

8. Close the Code window and do not save your changes. Leave the project open for the next Step-by-Step.

Event Procedure Solutions

There is one statement, the `Application.DoEvents` statement, which can prevent both of the problems illustrated above. This statement, however, introduces the potential for repetitive `Click` event procedures. The following sections illustrate the use of the `Application.DoEvents` statement and explain how to disable a button at the beginning of an event procedure to prevent a repetitive `Click` event.

> ### Computer Concepts
>
> Pressing the **Break All** button while a program is in an endless loop does not end the program. It suspends the execution so that you can see the line of code being executed. It also gives you the opportunity to end the program with the **Stop Debugging** button.

The Application.DoEvents Statement

The `Application.DoEvents` subroutine allows the computer to process other events, even though the current event procedure is not yet complete. By adding the `Application.DoEvents` subroutine inside a loop that may occupy significant processing time, you make it possible to handle other events while the loop is finishing its work. Let's look at the difference the `Application.DoEvents` subroutine makes.

STEP-BY-STEP 10.8

1. Double-click the **Go** button and add **Application.DoEvents()** as the first instruction of the loop, as shown in Figure 10-8.

FIGURE 10-8
Adding the `Application.DoEvents` code allows the computer to process other events while a loop is still taking place

2. Close the Code window and start debugging the program.

3. Click **Go**. The long loop starts again; however, by using `Application.DoEvents`, the computer allows other events to take place. The `Application.DoEvents` subroutine actually slows down the loop, making it take a long time to reach 500 million.

STEP-BY-STEP 10.8 Continued

4. Wait until the loop completes and click **Exit**. The program closes.

Note

The time required to complete the loop will vary between machines.

5. Change the value in the loop condition to **1000000** and run the program again. The event procedure now completes in a shorter amount of time.

6. End the program and save your changes. Leave the project open for the next Step-by-Step.

Preventing Repetitive Click Event Procedures

There is one more thing you should understand about using `Application.DoEvents`. When the `Application.DoEvents.` subroutine is executed, the computer can process whatever other events are waiting to be processed, including the event that is not yet complete. For example, suppose the user clicks a button to begin processing data. If the button's `Click` event procedure includes the `Application.DoEvents` statement, the user could actually click the same button again, causing the same process to begin again. This can have unpredictable and possibly disastrous results.

How do you prevent this from happening? It is a good idea to disable the button at the beginning of the event procedure to prevent the user from clicking the button again until the event processing is completed. Of course, you will want to enable the button again at the end of the procedure. Remember, the purpose of the `Application.DoEvents` subroutine is to allow other events to be processed, not to allow the same event to be processed simultaneously.

STEP-BY-STEP 10.9

1. Double-click the **Go** button and, above the loop, add the following code to disable the Go button.

```
cmdGo.Enabled = False
```

2. Below the loop, add the following code to enable the Go button.

```
cmdGo.Enabled = True
```

3. Close the Code window and start debugging the program.

4. Click **Go**. Notice that the Go button becomes disabled until the loop finishes counting, as shown in Figure 10-9.

FIGURE 10-9
Disabling the Go button prevents the same event procedure from being restarted before it is complete

STEP-BY-STEP 10.9 Continued

5. When the Go button is enabled again, click **Exit**.

6. Save your changes and close the project. Leave Visual Studio 2005 open for the next Step-by-Step.

Using Nested Loops

Like If statements, loops may be nested. It is not uncommon for a program to require a loop within a loop. For example, suppose you have a program that counts from 1 to 1000 on the screen. The program is executing so fast that the first value that appears is 1000. Inside the loop that is doing the counting, you can place another loop that simply slows the computer down.

STEP-BY-STEP 10.10

1. Open **Counter** from the **step10-10** folder in the data files for this lesson and, if necessary, open the form.

2. Start debugging the program and click **Go**. Notice that the program counts to 1000 too quickly to see that it is counting.

3. End the program.

4. Double-click the **Go** button and add the following code between the line *intDelay = 1* and the line *Loop 'End of outer loop.*

```
'Begin nested loop
Do While intDelay <= 100
    Application.DoEvents()
    intDelay = intDelay + 1
Loop 'End of nested loop
```

5. Close the Code window and start debugging the program again. You will be able to watch the numbers increase toward 1000. The Go button is disabled while the event is handled. After the count reaches 1000, the Go button is enabled again.

6. End the program, save your changes, and exit Visual Studio 2005.

SUMMARY

In this lesson, you learned:

■ Much of the work a computer does is repeated many times. This repetition in programs is accomplished using loops.

■ A Do loop condition applies a test to determine either a True or False result. A Do While loop tests the condition at the top of the loop and repeats a group of statements *while* a certain condition is True. A Do Until loop tests the condition at the bottom of the loop and repeats a group of statements *until* a certain condition becomes True. The code in a `Do Until` loop is always executed at least once.

■ The `InputBox` function creates a window that prompts the user for input. To use the `InputBox` function, you supply the text for the prompt, the title for the window's title bar, and the optional default text for the text box.

■ Sometimes, long event procedures can make a program unresponsive to other events.

■ An endless loop is a loop in which the condition that stops the loop is never met. Clicking the Break All button in the IDE will pause a program with an endless loop and will highlight the code where the program stopped.

■ The `Application.DoEvents` subroutine allows the program to process other events while an event procedure is executing.

■ Loops can be nested in the same way that `If` statements are nested.

VOCABULARY *Review*

Define the following terms:

`Do Until` loop	Endless loop	Loop
`Do While` loop	Iteration structure	

REVIEW *Questions*

TRUE / FALSE

Circle T if the statement is true or F if the statement is false.

T F **1.** A loop will repeat a specified block of code a number of times.

T F **2.** Both types of `Do` loops rely on a condition to be either True or False.

T F **3.** A `Do While` loop tests the condition at the bottom of the loop.

T F **4.** In a `Do Until` loop, the code in the loop is executed at least once.

T F **5.** The `MsgBox` function displays a window to ask the user for input.

T F **6.** In an endless loop, the condition that will stop the loop from repeating never becomes true.

T F **7.** Unlike `If` statements, loops cannot be nested.

T F **8.** Using `Application.DoEvents` prevents the computer from running multiple programs.

T F **9.** You can use the Break All button to pause a program that has entered an endless loop.

T F **10.** A loop can contain only one statement.

WRITTEN QUESTIONS

Write a brief answer to each of the following questions.

1. What is another name for the code required to create a loop?

2. What is the main difference between a Do While loop and a Do Until loop?

3. What keyword marks the end of the block of code contained within a loop?

4. Where is the condition of a Do Until loop tested?

5. What are the three parameters of the InputBox function?

6. What is the purpose of using the Application.DoEvents statement?

7. How can you prevent the Application.DoEvents subroutine from allowing a routine to be executed a second time before the first routine is completed?

8. How many times will the following loop be executed?

```
intCount = 0
Do While intCount <= 5
    intCount = intCount + 1
Loop
```

9. How many times will the following loop be executed?

```
intCount = 7
Do While Count < 5
    intCount = intCount - 1
Loop
```

10. How many times will the following loop be executed?

```
intCount = 9
Do
    intCount = intCount - 1
Loop Until intCount <= 5
```

PROJECTS

PROJECT 10-1

1. Start Visual Studio 2005 and open **Multiply** from the **proj10-01** folder in the data files for this lesson. If necessary, open the form.

2. Add the following code to the **Enter Number** button to create two input boxes.

```
Dim intNumber As Integer
Dim intTimes As Integer
Dim intCounter As Integer
Dim lngTimeWaster As Long
intCounter = 0
intNumber = Val(InputBox("Enter a number:", "Enter Number"))
intTimes = Val(InputBox("Multiply number by 2 how many times?", _
        "Multiply"))
```

3. Add the following code to create a loop that will multiply `intNumber` by 2, for `intTimes` number of times.

```
Do While intCounter < intTimes
    Application.DoEvents()
    intNumber = intNumber * 2
    lblAnswer.Text = intNumber
    lngTimeWaster = 0
    'Slow program
    Do While lngTimeWaster < 500000
        lngTimeWaster = lngTimeWaster + 1
    Loop
    intCounter = intCounter + 1
Loop
```

4. Close the Code window and start debugging the program to verify that it works correctly. (Remember that the maximum integer value is 2,147,483,647.)

5. Save your changes and close the project. Leave Visual Studio 2005 open for the next Project.

PROJECT 10-2

1. Open **Ball** from the **proj10-02** folder in the data files for this lesson and, if necessary, open the form.

2. Add the following code to the **Go** button to create an input box that will determine the number of times the ball will bounce.

```
Dim intBounces As Integer
Dim intCounter As Integer
intCounter = 0
'Input bounces
intBounces = Val(InputBox _
    ("How many times should the ball bounce back and forth?", _
    "Input Bounces"))
```

3. Add the following code below the code for the input box to move the ball on the form.

```
'Bounce ball
Do
    Application.DoEvents()
    'Move ball right
    Do While lblBall.Left < 300
        Application.DoEvents()
        lblBall.Left = lblBall.Left + 1
    Loop
    'Move ball left
    Do While lblBall.Left > 0
        Application.DoEvents()
        lblBall.Left = lblBall.Left - 1
    Loop
    intCounter = intCounter + 1
Loop Until intCounter = intBounces
```

4. Close the Code window and start debugging the program.

5. Click **Go** and enter data into the input box to verify that the ball will bounce back and forth across the screen.

6. End the program and save your changes. Leave the project open for the next Project.

PROJECT 10-3

1. If necessary, open the **Ball** program from the previous Project. Open the form.

2. Double-click the **Go** button and create an integer variable named `intTimeWaster`.

3. Add the following code within each loop that moves the ball to slow down the speed of the ball.

```
'Slow the speed of the ball
intTimeWaster = 0
Do While intTimeWaster < 1000
    Application.DoEvents()
    intTimeWaster = intTimeWaster + 1
Loop
```

4. Close the Code window and start debugging the program to verify that the speed of the ball has decreased.

5. End the program and save your changes, then exit Visual Studio 2005.

CRITICAL *Thinking*

Extend the **Numbers10** program you worked with in Step-by-Step 10.5 to do additional calculations. The program should also find the largest and smallest numbers entered by the user. (*Hint:* Set the largest number variable equal to the smallest possible integer, and set the smallest number variable equal to the largest possible integer.)

LIST BOXES, FOR NEXT LOOPS, AND LABEL SETTINGS

Using the ListBox Control

Label boxes are very useful to display an individual piece of information, but often you have a list of items that you need to display. Visual Basic includes the ***ListBox control***, which enables you to display a list of items to the user. Information is added to a `ListBox` using the `Items.Add` method. The following statement adds the message "First Item" to a list box named ListBox1.

```
ListBox1.Items.Add("First Item")
```

Any object type can be added to a list box, but you will mostly be using strings.

The items added to a `ListBox` object can be removed all at once by using the `Items.Clear` method. This can be useful when you want to add a completely new set of items to a list.

In the following exercise, you will create a simple program that uses the `Items.Add` and `Items.Clear` methods with a `ListBox` object.

STEP-BY-STEP 11.1

1. Start Visual Studio 2005 and create a new Visual Basic Windows Application. Name it **Sample ListBox**.

2. Create one command button near the bottom of the form. Name the button **cmdDisplay** and change the text property to **Display**.

STEP-BY-STEP 11.1 Continued

3. Create a `ListBox` on the form and name it **lstDisplay**. If necessary, resize the `ListBox` so it appears similar in size to Figure 11-1. (Note that the text shown will not appear in your list box yet.)

4. Add the following code to the `Click` event procedure of the Display button:

```
lstDisplay.Items.Add("This text was added to the list box.")
lstDisplay.Items.Add(" ") 'This statement inserts a blank line
        'on the list.
lstDisplay.Items.Add("The text appears at the left " _
        & "edge of the list box,")
lstDisplay.Items.Add("beginning at the top.")
```

5. Close the Code window and start debugging the program.

6. Click **Display**. The text appears in the window, as shown in Figure 11-1.

FIGURE 11-1
The `Items.Add` method adds lines of text to the `ListBox` object

7. Click **Display** again. The text displays again, below the original text.

8. Click **Display** several more times. The text extends below the bottom of the list box, but a scroll bar appears on the right side of the list box.

9. Close the program.

10. Add the following code to the top of the Display button's `Click` event procedure.

```
lstDisplay.Items.Clear()
```

11. Close the Code window and start debugging the program again. Click **Display** several times to verify that the `Items.Clear` statement is clearing the window each time the button is clicked.

12. Close the program.

13. Close the project, but leave Visual Studio 2005 open for the next Step-by-Step.

Using For Next Loops

The Do loops that you used in Lesson 10 repeat while a certain condition is True or until a certain condition is True. Sometimes, however, you simply want to repeat a block of code a specific number of times. For example, you might have some code that you would like to repeat ten times. You can do this with a Do While loop, using code like the following.

```
intCounter = 1
Do While intCounter <= 10
    'code that you want to repeat ten times would go here
    intCounter = intCounter + 1
Loop
```

There is nothing wrong with using a Do While loop like the one above. However, Visual Basic provides another kind of loop, the *For Next loop*, which is specifically designed for repeating a block of code a specific number of times. Using a For Next loop, the same task provided by the Do While loop shown above can be achieved with code that is simpler and easier to read, like in the next example.

```
For intCounter = 1 To 10
    'code that you want to repeat ten times would go here
Next
```

A For Next loop always begins with a For statement and ends with a Next statement. The statements between the For and Next statements are repeated the number of times specified in the For Next loop.

For Next loops always involve a Counter variable. This variable is usually an integer. While the loop is repeating, the value of the Counter variable automatically changes with each iteration of the loop.

> **Computer Concepts**
>
> In Visual Studio 2005 and Visual Studio .NET 2003, a loop control variable can be declared in the For statement. For example:
> ```
> For intCnt as Integer = 1 to 10
> ```

STEP-BY-STEP 11.2

1. Open **ForNext** from the **step11-02** folder in the data files for this lesson and, if necessary, open the form.

2. Add the following code to the Count by One button's click event procedure.

```
Dim intCounter As Integer

lstNumbers.Items.Clear()

For intCounter = 1 To 10
    lstNumbers.Items.Add(intCounter)
Next
```

3. Close the Code window and start debugging the program.

STEP-BY-STEP 11.2 Continued

4. Click **Count by One**. The `For Next` loop displays the numbers 1 through 10 in the window, as shown in Figure 11-2.

FIGURE 11-2
The `For Next` loop causes the numbers 1 to 10 to appear in the list box

5. Close the program and save your changes. Leave the project open for the next Step-by-Step.

Using the Step Keyword to Count Forward

Another useful feature of the `For Next` loop is the ability to specify the way the `For Next` loop counts. The *Step keyword* is used to cause the loop counter to count by an increment other than one. For example, the `For Next` loop that follows will count from 2 to 10 by twos.

```
For intCounter = 2 To 10 Step 2
    lstNumbers.Items.Add(intCounter)
Next
```

STEP-BY-STEP 11.3

1. Add the following code to the Count by Two button's `Click` event procedure.

```
Dim intCounter As Integer

lstNumbers.Items.Clear()

For intCounter = 2 To 10 Step 2
    lstNumbers.Items.Add(intCounter)
Next
```

2. Close the Code window and start debugging the program.

STEP-BY-STEP 11.3 Continued

3. Click **Count by Two**. The counter counts by two, as shown in Figure 11-3.

FIGURE 11-3
The Step keyword can be used to cause the loop to count by two

4. Close the program and save your changes, but leave the project open for the next Step-by-Step.

Using the Step Keyword to Count Backward

Would you like to count backwards? The Step keyword will allow you to do that, too. Just use a negative value after the Step keyword. If you use a negative Step value, make sure that the value on the left of the To keyword is greater than the value to the right of the To keyword. For example, in the code below, the For Next loop counts from 10 to 0.

```
For intCounter = 10 To 0 Step -1
    lstNumbers.Items.Add(intCounter)
Next
```

STEP-BY-STEP 11.4

1. Add the following code to the Count Down button's Click event procedure.

```
Dim intCounter As Integer

lstNumbers.Items.Clear()

For intCounter = 10 To 1 Step -1
    lstNumbers.Items.Add(intCounter)
Next
```

2. Close the code window and start debugging the program.

3. Click **Count Down**. The counter counts backwards from 10, as shown in Figure 11-4.

FIGURE 11-4
The Step keyword can be used to cause the loop to count backwards

4. Close the program and save your changes. Close the project, but leave Visual Studio 2005 open for the next Step-by-Step.

Nesting For Next Loops

For Next loops can be nested within other For Next loops or within Do loops. When you nest For Next loops, each nested loop must be completely contained within the outer loop. For example, in the code below, two For Next loops are nested within an outer For Next loop.

```
For intOuter = 1 To 10
    For intInner1 = 1 To 2
        'Code goes here
    Next
    For intInner2 = 1 To 4
        'Code goes here
    Next
Next
```

The indentation of the code helps you to identify which Next statement is paired with each For statement. However, there is an optional feature that can be used to make code for nested loops clearer. Following the Next keyword, you can specify which loop the Next keyword is ending by including the counter variable name. For example, the nested loops just shown could be coded as follows to increase readability.

```
For intOuter = 1 To 10
    For intInner1 = 1 To 2
        'Code goes here
    Next intInner1
    For intInner2 = 1 To 4
        'Code goes here
    Next intInner2
Next intOuter
```

In Step-by-Step 11.5, you will create a set of nested loops that will generate a pattern of the letters A, B, and C in a window. You may have noticed in your use of the `Items.Add` method that each item is added to a new line of the list box. In the code in the next Step-by-Step, you will use concatenation to build a string to add to the list box.

S TEP-BY-STEP 11.5

1. Open **NestedFor** from the **step11-05** folder in the data files for this lesson and, if necessary, open the form. The Clear List and Exit buttons have already been coded for you.

2. Add the following code to create the `click` event procedure for the Begin Loop button.

```
'Declare loop counters
Dim intA As Integer
Dim intB As Integer
Dim intC As Integer
Dim strTemp As String

'Build the character pattern
For intA = 1 To 4
    strTemp = strTemp & "A"
    For intB = 1 To 3
        strTemp = strTemp & "B"
        For intC = 1 To 2
            strTemp = strTemp & "C"
        Next intC
    Next intB
    ' Add the string to the list box
    lstOutput.Items.Add(strTemp)
Next intA
```

3. Try to predict the pattern that will be created by the nested loops. Write your prediction on paper.

4. Close the Code window and start debugging the program.

5. Click **Begin Loop**. The pattern appears at the top of the window. Was your prediction correct? Were you expecting it to look like Figure 11-5?

FIGURE 11-5
The nested loops display four rows of a growing pattern

STEP-BY-STEP 11.5 Continued

6. Click the **Begin Loop** button again. The pattern is repeated below the first pattern.

7. Click the **Clear List** button. The list box is now empty.

8. Close the program and save your changes. Close the project and leave Visual Studio 2005 open for the next Step-by-Step.

Changing Label Font Settings

When you create label controls on forms, you can use the Font property of the label control to select the font, style, and size. You can make labels appear in any font installed on your computer. You should use standard fonts in your programs. If a font that you use in your program is not installed on other computers, the system will substitute another font, and your program may not look the same as you intended it to look.

To set the Font property of a label, select the label and click the ellipsis (...) in the Font property field in the Properties list. The Font dialog box appears, similar to that shown in Figure 11-6.

FIGURE 11-6
The Font dialog box allows you to set the font, style, and size of a label

STEP-BY-STEP 11.6

1. Choose **New** > **Project**, or **New Project**, from the **File** menu and create a new Visual Basic Windows Application. Name it **LabelFont**.

2. Create a new label control on the form.

3. Name the label **lblLarge** and set the Text to **Large Label**.

STEP-BY-STEP 11.6 Continued

4. With the label control selected, click the **Font** property field in the Properties list. Then click the ellipsis (**...**) that appears at the end of the field. The Font dialog box appears.

5. Select **Arial** as the Font, **Bold Italic** as the Font style, and **18** for the Size. If your computer does not have Arial installed, select another font.

6. Click **OK**. The label's text appears in the larger font. Because the label control's AutoSize property is set to True, the label is resized, as shown in Figure 11-7.

FIGURE 11-7
The label appears in the new font

7. Save and close the project, then exit Visual Studio 2005.

 Programming Skills

GOOD PRACTICE FOR FOR NEXT STATEMENTS

There is no set number of lines that may appear between the For and Next statements. Good coding practice, however, suggests that any section of code that does not fit on one or at most two screens should be examined to see if it could be broken up into one or more new subroutines. Long strings of code are difficult to maintain and to debug. If the contents of a loop cannot be examined easily, there is always a greater possibility of logic errors.

SUMMARY

In this lesson, you learned:

■ Visual Basic 2005 includes a `ListBox` control for displaying lists of information. The `Items.Add` method adds items to a `ListBox` control. The `Items.Clear` method removes all the entries in a `ListBox` control.

■ A `For Next` loop is specifically designed for repeating a block of code a specific number of times.

■ A `For Next` loop always begins with a `For` statement and ends with a `Next` statement. The statements between the `For` and `Next` statements are repeated the number of times specified in the `For Next` loop.

■ `For Next` loops always involve a `Counter` variable.

■ If you want a `For Next` loop to count by an increment other than 1, you can use the `Step` keyword. The `Step` keyword can also be used to make a `For Next` loop count backwards.

■ `For Next` loops can be nested.

■ Indenting your code can help make nested `For Next` loops easier to read. You can also use `Next` statements that specify the counter variable of the loop.

■ You can use the Font property to change the font, style, and size of a label.

VOCABULARY *Review*

Define the following terms:

`For Next` loop	`ListBox` control	Step keyword

REVIEW *Questions*

TRUE / FALSE

Circle T if the statement is true or F if the statement is false.

T   F   1. A `ListBox` can only hold one piece of information.

T   F   2. A `Do While` loop cannot be used to repeat a block of code a specific number of times.

T   F   3. A `For Next` loop always begins with a `For` statement and ends with a `Next` statement.

T   F   4. A `For Next` loop always involves a `Counter` variable.

T   F   **5.** You cannot count backwards with a `For Next` loop.

T   F   **6.** When `For Next` loops are nested, each nested loop must be completely contained within the outer loop.

T   F   **7.** The loop control variable must always be named in the `For` statement and the `Next` statement.

T   F   **8.** A label's Font property can be used to control its appearance on a form.

T   F   **9.** A `ListBox` cannot be emptied once information has been placed in it.

T   F   **10.** A `ListBox` always has a slider bar.

WRITTEN QUESTIONS

Write a brief answer to each of the following questions.

1. What types of objects can be added to a `ListBox`?

2. What statement or method is used to add information to a `ListBox`?

3. How can multiple pieces of information be added to a single line in a `ListBox`?

4. For what purpose is the `For Next` loop specifically designed?

5. What keyword allows you to count by an increment other than 1 when used with a `For Next` loop?

6. Why might you include a `Counter` variable name after the `Next` statement of a `For Next` loop?

7. What are three appearance attributes that can be changed in a Font dialog box?

8. Where is the loop control variable initialized for a `For Next` loop?

9. How many lines of code may be between the `For` and `Next` statements?

10. What fonts can be used in a label box?

PROJECTS

PROJECT 11-1

1. Start Visual Studio 2005 and open **NameProject** from the **proj11-01** folder in the data files for this lesson. If necessary, open the form.

2. Add the following code to the OK button so a Print statement will display on the form using the name that is entered in the text box.

```
lstMessage.Items.Clear()
lstMessage.Items.Add("Hello " & txtName.Text & "!")
lstMessage.Items.Add(" ")
lstMessage.Items.Add("How are you today?")
```

3. Close the Code window and start debugging the program.

4. Key your first name and click **OK** to verify that the program works.

5. Close the program and save the changes. Close the project and leave Visual Studio 2005 open for the next Project.

PROJECT 11-2

1. Open **ForNextLoops** from the **proj11-02** folder in the data files for this lesson and, if necessary, open the form.

2. Add the following code to the Count by Three button.

```
Dim intCounter As Integer
lstCounter.Items.Clear()
For intCounter = 3 To 21 Step 3
    lstCounter.Items.Add(intCounter)
Next
```

3. Add the following code to the Count Down by Four button.

```
Dim intCounter As Integer
lstCounter.Items.Clear()
For intCounter = 24 To 0 Step −4
    lstCounter.Items.Add(intCounter)
Next
```

4. Close the Code window and start debugging the program.

5. Before clicking each button, try to determine what the output is going to be.

6. Click both buttons to verify whether you were correct.

7. Close the program and save your changes. Close the project and leave Visual Studio 2005 open for the next Project.

PROJECT 11-3

1. Open the **QuestionBox** program you worked with in Lesson 10. (If you do not have this program completed, ask your instructor for a program.)

2. Find the lblName label in the Property window. Change the font size to **12** and change the font style to **Bold**. Change the AutoSize value to **false**. If necessary, resize the label so that the text will fit.

3. Start debugging the program.

4. Enter data into the input box and notice how, when you click OK, the font size and style of the name on the form has changed.

5. End the program and save your changes. Close the project and leave Visual Studio 2005 open for the next Project.

PROJECT 11-4

1. Open **Pattern** from the **proj11-04** folder in the data files for this lesson and, if necessary, open the form.

2. Add the following code for the Create Pattern button to create a pattern using the letters A, B, and C.

```
'Declare loop counters
Dim intA As Integer
Dim intB As Integer
Dim intC As Integer

'Declare a working string variable
Dim strOutput As String

'Create a blank line in the list box
lstPattern.Items.Add("")
'Print the character pattern
For intA = 1 To 3
        strOutput += "A"
        For intB = 1 To 4 Step 2
                strOutput += "B"
        Next intB
        For intC = 3 To 9 Step 3
                strOutput += "C"
        Next intC
Next intA
lstPattern.Items.Add(strOutput)
lstPattern.Items.Add("    --- End ---")
```

3. Close the Code window and start debugging the program.

4. Try to determine what the output is going to be, then click **Create Pattern** to verify if you are correct. (ABBCCC three times)

5. Close the program, save your changes, and exit Visual Studio 2005.

CRITICAL*Thinking*

Create a program that builds a triangle composed of lines in a list box by using nested loops. The program should accept a number from the user that says how many lines the triangle should have. The first line in the list box would have one character, the second line two characters, and so on until the triangle is complete. Figure 11-8 shows what a solution might look like.

FIGURE 11-8
Sample solution for Activity 11-1

ARRAYS

OBJECTIVES

Upon completion of this lesson, you should be able to:

■ Declare an array.

■ Enter information into an array.

■ Access the information in an array.

■ Use loops with arrays.

■ Use parallel arrays.

Estimated Time: 2 hours

VOCABULARY

Array

Element

Index

Initialization list

Lower bound

Parallel array

Subscript

Upper bound

Zero-based array

Declaring and Accessing Arrays

In previous lessons, every individual piece of information had its own variable to hold it. Sometimes we have lots of information that would be easier to handle as a group. Within that group there may be several pieces of information that are the same type of information (for example, they are all grades), but there are many values. In this lesson, you will learn how to use arrays to gather and manipulate different pieces of information of the same type.

We will start by declaring individual variables for each piece of information. Then we will learn how to set up an array to allow us to deal with that information in a much easier way.

Declaring a Variable

Imagine that you have a set of very similar data you need to store or process. For example, suppose you have the grades that a class of 10 students achieved on a test. One way you can write a program to store and average the grades is to declare a variable for each student's grade, as you learned to do in previous lessons. As you will see in the next Step-by-Step, this approach works, but is not very convenient or flexible.

STEP-BY-STEP 12.1

1. Start Visual Studio 2005 and open **TestGrades** from the **step12-01** folder in the data files for this lesson and, if necessary, open the form.

2. Enter the following code in the (Declarations) section.

```
' Declare ten variables to hold grades
Dim Grade1 As Integer
Dim Grade2 As Integer
Dim Grade3 As Integer
Dim Grade4 As Integer
Dim Grade5 As Integer
Dim Grade6 As Integer
Dim Grade7 As Integer
Dim Grade8 As Integer
Dim Grade9 As Integer
Dim Grade10 As Integer
```

3. Add the following code to the `click` event procedure of the Input Grades button.

```
' Use input boxes to get the grades for each student
Grade1 = InputBox("Enter grade 1", "Grade Entry", "100")
Grade2 = InputBox("Enter grade 2", "Grade Entry", "100")
Grade3 = InputBox("Enter grade 3", "Grade Entry", "100")
Grade4 = InputBox("Enter grade 4", "Grade Entry", "100")
Grade5 = InputBox("Enter grade 5", "Grade Entry", "100")
Grade6 = InputBox("Enter grade 6", "Grade Entry", "100")
Grade7 = InputBox("Enter grade 7", "Grade Entry", "100")
Grade8 = InputBox("Enter grade 8", "Grade Entry", "100")
Grade9 = InputBox("Enter grade 9", "Grade Entry", "100")
Grade10 = InputBox("Enter grade 10", "Grade Entry", "100")
```

4. Add the following code to the `click` event procedure of the Calculate Average button.

```
' Declare variable for the total and the average
Dim sglTotal As Single
Dim sglAverage As Single

' Add all the individual grades to get a total
sglTotal = Grade1 + Grade2 + Grade3 + Grade4 + Grade5 _
    + Grade6 + Grade7 + Grade8 + Grade9 + Grade10
' Calculate the average
sglAverage = sglTotal / 10

' Display the average grade
lblAverage.Text = sglAverage
lblAveragelbl.Visible = True
lblAverage.Visible = True
```

5. Start debugging the program.

STEP-BY-STEP 12.1 Continued

6. Click **Input Grades** and enter the following values.

75

80

90

100

100

95

85

70

60

100

7. Click **Calculate Average**. The average is calculated and displayed using label boxes, as shown in Figure 12-1.

FIGURE 12-1
The average grade is displayed in label boxes

8. Stop debugging the program and save the project. Close the project, but leave Visual Studio 2005 open for the next Step-by-Step.

Difficulties with Using Variables

This program works, but there are several difficulties with it. For one thing, it is very tedious to enter all these variables. It is very easy to make a mistake by using the same variable name twice or leaving a number out completely. Also consider that, as problematic as ten grades can be, it would be that much worse for 30 grades, or 100 grades. It would be almost impossible to write a program this way for 1000 grades. Fortunately there is a better way—using a data structure called an array.

Declaring Arrays

An *array* allows you to refer to a series of variables by the same name and to use a number, called an *index* or *subscript*, to tell them apart. You will notice that the variable names we used in the last Step-by-Step differ from each other only by the number at the end of the name. Indexes or subscripts are very similar to those numbers, except that the syntax for using them is a little different.

Visual Studio 2005 arrays are referred to as *zero-based arrays* because the index values start at zero. The number of elements in the array is always the upper bound (explained below) plus one, because the zero element can be used to store information.

Like variables, arrays must be declared. As with other variables, you declare the name and type of an array. An array, however, also has additional information that must be declared.

■ The number of values in the array must be declared. Each value in the array is called an *element* of the array.

■ When an array is declared, you specify the upper bound of the array. The *upper bound* is the largest index value that can be used to access an element of the array. The *lower bound*, the smallest index value that can be used to access an element of an array, is always zero.

The upper bound of an array is enclosed in parentheses after the name of the variable. The following declaration declares an array with 12 elements.

```
Dim intMonth(11) As Integer    ' Reserves 12 elements -- (0) through (11)
```

The length of an array is limited to the maximum value of a Long data type, which is 9,223,372,036,854,775,807. Arrays that do not fit into memory will still work, but will be much slower than smaller arrays.

An array can also be declared with a list of initial values called an *initialization list*. If a list of values is used, the upper bound is not specified. Visual Studio 2005 will set the upper bound based on the number of elements in the initialization list.

The initialization list follows the type declaration and an equal sign. The list is enclosed in a set of curly braces ({ }). The following code declares a string array with the names of the months. It has 12 elements with the lower bound of zero holding "January" and the upper bound of 11 holding "December".

```
Dim strMonth() As String = {"January", "February", "March", "April", "May",
"June", "July", "August", _
   "September", "October", "November", "December"}
```

STEP-BY-STEP 12.2

1. Start Visual Studio 2005 and open **Months** from the **step12-02** folder in the data files for this lesson. Open the form, if necessary.

2. Enter the following code in the `Click` event procedure for the Display command button.

```
' Declare a string array with the names of the months
Dim strMonth() As String = {"January", "February", "March", "April", _
   "May", "June", "July", "August", _
   "September", "October", "November", "December"}
```

3. Save the project and leave Visual Studio open for the next Step-by-Step.

Entering and Accessing the Elements in an Array

After an array is declared, the program must be able to place information into the array and get information from the array. The index, or subscript, is used to identify the element to be processed. The index is specified inside a set of parentheses that follow the name of the array. For example, the following code copies the fifth element in an array into the text property of a label box.

```
lblMonth.Text = strMonth(5)
```

The index can also be specified using a variable or an equation, provided that the result is an integer value that is lower than or equal to the upper bound of the array. The following code copies the sixth element of an array into a label box.

```
intMonth = 5
lblMonth.Text = strMonth(intMonth + 1)
```

However you specify the index, it must be a value between zero and the upper bound. Visual Studio 2005 will give you an error message if you try to use an index below zero or greater than the upper bound. Figure 12-2 shows the message that will appear if a bad index is attempted.

FIGURE 12-2
An index outside the bounds of an array returns an error

STEP-BY-STEP 12.3

1. Enter the following code in the `click` event procedure for the Display command button underneath the array declaration you entered in the previous Step-by-Step.

```
' Declare an integer value to use as an index
Dim intMonth As Integer

' Get the month number from the text box
intMonth = Val(txtMonth.Text)

' Display the name of the month
lblMonth.Text = strMonth(intMonth)
```

STEP-BY-STEP 12.3 Continued

2. Start debugging the program and click **Display**. January should be displayed as the name of the month, as shown in Figure 12-3.

FIGURE 12-3
The name of the "zero" month is displayed

3. Enter **12** in the text box and click **Display**. An error should be displayed.

4. Click **Stop Debugging** from the Debug menu of the IDE.

5. Save the project and leave Visual Studio open for the next Step-by-Step.

Making an Array User-Friendly

The previous Step-by-Step demonstrates two important issues of which you should be aware when working with arrays. The most obvious of these is that it is important to trap errors when using arrays. Before an index is used with an array, the program should verify that the index is in the allowable range of indexes.

The second issue is that a zero-based array does not always fit with the way users are accustomed to thinking. Most people do not think of January as month zero or December as month 11. Sometimes a programmer will want to hide the actual way information is stored from the user to make the program easier to use. This can be done by allowing users to enter values in the way they think of the data and then having the program add or subtract numbers to correctly index into the array.

STEP-BY-STEP 12.4

1. Replace the code in your **Months** program that gets the index from the text box with the following code.

```
' Get the month number from the text box
' Subtract one to match zero-based array
intMonth = Val(txtMonth.Text) - 1
```

2. Add the following code to check that the user has entered a valid month number.

```
If intMonth < 0 Or intMonth > 11 Then
    MessageBox.Show("Months must be between 1 and 12")
    Exit Sub
End If
```

Your program should look like Figure 12-4.

STEP-BY-STEP 12.4 Continued

FIGURE 12-4
Program modified for range checking

3. Start debugging the program. Test your program with numbers that are between one and twelve as well as with numbers that are outside the range.

4. Stop debugging the program and save the project. Close the project, but leave Visual Studio open for the next Step-by-Step.

> **Did You Know?**
>
> We could have set up our month array with an empty element in the first, or zero, position. This would have given us 13 elements, but elements one through 12 would have matched user expectations. Then we would want to make sure that we do not allow the user to display the zero element.

Array Methods and Properties

All arrays have a number of methods and properties that make using them easier. The Length property is very useful when an array is declared with an initialization list. The Length property returns the number of elements in an array. Remember that the number of elements is one more than the upper bound. If the length of an array is 20, that means the upper bound is 19. The following code adds the elements of an array to a list box.

```
For intIndex = 0 To strNames.Length - 1
    lstStudent.Items.Add(strNames(intIndex))
Next
```

The GetLowerBound and GetUpperBound methods return integers representing the lower and upper bounds of an array. The following code checks to make sure that an index value is within the range of indexes for the strNames array.

```
If intIndex >= strNames.GetLowerBound(0) And _
intIndex <= strNames.GetUpperBound(0) Then
    ' Process index value
End If
```

Arrays can be passed to subroutines as parameters. Subroutines that accept arrays often use the Length property and `GetLowerBound` and `GetUpperBound` methods to determine how to process these arrays. By using these features of arrays, programmers do not have to know the size of an array when they write the subroutine. We will be using this in a later Step-by-Step.

Using Loops with Arrays

One of the great advantages of arrays is that they can be easily used with loops. A loop cannot process a group of variables with different names, but a loop control variable can be used as an index to process the values in an array.

There are several common ways that arrays and loops are used together.

■ A loop can be used to apply the same process to each element in an array. For example, a loop can be used to set each element in an array to a specific value.

■ A loop can be used to prompt for input for each element in an array and set its value.

■ An array can be searched by using an `if` statement in a loop that compares each element of the array with a specific value.

Programs often use several loops to apply different processes to an array. For example, one loop may calculate an average value, and a second loop may place the values that are above average into a list box.

STEP-BY-STEP 12.5

1. Open the **TestGrades** project that you saved in Step-by-Step 12.1. Open the form, if necessary.

2. Replace the ten variable declarations in the (Declarations) section with the following code. (To simplify usage of the array, we will declare an array of 0 to 10 and ignore the zero (0) element.)

```
' Declare an array to hold grades
Dim Grade(10) As Integer
```

3. Replace the code in the `click` event procedure for the Input Grades command button with the following code.

```
' Declare an index variable
Dim intIndex As Integer

' Use input boxes to get the grades for each student
For intIndex = 1 To 10
    Grade(intIndex) = InputBox("Enter grade " & intIndex, "Grade Entry", "100")
Next intIndex
```

4. Add the following declaration to the `click` event procedure for the Calculate Average command button.

```
Dim intIndex As Integer
```

STEP-BY-STEP 12.5 Continued

5. Replace the code in the `click` event procedure for the Calculate Average command button (which calculates the total of the grades) with the following code.

```
' Add all the individual grades to get a total
For intIndex = 1 To 10
   sglTotal += Grade(intIndex)
Next intIndex
```

Your program should now look like Figure 12-5.

FIGURE 12-5
Updated program code

6. Start debugging the program. Click **Input Grades** and enter the following values.

75

80

90

100

100

95

85

70

60

100

Extra for Experts

Compare this program to the program in Step-by-Step 12.1. Which program is simpler? Which one would you rather modify to handle ten more grades? Which one is more likely to have errors when you add more grades?

7. Click **Calculate Average**. The average is calculated and displayed. The average should be 85.5.

8. Stop debugging the program, then save and close the project. Leave Visual Studio open for the next Step-by-Step.

Parallel Arrays

All elements in an array hold information of the same type. There are many applications in which you want to have several pieces of related information of different types. For example, you may want to have a student's name associated with each grade. Names are strings; grades are generally integer or single values. One way to implement a solution is to use parallel arrays.

Parallel arrays are arrays of the same length in which each element in one array is related to an element in the second array with the same index value. A string array with student names could be used with an integer array holding student grades. The name in the fifth element of the name array would be the name of the student who achieved the grade held in the fifth element on the grade array.

> **Did You Know?**
>
> Parallel arrays can be used with many more than two arrays, as long as all information is placed in the correct index locations in all the arrays.

STEP-BY-STEP 12.6

1. Open the **ClassReport** project from the **step12-06** folder in the data files for this lesson. Open the form, if necessary.

2. Enter the following code in the (Declarations) section of the program.

```
' Declare and initialize the name array
Dim strNames() As String = {"John", "Paul", "Mary", "Jane", "Peter", _
   "Sam", "Andrew", "Laura", "Juan", "Rachel", "Clifford", "Thomas", _
   "Rebecca", "Susan", "Roberto", "Stefano", "Sara", "Jean", "Fred", _
   "Roseann"}

' Declare and initialize the grade array
Dim intGrades() As Integer = {75, 85, 95, 100, 87, 77, 65, 73, 99, 100, _
   83, 88, 92, 93, 90, 80, 70, 97, 76, 88}
```

3. Enter the following code in the `click` event procedure for the Find command button.

```
' Declare an index variable
Dim intIndex As Integer

' Set the index to the lower bound
intIndex = strNames.GetLowerBound(0)
```

4. Enter the following code to move through the array comparing each element to the name in the `txtName` text box.

```
' while the index is in range compare an element
'in the array with the search text
While ((intIndex < strNames.GetUpperBound(0)) And _
  (strNames(intIndex) <> txtName.Text))
   intIndex += 1       ' Increment the index
End While
```

STEP-BY-STEP 12.6 Continued

5. Enter the following code to compare the name in the element pointed to by the index value to the name in the text box. If there is a match, the index value will be used to return a value from the `intGrades` array. If no match was found, the message "Not Found" will be displayed.

```
' Check to see if the name has been found
If strNames(intIndex) = txtName.Text Then
   lblGrade.Text = intGrades(intIndex)
Else
   lblGrade.Text = "Not Found"
End If
```

6. Start debugging the program. Enter **Jane** in the Name text box and click **Find**. The grade *100* should be displayed in the label box, as shown in Figure 12-6.

FIGURE 12-6
Sample student found result

7. Enter **George** in the Name text box and click **Find**. The message *Not Found* should be displayed in the label box, as shown in Figure 12-7.

FIGURE 12-7
Sample student not found result

8. Stop debugging the program, save and close the project, then close Visual Studio 2005.

SUMMARY

In this lesson, you learned:

■ Visual Studio 2005 supports arrays that use an index or subscript to access different variables with the same name.

■ All elements of an array are of the same data type.

■ Arrays are declared by specifying the upper bound of the array.

- Arrays can be declared using initialization lists that set the starting values of the array. When arrays are declared using initialization lists, the upper bound is calculated by the system based on the number of items in the list.

- Individual elements in an array are read or changed by using an index value in parentheses to identify the element to use.

- The GetLowerBound and GetUpperBound methods can be used to check that an index value is in the allowable range.

- The Length method of an array returns the number of elements in an array.

- Arrays can be processed sequentially using a loop.

- Parallel arrays are any number of arrays, which may be of different data types, which hold information in corresponding elements.

VOCABULARY *Review*

Define the following terms:

Array	Initialization list	Subscript
Element	Lower bound	Upper bound
Index	Parallel array	Zero-based array

REVIEW *Questions*

TRUE / FALSE

Circle T if the statement is true or F if the statement is false.

T   F   **1.** An array uses variables with different names.

T   F   **2.** While loops can be used to search an array.

T   F   **3.** Arrays must always be initialized using an initialization list.

T   F   **4.** The lower bound of an array (in Visual Studio 2005) is always zero.

T   F   **5.** The Length property returns the upper bound of an array.

T   F   **6.** Parallel arrays must be of the same length.

T   F   **7.** Loop control variables may not be used to index through a loop.

T   F   **8.** An equation may be used as the index into an array.

T   F   **9.** Index values greater than the upper bound can be used to fit more information in an array.

T   F   **10.** The same variable that is used to index in one array can be used to index into a parallel array.

WRITTEN QUESTIONS

Write a brief answer to each of the following questions.

1. What characters are used to enclose the items in an initialization list?

2. How many items are there in an array with an upper bound of 25?

3. What is the upper bound of an array with a length of 24?

4. What important consideration must you make when entering information into parallel arrays?

5. How can you find out the number of elements in an array?

6. What is used to set starting values for an array during the array declaration?

7. Name the methods that are used to find out the upper and lower allowable index values for an array.

8. How is the upper bound determined for an array that is declared using an initialization list?

9. What is the maximum length of an array?

10. Why are Visual Studio 2005 arrays called zero-based arrays?

PROJECTS

PROJECT 12-1

1. Open the **TestGrades** program you worked with in Step-by-Step 12.1 and 12.5. Open the form, if necessary.

2. Add a command button above the *Calculate Average* button. Name the command button **cmdHigh** and change the text property to **High Grade**.

3. The command buttons that process the array should not be used until the array has values in it, so set the Visible property of the cmdAverage and cmdHigh command buttons to **False**.

4. Enter the following code for the Click event procedure of the cmdHigh command button. It will search the array for the highest grade in the array.

```
' Declare an index variable
Dim intIndex As Integer

'Declare a variable to hold the highest grade
' and set it to the first value in the array
Dim intHigh As Integer = Grade(0)

' Compare each grade to the highest grade seen so far
For intIndex = 1 To Grade.Length - 1
   If Grade(intIndex) > intHigh Then
      intHigh = Grade(intIndex)     ' Save the new highest grade
   End If
Next

' Show the high grade in a message box
MessageBox.Show("The highest grade is " & Format(intHigh))
```

5. Add the following code to the bottom of the click event procedure for the cmdGrades command button to make the other command buttons visible.

```
' Make processing commands visible
cmdAverage.Visible = True
cmdHigh.Visible = True
```

6. Start debugging the program.

7. Click **Input Grades** and enter ten grades.

8. Click **High Grade** and verify that the message box displays the highest grade you entered.

9. Stop debugging the program and save your changes. Close the project, but leave Visual Studio 2005 open.

PROJECT 12-2

1. Open **TimesTable** from the **proj12-02** folder in the data files for this lesson and, if necessary, open the form.

2. Enter the following code into the (Declarations) section of the program.

```
' Declare an array to hold the answer key
Dim intTable(12) As Integer
```

3. Enter the following code into the click event procedure for the mnuFileNewTable menu item.

```
' Declare integer variables
Dim intMultiplier As Integer
Dim intIndex As Integer

' Ask the user for a number
intMultiplier = Val(InputBox("Enter a number between 1 and 12", _
    "Multiplier", "5"))

' Check the range of the user input
If intMultiplier >= 1 And intMultiplier <= 12 Then
    ' Build the answer table
    For intIndex = 1 To 12
        intTable(intIndex) = intIndex * intMultiplier
    Next
    ' Display the number entered
    lblMultiplier.Text = intMultiplier
    ' Make the command button visible so it can be used
    cmdMultiply.Visible = True
Else
    ' Display error message
    MessageBox.Show("An integer between 1 and 12 must be entered.")
End If
```

4. Enter the following code into the click event procedure for the cmdMultiply command button.

```
' Declare an integer to use as an index
Dim intIndex As Integer

' Get the number from the text box
intIndex = Val(txtTimes.Text)

' Check that the index entered is in the correct range
If intIndex >= 1 And intIndex <= 12 Then
    ' Display the answer from the array
    lblResult.Text = Format(intTable(intIndex))
Else
    ' Display error message
    MessageBox.Show("An integer between 1 and 12 must be entered.")
End If
```

5. Start debugging the program and select the **New Table** option from the **File** menu.

6. Enter **12** into the InputBox and click **OK**. The number should display in a label as part of a formula. The number 12 also appears in the form's textbox. The Multiply button will appear.

7. Enter a new number into the text box, click **Multiply**, and verify that the correct answer is displayed.

8. Stop debugging the program, save your changes, and exit Visual Studio.

PROJECT 12-3

This project will use three parallel arrays to create a report of a sale at a concession stand. The first array is a string array with the name of the items that were for sale. The second array holds the quantity of each item that was available for sale at the opening of the stand. The third array holds the quantity of each item sold during the sale.

1. Start Visual Studio 2005 and open **SalesData** from the **proj12-03** folder in the data files for this lesson. If necessary, open the form.

2. Add a list box to the form under the label that says *Items Remaining*. Rename it to **lstRemaining**.

3. Add the following code to the click event procedure for the Report command button. The code will compare the quantity of each item sold to the quantity of items that were available for sale and add the item names and remaining count of those items not sold to the list box.

```
' Declare a loop control variable to use as an index
Dim intIndex As Integer

' Process each item in the list
For intIndex = 0 To intStarting.Length - 1
    ' Subtract the number sold from the number available _
    ' and see if there are any left
    If intStarting(intIndex) - intSold(intIndex) > 0 Then
        ' Add the name of the item and the amount left to the text box
        lstRemaining.Items.Add(strItems(intIndex) & " " & _
        Format(intStarting(intIndex) - intSold(intIndex)))
    End If
Next
```

4. Start debugging the program and click **Report**. The result should look something like Figure 12-8.

FIGURE 12-8
Items still in inventory are displayed

5. Stop debugging the program and save your changes. Close the project but leave Visual Studio 2005 open.

CRITICAL*Thinking*

The **NestedFor** project in the **crit12-01** folder in the data files for this lesson includes definitions for a pair of parallel arrays. The first array lists names, and the second array holds the gender of each person. There is an *M* for male names and an *F* for female names. Add a list box and command buttons with code that lets the user get a list of male names or female names in the list box. Your solution may look something like Figure 12-9.

FIGURE 12-9
Sample solution for Critical Thinking activity

LOOPS AND ARRAYS

REVIEW *Questions*

TRUE / FALSE

Circle T if the statement is true or F if the statement is false.

T   F   **1.** As a rule, a `Do` loop cannot be nested within a `For Next` loop.

T   F   **2.** The *Loop* keyword marks the end of a block of code contained within a `For` loop.

T   F   **3.** The `For Next` loop allows you to count by an increment other than one.

T   F   **4.** Arrays cannot be used with `For Next` loops.

T   F   **5.** An `InputBox` can only be used to read integer values.

T   F   **6.** All elements of an array must be of the same type.

T   F   **7.** The lower bound of an array is always zero.

T   F   **8.** The upper bound of an array cannot be determined using program code.

T   F   **9.** The upper bound and length of an array are the same.

T   F   **10.** The `Loop Until` loop continues until a condition is false.

MATCHING

Match the correct term in Column 1 to its description in Column 2.

Column 1	Column 2
___ 1. array	**A.** the value that identifies an element in an array
___ 2. iteration structure	**B.** properties that define how text in a label box appears
___ 3. index	**C.** one variable name with multiple values
___ 4. font settings	**D.** placing one control structure (loop or If...Else) inside of another
___ 5. nesting	**E.** the code required to create a loop

WRITTEN QUESTIONS

Write a brief answer to each of the following questions.

1. What type of Do loop should you use if you want the code within the loop to be executed at least once?

2. Why is a Counter variable necessary in a For Next loop?

3. How could you use a For Next loop to count backwards?

4. What is an endless loop?

5. Why might it be dangerous to use the Application.DoEvents method in an event procedure?

6. What function displays a window to prompt the user for input?

7. What property is used to find the number of elements in an array?

8. How can a For Next loop be used to process all the elements in an array?

9. What method is used to empty a ListBox?

10. Why is it good practice to name the counter variable in a Next statement?

SIMULATIONS

As an intern for a software development firm, you often get assigned the tasks of cleaning up code, writing small segments of code, or verifying that code will work as expected. Testing and modifying is an important part of on-the-job training at most companies. It is also how companies evaluate interns for consideration for future full-time employment. Today you have been asked to do several such jobs, which are outlined below.

JOB 4-1

Your supervisor has identified some faulty code segments as part of the formal code review of a large project and wants you to verify the problems and correct them. There is a problem in each of the following code segments. State the problem and then correct the code.

1.
```
Dim I As Integer
I = 1
Do While I <= 10
    lstDisplay.Items.Add( "Iteration Number: " & Format(I))
Loop
```

2.
```
Dim I As Integer
I = 10
Do
    lstDisplay.Items.Add( "Iteration Number: " & Format(I))
    I = I + 1
Loop Until I = 10
```

3.
```
Dim intCounter As Integer
For intCounter = 1 To 10
     Sum = Sum + 1
Next Sum
```

JOB 4-2

Your supervisor would like you to add code to a program so it will calculate the factorial of a number entered by the user. The factorial of a number *n* is the product of all the positive whole numbers from 1 to *n*. Factorials are used as part of several other complex calculations, so it is important that your code work correctly. The symbol for factorial is *!*.

1. Open **Factorial** from the **job04-02** folder in the data files for this unit review.

2. Add the following code to the Calculate event procedure.

```
Dim strMessage As String
Dim dblNumber As Double
Dim dblResult As Double
dblNumber = Val(txtNumber.Text)
If dblNumber > 17 Then
     MsgBox "The value is too big.  Please enter another number."
Else
     Dim I As Integer
     dblResult = dblNumber
     For I = dblNumber - 1 To 1 Step -1
          dblResult = dblResult * I
     Next I
     strMessage = dblNumber & "! = " & dblResult
     MsgBox strMessage
End If
```

3. Add code for the text box that will highlight the text when the text box is clicked.

4. Test the program for several numbers. For each number, enter the value and click **Calculate**. Verify that the code displays a message when a number greater than 17 is entered.

5. Stop debugging the program by choosing **Exit** from the **File** menu.

6. Save the changes, and then close the project.

JOB 4-3

In order to verify that the following code is correct, your supervisor would like you to study the code, and then answer the questions.

```
Dim intGrades() As Integer = {75, 85, 95}
Dim intAverage As Integer
Dim intTotal As Integer
Dim intIndex As Integer

For intIndex = 0 To intGrades.GetUpperBound(0)
      intTotal = intTotal + intGrades(intIndex)
Next

intAverage = intTotal / intGrades.Length
```

1. What is the value of `intGrades(2)`?

2. What is the value of `intTotal`?

3. What is the value of `intAverage`?

4. What is the value of `intGrades.GetUpperBound(0)`?

5. What is the value of `intGrades.Length`?

MULTIPLE FORMS, MENUS, AND PRINTING

Unit 5

Estimated Time for Unit: 4 hours

MULTIPLE FORMS

Using Multiple Forms

The programs you have been working with up to this point have involved only one form. Visual Studio 2005 allows you to work with multiple forms. Common uses for additional forms include program instructions, dialog boxes, splash screens, and About boxes.

You have seen many examples of dialog boxes. Dialog boxes appear often in Windows programs. A *splash screen* is a window that appears briefly when a program is started. Programs like Microsoft Word have a splash screen that appears while the program loads. An About box is a window that provides information about the program. An *About box* might include information like a registration number, version number, copyright, and details about the developer of the software.

STEP-BY-STEP 13.1

1. Start Visual Studio 2005. Watch closely to see the splash screen that appears as Visual Studio 2005 loads. Figure 13-1 is an example of the Visual Studio 2005 splash screen. Your splash screen may differ from this figure.

FIGURE 13-1
A splash screen is a window that appears briefly as a program loads

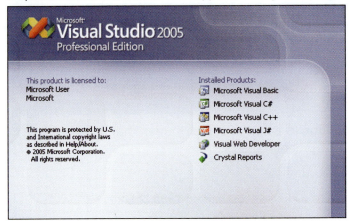

The New Project dialog box that appears when you start a new project with Visual Studio 2005 is a good example of a dialog box.

2. Choose **About Microsoft Visual Studio** from the **Help** menu. An About box opens, as shown in Figure 13-2. Your About box may vary from the figure, depending on what version of Visual Studio you have installed.

FIGURE 13-2
An About box tells you something about the program itself

STEP-BY-STEP 13.1 Continued

3. Click **OK**. The About box closes. Leave Visual Studio 2005 open for the next Step-by-Step.

Visual Studio 2005 makes it easy to add additional forms to your programs. While there are many things that can be done with multiple forms, we will focus on two uses for multiple forms: splash screens and About boxes.

Creating a New Form

The first step in using additional forms in your project is to create the new form. Once a new form is added to a project, other objects—such as label boxes and command buttons—can be added to it. This form can then be loaded and unloaded by your program.

STEP-BY-STEP 13.2

1. Open the **Pattern** project you created in Project 11-4 of Lesson 11 and, if necessary, open the form. (If you did not complete this project, ask your instructor for the completed Pattern project.)

2. Choose **Add Windows Form** from the **Project** menu. The Add New Item dialog box, shown in Figure 13-3, appears.

FIGURE 13-3
The Add New Item dialog box is used to create a new Windows form

Windows
Form
template
selected

STEP-BY-STEP 13.2 Continued

3. Select **Windows Form** from the *Templates* section of the dialog box. Change the text in the Name text box to **frmAbout.vb** and click **Add**. A new, empty form appears, as shown in Figure 13-4.

FIGURE 13-4
A new form is added to the project

4. Change the Text property of the new form to **About Pattern**.

5. Add two label boxes and a command button to the new form.

6. Name one label box **lblProgram** and the other **lblAuthor**. Change the font size to **18** and the AutoSize property to **True** for both label boxes.

7. Enter **Pattern** in the Text property for the program label and your own name in the author label.

8. Add the text **OK** to the command button and name it **cmdOK**.

9. Resize your form to avoid wasted space. Your form should look something like Figure 13-5.

FIGURE 13-5
The About screen form is now ready

STEP-BY-STEP 13.2 Continued

10. In the click event handling routine for the command button, enter the following code.

```
Close()
```

11. Start debugging the program. The About box does not appear. Why not?

12. Stop debugging the program. Leave the project open for the next Step-by-Step.

> **Note**
>
> The Close statement is used to close forms without shutting the whole program down. The End statement would shut down all forms in a project.

To get the About form to appear, some command must be issued, and the form must be loaded. Forms and dialog boxes have one of two characteristics: modal or modeless. A *modal form* or dialog box must be dismissed before you can continue working with the application. A *modeless form* or dialog box can stay on the screen and be moved behind other forms in a project. About boxes are loaded as modal forms by default.

If you have ever tried to ignore a dialog box and had the system beep at you when you tried to change the focus to another part of the application, you experienced a modal dialog box. Modeless dialog boxes, such as the Find dialog box, allow you to switch to another part of the application and come back later to deal with the dialog box. Often, tool windows or information windows are shown in a modeless fashion.

The form that we have created is a control. An object of that control type must be declared before the form is displayed. A Dim statement is used to declare this object. The ShowDialog method is used to display a modal form. The Show method is used to display a modeless form. The code to display our About box includes the Dim statement and the call to the ShowDialog method, as in the following code.

```
Dim fAboutMe As frmAbout = New frmAbout
fAboutMe.ShowDialog()
```

Note that the name of our form is used as the type of object created, but that we have a new name for the object. The single letter f is often used for the form variable name instead of frm to differentiate it from the control. In the next Step-by-Step, we will add these lines of code to display the About box.

STEP-BY-STEP 13.3

1. Double-click on the **Form1.vb** icon in the Solutions Explorer to return to the main form design window.

2. Add a new command button to the form under the Exit button. You may have to increase the size of the form for the button to fit.

3. Name the new command button **cmdAbout** and change the text to read **About**.

4. Add the following code to the click event routine for cmdAbout.

```
Dim fAboutMe As frmAbout = New frmAbout
fAboutMe.ShowDialog()
```

5. Start debugging the program and click **About**. The About Pattern box appears.

6. Try to click the buttons on the main form. You may have to move the About box. Why does the main form not respond?

7. Click **OK** on the About Pattern box, and it disappears. The main form will respond to you now.

8. Stop debugging the program and save your changes, but leave the project open for the next Step-by-Step.

This is a very simple About box. By adding more labels you can add as much information about your program as you wish. In the next lesson, you will learn how to add menus so that your About box can be opened from a menu option.

Adding a Splash Screen

As you read at the beginning of the lesson, a splash screen is a window that appears briefly when a program starts. Splash screens do not generally have title bars and resizable borders, and they usually appear in the center of the screen.

Adding a splash screen is similar to adding an About box. You follow the same steps to create a form for a splash screen; however, you set a few of the form's properties differently. Also, the splash screen must be loaded before your main screen is loaded. This means that you have to add a new code module that will load both your splash screen and your main screen. This code module will be the first thing that Visual Studio 2005 starts when it runs your program.

Unlike an About box, a splash screen does not have a command button to close it. The splash screen only has information to be displayed. The module that displays the splash screen will also close it.

STEP-BY-STEP 13.4

1. Choose **Add Windows Form** from the **Project** menu. The Add New Item dialog box appears.

2. Select the **Windows Form** template from the dialog box, change the Name to **frmSplash.vb**, and click **Add**. A new, empty form appears.

3. To remove the title bar and resizable borders, change the FormBorderStyle property to **None**.

4. Set the StartPosition property to **CenterScreen**.

5. Add two label boxes to the new form.

6. Name one label box **lblProgram** and the other **lblAuthor**. Change the font size to **24** and the AutoSize property to **True** for both label boxes.

STEP-BY-STEP 13.4 Continued

7. Enter **Pattern** in the Text property of the program label and your own name in the author label.

8. Start debugging the program. The splash screen does not appear. Why?

9. Stop debugging the program and save your changes. Leave the project open for the next Step-by-Step.

Now that the splash screen has been created, it must be run.

Loading a Splash Screen

A code module is created using the Add Module option from the Project menu. This option opens the Add New Item dialog box with the Module template selected, as shown in Figure 13-6.

FIGURE 13-6
The Add New Item dialog box is also used to create a new module

A module file includes only program code. There is no form to design with it. The code in the module can open and control forms that are part of the project. The main routine in a module must be set up as the `Startup` object in the project's properties. The following Step-by-Step shows how to create a module, add code to it, and then set the project so that this code is run first. This will cause the program to load the splash screen and then load the main form.

STEP-BY-STEP 13.5

1. Choose **Add Module** from the **Project** menu. The Add New Item dialog box appears.

STEP-BY-STEP 13.5 Continued

2. Make sure that the **Module** template is selected, change the Name to **modMain.vb**, and click **Add**. A new code window appears, as shown in Figure 13-7.

FIGURE 13-7
A new code window is opened for the module

3. In the declarations section of the module, declare variables for the splash form and the main form of the program using the following code. (If you changed the Name of the main form in the frmPattern.vb file to something other than Form1, you will need to use that name in the last line of code.)

```
' Declare objects for the splash and main form
Dim fSplash As frmSplash = New frmSplash
Dim fPattern As Form1 = New Form1
```

4. Key **Sub main()** to create a main subroutine for the module and press **Enter**. The IDE will automatically create the End Sub statement after you press Enter.

5. Key the following code to display the splash screen as a modeless form.

```
' Display the splash screen
fSplash.Show()
Application.DoEvents()
```

6. Key the following code to wait one second (1000 milliseconds) and close the splash screen.

```
' Wait one second
Threading.Thread.Sleep(1000)
' Close the splash screen
fSplash.Close()
```

7. Key the following code to start the main form as a modal form. When the main form exits, the program will automatically shut down.

```
' Load the main form
fPattern.ShowDialog()
```

STEP-BY-STEP 13.5 Continued

Your completed module should look like Figure 13-8.

FIGURE 13-8
The completed code module

8. Select **Pattern** (the project name) in the Solutions Explorer, and then select the **Property Pages** option from the **View** menu to open the Property Pages window.

9. Deselect the **Enable application framework** checkbox if necessary. Select **Sub Main** as the *Startup object* (as shown in Figure 13-9), save the settings by selecting the **Save All** option from the **File** menu, and then close the Property Pages window.

FIGURE 13-9
Selecting the `Startup` object

10. Start debugging the program. The splash screen should appear in the middle of the screen, stay for one second, and disappear as the main form appears. Exit the form.

11. Save your program and leave it open for the next Step-by-Step.

You can build on a simple splash screen like this one by adding more labels with more information, changing the background color, or by making many other cosmetic changes. But remember that the splash screen only appears for a short time; your main form does the real work, and this is where you should spend most of your time and effort.

Modifying a Form at Run Time

Just as the objects on a form can be modified while the form is being displayed, form objects can also be modified before the form is displayed. This is useful for creating general purpose information forms. For example, you could create a basic form for displaying help messages and then load different information in it depending on what information the user requests. You could, therefore, use one form for multiple purposes.

The objects on a form are accessed by using the name of the form connected with a dot to the name of the object. For example, to set a value in a label box named lblProgram on a form called fAbout, you would use a statement like the following.

```
fAbout.lblProgram.Text = "Push Buttons"
```

In the next Step-by-Step, we will reuse the About box form to display a different set of information.

STEP-BY-STEP 13.6

1. Add a new command button to the frmPattern form. Place it under the Create Pattern button.

2. Change the Name of the command button to **cmdDirections** and the Text property to **Directions**.

3. Add the following code to the click event procedure for cmdDirections to declare a new form.

```
' Declare an object of the type of the About box form
Dim fDirections As frmAbout = New frmAbout
```

4. Add the following code to change the title bar of the form to be displayed.

```
' Change the forms text property
fDirections.Text = "What to do?"
```

5. Add the following code to change the values in the text properties of the label boxes.

```
' Change the text values in the label boxes on the form
fDirections.lblProgram.Text = "Push Buttons"
fDirections.lblAuthor.Text = ""
```

STEP-BY-STEP 13.6 Continued

6. Add the following code to display the modified form.

```
'Display the form
fDirections.ShowDialog()
```

7. Start debugging the program and click **Directions**. The modified form will be displayed and should look something like Figure 13-10.

FIGURE 13-10
A new About form has been created

8. Close the information box.

9. Click **About** to display the About box. Notice that it appears unchanged.

10. Close the About box. Close the Pattern program.

11. Save the Pattern program, and then exit Visual Studio 2005.

SUMMARY

In this lesson, you learned:

■ Visual Basic programs can include multiple forms. Splash screens and About boxes are two common uses for additional forms in a program.

■ Modal forms must be closed before other windows in a program can be used.

■ Modeless forms can remain open, and a program can switch back and forth between several modeless forms.

■ The Close method is used to shut down a form and leave the program running.

■ A program module that includes only code can be used to control several forms.

■ Forms can be created without any border and placed in the center of the screen.

■ The Property Pages window lets you select which form or module starts up the program when it runs.

■ The properties of a form and the object on the form can be changed under program control before the form is displayed.

VOCABULARY *Review*

Define the following terms:

About box   Modeless form   Splash screen
Modal form

REVIEW *Questions*

TRUE / FALSE

Circle T if the statement is true or F if the statement is false.

T   F   **1.** About boxes can hold many different label boxes to display information about a program.

T   F   **2.** A code module may only control one form in the project.

T   F   **3.** Splash screens may be created without any title bar or border, using the `FormBorderStyle` property.

T   F   **4.** Modeless forms are displayed using the `ShowDialog` method.

T   F   **5.** Splash screens are closed when a command button is clicked.

T   F   **6.** An object of a form type must be declared before it can be displayed by a program.

T   F   **7.** The `Close` method is used to exit an About box form.

T   F   **8.** The `StartPosition` property of a form allows you to force the form to be displayed in the center of the screen.

T   F   **9.** An About box is a window that appears briefly when a program is started.

T   F   **10.** Splash screens must be displayed by a command button.

WRITTEN QUESTIONS

Write a brief answer to each of the following questions.

1. Where is Sub Main identified as the `Startup` object?

2. How is a module file different from a form file?

3. What statement is used to close a form without shutting down the whole program?

4. What kind of form would be used to show a user the version number of a program?

5. What method would you use to display a modal form?

6. Which property determines where on the screen a form is displayed?

7. How are the objects on a form identified so that they can be accessed from a code module?

8. What are three uses of multiple forms in a project?

9. When is a splash screen displayed?

10. What step must be taken before a form can be loaded under program control?

PROJECTS

PROJECT 13-1

1. Start Visual Studio 2005 and open **Name** from the **proj13-01** folder in the data files for this lesson.

2. Add a new Windows form named **frmHello** to the project.

3. Set the Text property of frmHello to **Hello**.

4. Add a label box called **lblHello** to the upper left of the frmHello form. Set the font size to **18** and the AutoSize property to **True**. Change the Text property to **Say Hello**.

5. Open the design window for **Form1** and add the following code to the Say Hello button so that a new form will be displayed using the name that is entered in the text box.

```
' Declare a form object
Dim fHello As frmHello = New frmHello

' Copy a message into the label box
fHello.lblHello.Text = "Hello " & txtName.Text

' Show the form
fHello.Show()
```

6. Start debugging the program.

7. Key your first name in the text box and click **Say Hello** to verify that the program works.

8. Move the new form so that it does not cover the main form, replace the name in the text box, and click **Say Hello** to verify that a new form is opened.

9. Close the forms and end the program. Save the changes. Close the project, but leave Visual Studio 2005 open.

PROJECT 13-2

1. Open the **ClassReport** project you created in Lesson 12. (If you did not complete this project, ask your instructor for the required program files.)

2. Using the **Add Windows Form** option from the **Project** menu, add a new form called **frmSplash** to the project.

3. Set the following property values for frmSplash.

```
FormBorderStyle:    None
StartPosition:      CenterScreen
```

4. Add two label boxes. Name one **lblProgram** and the other **lblProgrammer**.

5. Set the Text property of lblProgram to **Class Report Project**. Set the font size to **18**. Resize and relocate the label box as needed to make it show the whole message and fit on the form.

6. Set the Text property of `lblProgrammer` to your name. Set the font size to **16**. Resize and relocate the label box as needed to make it show the whole message and fit on the form.

7. Using the **Add Module** option from the **Project** menu, add a code module named **modMain**.

8. Add the following code to the code module to display the splash screen and load the main program.

```
Sub main()
    ' Declare the forms to be used
    Dim fSplash As frmSplash = New frmSplash
    Dim fMain As Form1 = New Form1
    ' Show the splash screen and wait one second
    fSplash.Show()
    Application.DoEvents()
    Threading.Thread.Sleep(1000)
    ' Unload the splash screen and load the main form
    fSplash.Close()
    fMain.ShowDialog()
End Sub
```

9. Select the project name in the Solution Explorer and open the Property Pages window from the **Property Pages** option in the **View** menu.

10. Deselect the **Enable application framework** checkbox if necessary. Set the `Startup` object to **Sub Main,** save the settings, and then close the Property Pages window.

11. Start debugging the program to verify that the splash screen is shown and the main form is loaded.

12. Stop debugging the program. Save the changes to the project and leave the project open for Project 13-3.

PROJECT 13-3

1. Choose **Add Windows Form** from the **Project** menu. Change the Name of the new form to **frmAbout.vb,** and click **Add**.

2. Change the Text property of the new form to **About Class Report**.

3. Add one label box named **lblProgram** and one label box named **lblAuthor**. Change the font size to **18** and resize and relocate the label boxes as needed on the form.

4. Set the Text property of `lblProgram` to **Class Report** and the Text property of `lblAuthor` to your name.

5. Add a command button to the form named **cmdOK**, and set the Text to **OK**.

6. In the `Click` event handling routine for `cmdOK`, enter the code necessary to close the About form. (*Hint:* You want to use either the `Close` statement or the `End` statement.)

7. Rename **Form1.vb** to **frmClassReport.vb** and open it in the design window. Add a new command button named **cmdAbout** to the form under the Exit button. Set its Text property to **About**.

8. Add the following code to the `Click` event routine of the new button.

```
Dim fAboutMe As frmAbout = New frmAbout
fAboutMe.ShowDialog()
```

9. Start debugging the program and check to make sure the new form appears when you click the **About** button. Verify that you cannot click the buttons on the main form. Click the **OK** button on the About form.

10. Stop debugging the program, save your changes, and exit Visual Studio 2005.

CRITICAL *Thinking*

Create a splash screen and an About box for the **NestedFor** project you worked with in Lesson 11. (If you did not complete this program, ask your instructor for the completed files.) You can decide what objects you need on the forms. Keep in mind the following items when completing this activity:

1. You will need to create a code module to load the splash screen and main form.

2. You will need to show the program name and program author on both the splash screen and the About box.

3. You will need to create an About button on the form.

4. You will need a description of the program in the About form.

MENUS AND PRINTING

Creating Menus Using the Menu Editor

In addition to buttons and other user interface elements, most Windows applications provide menus. A *menu* is a list of related items that can be selected to cause an event. In most programs, the menus provide the most complete set of options. Toolbars and other buttons are usually just shortcuts to what is available on menus.

Visual Studio 2005 allows you to create standard menus that pull down from the menu bar. Like most other elements of the user interface, Visual Studio allows you to create menus without writing code. As with buttons, choosing a menu command triggers an event. The only coding required is writing the event procedure.

To make creating menus easy, Visual Studio includes a `MenuStrip` object. The `MenuStrip` object is a simple, yet powerful tool for quickly creating menus. It even allows you to create menus with submenus, like the one shown in Figure 14-1.

FIGURE 14-1
Menus created in Visual Studio can include all the features of Windows menus, including submenus

Because menus pull down from a menu bar, they are always associated with a form. The `MenuStrip` object is added to a form by selecting it from the Toolbox, just like any other object. When a `MenuStrip` object is added to a project, the **Menu Designer** is added to the form (displaying the text *Type Here*), and the `MenuStrip` control is shown in a special area called the **component tray**, as shown in Figure 14-2. The component tray is an area at the bottom of the design window where non-visual items appear. Once a control has been added to the component tray, you can select the component and set its properties as you would any other control on the form.

Hot Tip

The `MenuStrip` object replaced the `MainMenu` object from previous versions of Visual Basic. Although the `MainMenu` object is still available for backwards compatibility and future use, the `MenuStrip` has added functionality built into it.

FIGURE 14-2
The MenuStrip object shows up on the form and on the component tray

Menu
Designer
on the form

Menu control
on the
component
tray

To learn about the MenuStrip object and how to make menus for your programs, we are going to create a simple program that allows you to manipulate the properties of a form and an image by using menus.

STEP-BY-STEP 14.1

1. Start Visual Studio and open **Amy** from the **step14-01** folder in your data files for this lesson. Open the form if necessary. Note that the form includes an image.

2. With the form open and selected, double-click the MenuStrip object on the Toolbox (in the Menus & Toolbars section) to add a menu to the form. Leave Visual Studio open for the next Step-by-Step.

When you select a MenuStrip control, you will see the text *Type Here* just below the caption bar of the form. Clicking this text and keying will create a menu item whose Text property is specified by the name you key. The menu structure of the form is represented by the Menu Designer. The Menu Designer allows you to create menus and submenus interactively.

Additionally, by clicking the drop-down arrow in the Menu Designer, you can insert new menu items and various other objects contained in the MenuStrip control, such as a *separator bar*. A separator bar is simply a horizontal line used to group related menu items to help make the menus more readable. The Properties window can be used to modify all of these menu objects.

Most applications that follow the standard Windows interface include a File menu. So the first menu we will create for our program is a File menu. The only command we are going to include on the File menu is the Exit command.

When you key a new value to replace *Type Here*, you are changing the Text property of the menu item. Once the Text value has been set, you should use the Properties window to set the name of the menu item. The standard prefix for a menu item is *mnu*. It is standard practice to name the menu item after the text value, so the File menu item would be mnuFile. An item under the main menu would include the name of the main menu as well as the item's text value. So, the Exit option under the File menu would be mnuFileExit.

When a top-level menu item is selected, you can use the right arrow on your keyboard to create another top-level menu item. When you have a menu item selected that is in a lower level of the structure, the right arrow will create a submenu for that item. You can also use the down arrow to create a new menu item. In Figure 14-3, a new menu item has been opened under the File menu.

FIGURE 14-3
A menu item has been opened under the File menu

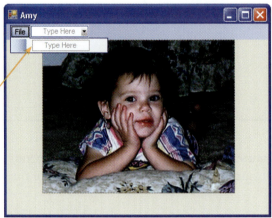

Menu item under the File menu

STEP-BY-STEP 14.2

1. Key the word **File** in the Text field of the Menu Designer at the top of the form, in place of the phrase *Type Here*.

2. Press the down arrow on the keyboard. The Menu Designer is ready for the next menu item to be created, with the text *Type Here* displayed.

3. Create the Exit command by keying **Exit** in the Text field.

4. Click the word **File** at the top of the menu. When the Properties window appears, key **mnuFile** as the Name of the menu item.

5. Use the Properties window to name the Exit command **mnuFileExit**. Your form should look something like the one shown in Figure 14-4.

STEP-BY-STEP 14.2 Continued

FIGURE 14-4
To add a menu item, enter Text and a name for the item

You can see that a menu bar now appears along the top of the form.

6. Start debugging the program. Pull down the **File** menu to reveal the Exit command.

7. Choose the **Exit** command. Note that nothing happens. As with command buttons, menu commands cannot carry out their commands until code is written.

8. Click **Close** to end the program.

9. Save your changes and leave the project open for the next Step-by-Step.

Writing Code for a Menu Command

Writing code for a menu command is much like writing code for a command button. When the user selects a menu command, a click event is triggered. When you code a menu command, you write an event procedure to handle the click event.

To write a menu event procedure, choose the menu command from the menu bar that appears on the form as you design your program (not as you run your program). The event procedure will be set up for you.

STEP-BY-STEP 14.3

1. While the program is stopped, click on the **File** menu item at the top of the form. The Exit command will appear.

2. Double-click the **Exit** command. The Code window opens. The `click` event procedure is ready for your code.

3. Add the **End** code to the `click` event procedure, as shown in Figure 14-5.

Hot Tip

If the Exit command opens in Text edit mode, then double-click the area just to the left of the text to open the Code window.

FIGURE 14-5
Event procedures for menu items are like those for command buttons

4. Start debugging the program and test the **Exit** command in the **File** menu. The Exit command should now end the program.

5. Save your changes and leave the project open for the next Step-by-Step.

Using Check Marks in Menus

Often, a menu command is used to toggle an item on and off. For example, a menu command might be used to make a toolbar appear or disappear. To help the user determine when the item is active, a check mark can be made to appear in the menu, as shown in Figure 14-6.

FIGURE 14-6
Check marks in menus can be used to determine when items are active

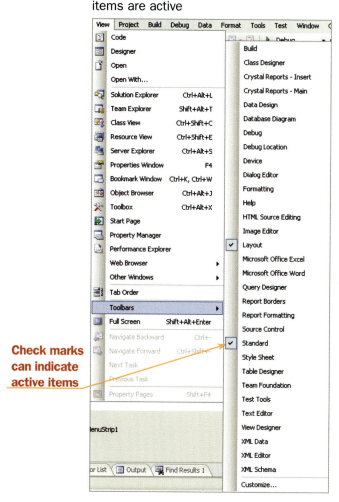

Check marks can indicate active items

You can add a check mark to a menu item in the Menu Designer by right-clicking the box to the left of the menu text and selecting the Checked option from the shortcut menu. You can also make the check mark appear and disappear by using Visual Basic code to modify the menu item's Checked property.

S TEP-BY-STEP 14.4

1. Click the **File** menu on your project's form to select it, and then press the right arrow on your keyboard to move to a new top-level menu item.

2. Key the word **Image** to replace the *Type Here* text. Press **Enter** to enter the new name, and then click the word **Image** to access the Properties window.

3. Key **mnuImage** in the Name field.

4. Select **Image** and press the down arrow on your keyboard to create a new menu item under Image.

STEP-BY-STEP 14.4 Continued

5. Key **Visible** as the text for the menu item, press **Enter**, select the word *Visible*, and change the Name of the item in the Properties window to **mnuImageVisible**.

6. Right-click the box to the left of the word *Visible* in the Menu Designer. A shortcut menu will appear. Choose the **Checked** property from the menu. This will set the menu item's Checked property to True. The form should appear similar to that shown in Figure 14-7.

FIGURE 14-7
The Checked value causes the menu item to be checked when the program is started

7. Start debugging the program.

8. Choose **Visible** from the **Image** menu.

9. Open the **Image** menu. Notice that *Visible* is still checked. Because no code has been written, the check mark remained unchanged.

10. Stop debugging the program and save your changes. Leave the project open for the next Step-by-Step.

The code for the Visible menu item will do two things: toggle the Visible property of the image and toggle the check mark. The **Not operator** can be used to reverse the current status of the properties. The Not operator will turn a True setting into False and a False setting into True.

S TEP-BY-STEP 14.5

1. Double-click the **Visible** command from the **Image** menu to access the Code window.

2. Add the following code to the Visible menu item's `click` event procedure.

```
'Change the visible property of the picture
'and the state of the checkmark
imgAmy.Visible = Not imgAmy.Visible
mnuImageVisible.Checked = Not mnuImageVisible.Checked
```

The first line of code uses the Not operator to set the image's Visible property to the opposite of what it is currently. The second line of code uses the Not operator to set the menu item's Checked property to the opposite of what it is currently.

3. Close the code window and start debugging the program.

4. Pull down the **Image** menu. Notice that Visible is checked.

5. Click **Visible**. The image disappears.

6. Pull down the **Image** menu again. Notice that the check mark for Visible has also disappeared.

7. Click **Visible** again. The image reappears.

8. Pull down the **Image** menu and notice that the check mark also returned.

9. Stop debugging the program and save your changes. Leave the project open for the next Step-by-Step.

Creating a Submenu

Submenus (also called cascading menus) are often used to further organize the options in a menu. In the next Step-by-Step, you will create a Size command in the Image menu and two submenus for the Size command.

S TEP-BY-STEP 14.6

1. Click the **Image** menu to select the **Menu Designer**.

2. Press the down arrow twice to create a new menu item just below the Visible menu item. Key **Size** as the text for the menu item and set the Name property to **mnuImageSize**.

3. Select **Size** and press the right arrow to create an indented menu item to the right of the Size menu item. Key **Small** as the text for the menu item and set the Name property to **mnuImageSizeSmall**.

4. Select **Small** and press the down arrow to create another indented item just below the Small menu item. Key **Large** as the text for the menu item, set the Name property to **mnuImageSizeLarge**, and set the Checked property to **True**.

STEP-BY-STEP 14.6 Continued

Your completed menu and submenu should look similar to Figure 14-8.

FIGURE 14-8
Submenus are created at the next level of indention

5. Double-click on **Small** to open the code window.

6. Add the following code to the **mnuImageSizeSmall** click event procedure. This event procedure will adjust the Height and Width properties to change the size of the image. The code will also change the Checked property to ensure that the Large menu item loses its check mark and the Small menu item becomes checked.

```
'Set the values for a small image
imgAmy.Height = 115
imgAmy.Width = 150
mnuImageSizeLarge.Checked = False
mnuImageSizeSmall.Checked = True
```

7. Add the following code to the **mnuImageSizeLarge** click event procedure. This event procedure is similar to the mnuImageSizeSmall event procedure. In this case, however, the image will be made larger, and the check mark will be switched to the Large menu item.

```
'Set the values for a large image
imgAmy.Height = 230
imgAmy.Width = 300
mnuImageSizeSmall.Checked = False
mnuImageSizeLarge.Checked = True
```

8. Close the Code window and start debugging the program.

9. Open the **Image** menu, access the **Size** submenu, and choose the **Small** command. The image becomes smaller.

STEP-BY-STEP 14.6 Continued

10. Open the **Image** menu and access the **Size** submenu. Notice the check mark is now on the Small menu item.

11. Choose **Large**. The image becomes large again.

12. Stop debugging the program and save your changes. Leave the project open for the next Step-by-Step.

Inserting Separator Bars in Menus

Often, especially on large menus, separator bars between some menu items can improve readability. For example, Figure 14-9 shows how the Visual Studio Help menu is separated into four sections. The separator bars group the items on the menu, making it more user-friendly. The separator bars cannot be selected by the user.

FIGURE 14-9
Separator bars can improve readability in menus

To create a separator bar, right-click the Menu Designer at the location you want the separator, select the Insert option, and then choose Separator. Give each separator bar a unique name in its Name property.

Note

Items shown in your Help menu may vary from those shown in Figure 14-9.

STEP-BY-STEP 14.7

1. Click the **Image** menu to access the Menu Designer.

2. Right-click the **Size** menu item to access the Menu Designer commands. Select the **Insert** option, and then choose **Separator**. A new separator bar appears above the Size menu item.

3. Modify the Name property of the separator bar to **mnuImageSeparator**.

4. Start debugging the program.

STEP-BY-STEP 14.7 Continued

5. Open the **Image** menu. Notice the separator bar that appears between the Visible and Size options, as shown in Figure 14-10.

FIGURE 14-10
The Insert Separator command creates a separator bar

6. Stop debugging the program, save your changes, and then close the project. Leave Visual Studio open for the next Step-by-Step.

Printing from Visual Studio

Even with highly-effective user interfaces on the screen, there are many instances in which you eventually need or want the information from a program on paper. Visual Studio actually provides a variety of ways to print. Most commercial software uses a set of Windows procedures that allow printing to any type of printer using many options. However, printing using this method is too complex to cover in this lesson.

A different and simpler way to send output to the printer is the PrintDocument object. The PrintDocument object is a collection of prewritten programming code that allows you to communicate with the printer. Many options are involved in using the PrintDocument object, and it requires a bit of setup to use. You will create an instance of the PrintDocument object by declaring a variable of that type. This allows you to set up any print properties you want, such as which printer to use or the default page margins to use. Then, you will use the Print event to start the printing process.

> **Note**
>
> The Step-by-Step exercises in this section assume that your computer has a printer attached, either directly or through a network. The Step-by-Step that follows may not work on all printer and network configurations.

The printing will be handled by a subroutine that you will create to handle the Print event. This routine will use the DrawString method to write text to the printed page. Lesson 15 will talk about other graphics methods which may also be used to draw on the printed page.

STEP-BY-STEP 14.8

1. Choose **New Project** from the **File** menu and create a new Windows Application project called **PrintDemo**.

2. Set the form's Text property to **Print**.

3. Create a command button.

4. Set the command button's Name property to **cmdPrint** and the Text property to **Print**.

5. Double-click the **Print** button to open the code window. At the very top of the program before the `Public Class` statement, enter the following line of code.

```
Imports System.Drawing.Printing
```

6. Inside the event handler for the `Click` event for the `cmdPrint` button, add the following code that will create a new `PrintDocument` object.

```
Dim pdPage As New PrintDocument
```

7. Below the `Click` event handler, enter the following code to handle the `Print` event for your `PrintDocument` object.

```
Private Sub PrintPage(ByVal sender As Object, ByVal ev As PrintPageEventArgs)
    ' Draw a message using the Tahoma font in 24 point size using a
    ' black brush at the top left corner of the page
    ev.Graphics.DrawString("Page Header", New Font("Tahoma", 24), _
        Brushes.Black, ev.MarginBounds.Left, ev.MarginBounds.Top)
    ' Draw a message using the Times New Roman font in 12 point size
    ' using a black brush at 200 pixels down and 200 pixels
    ' from the left of the page
    ev.Graphics.DrawString("Hello World", New Font("Times New Roman", 12), _
        Brushes.Black, 200, 200)
End Sub
```

8. Enter the following lines of code in the `Click` event handler to set up the event handler for the `Print` event and to call the `Print` event.

```
AddHandler pdPage.PrintPage, AddressOf PrintPage
pdPage.Print()
```

> **Hot Tip**
>
> If no specific printer is set for the `PrintDocument` object, it will automatically be sent to the system's default printer.

STEP-BY-STEP 14.8 Continued

Your program should look like Figure 14-11.

FIGURE 14-11
The completed PrintDemo code

```
Form1.vb   Form1.vb [Design]
Form1                                          PrintPage
    Imports System.Drawing.Printing

  Public Class Form1

      Private Sub cmdPrint_Click(ByVal sender As System.Object, ByVal e As System.EventArgs)
          Dim pdPage As New PrintDocument
          AddHandler pdPage.PrintPage, AddressOf PrintPage
          pdPage.Print()
      End Sub

      Private Sub PrintPage(ByVal sender As Object, ByVal ev As PrintPageEventArgs)
          ' Draw a message using the Tahoma font in 24 point size using a
          ' black brush at the top left corner of the page
          ev.Graphics.DrawString("Page Header", New Font("Tahoma", 24), _
              Brushes.Black, ev.MarginBounds.Left, ev.MarginBounds.Top)
          ' Draw a message using the Times New Roman font in 12 point size
          ' using a black brush at 200 pixels down and 200 pixels
          ' from the left of the page
          ev.Graphics.DrawString("Hello World", New Font("Times New Roman", 12), _
              Brushes.Black, 200, 200)
      End Sub
  End Class
```

9. Close the Code window and start debugging the program.

10. Click **Print**. After a couple of seconds, your printer should begin printing your sample page.

11. Save and close the project, and then exit Visual Studio 2005.

SUMMARY

In this lesson, you learned:

■ Visual Studio allows you to create menus without writing code by using the Menu Designer.

■ The component tray is an area that displays nonvisual items and allows you to set their properties.

■ A menu item's Text property specifies the text that will appear on the menu.

■ Menu items also have a Name property that is used to identify the menu item in code.

■ When the user selects a command from a menu, a Click event is triggered. Writing code for a menu item is like writing any other Click event procedure.

■ Check marks may be added to the items in a menu to indicate that an option is on or off.

■ To better organize menus, you can insert separator bars from the Menu Designer. Separator bars cannot be selected by the user, but they can help group menu items.

■ You can print text to the printer using the PrintDocument object. The PrintDocument object allows you to draw text strings to a printer.

VOCABULARY *Review*

Define the following terms:

Component tray	Not operator	Submenus
Menu	PrintDocument object	
Menu Designer	Separator bars	

REVIEW *Questions*

TRUE / FALSE

Circle T if the statement is true or F if the statement is false.

T F 1. In most programs, menus provide the least complete set of options.

T F 2. The command performed by a toolbar button is usually also found on a menu.

T F 3. Visual Studio allows you to create the standard menus that open from the Menu bar.

T F 4. A menu item you create will be fully functional without any additional code.

T F 5. Because menus open from their own Menu bar, they do not need to be associated with a form.

T F 6. It is common practice to name menu items after their Text property.

T F 7. You cannot use code to modify the presence of a check mark next to a menu item.

T F 8. Separator bars are used to improve the readability of a menu.

T F 9. The PrintDocument object is used with a Print event handler.

T F 10. The PrintDocument object is only able to print to the default printer.

WRITTEN QUESTIONS

Write a brief answer to each of the following questions.

1. What type of event is triggered when a user chooses a menu command?

2. What does Visual Studio provide to help you create menus?

3. Where can you include code for the menu item?

4. Which field provides the text that will appear in the menu?

5. What prefix is commonly used when naming menu items?

6. How do you create a new menu item using the Menu Designer?

7. How do you create a checked menu item using the Menu Designer?

8. What is another name for submenus?

9. How do you add a separator bar to a menu?

10. What method is used to place text in the `PrintDocument` object?

PROJECTS

PROJECT 14-1

1. Start Visual Studio 2005 and create a new Visual Basic project.

2. Give your form the Text property **Menu Test**.

3. Create a **File** menu.

4. Create an **Exit** menu item under the File menu.

5. Add code to the Exit menu item that will end the program.

6. Start debugging the program to verify that it works.

7. Close the project, but leave Visual Studio open.

PROJECT 14-2

1. Open **Print Name** from the **proj14-02** folder in the data files for this lesson and, if necessary, open the form.

2. Open the code window and add the following `Print` event handler method.

```
Private Sub PrintPage(ByVal sender As Object, _
  ByVal ev As PrintPageEventArgs)
' Print the name in the textbox onto the PrintDocument object
ev.Graphics.DrawString(txtName.Text, _
  New Font("Times New Roman", 24), _
  Brushes.Black, 100, 100)
End Sub
```

3. Add the following code to the `Click` event procedure of the Print Name to Printer button.

```
Dim pdDocument As New PrintDocument
AddHandler pdDocument.PrintPage, AddressOf PrintPage
pdDocument.Print()
```

4. Close the code window and create a new menu item with the following properties.
Text: **File**
Name: **mnuFile**

5. Create a menu item just below the File menu item with the following properties.
Text: **Print Name**
Name: **mnuFilePrintName**

6. Create a menu item just below the Print Name menu item with the following properties.
Text: **Exit**
Name: **mnuFileExit**

7. Create a separator bar between the Print Name and Exit menu items.

8. Copy the code for the `cmdPrint` `Click` event procedure to the `Click` event procedure for `mnuFilePrintName`.

9. Add code to `mnuFileExit`, which will end the program.

10. Debug the program to test the code for the command button and the two submenu items.

11. Stop debugging the program and save your changes. Close the project, but leave Visual Studio open.

PROJECT 14-3

1. Open the project **Amy** that you worked with earlier in this lesson. (If you did not complete this project, ask your instructor for files with which to work.)

2. Click the **Image** menu item, and use the right arrow key to create a new menu item to the right of the Image menu with the following properties.
   Text: **Color**
   Name: **mnuColor**

3. Create a menu item just below the Color menu item with the following properties.
   Text: **White**
   Name: **mnuColorWhite**

4. Create a menu item just below the White menu item with the following properties.
   Text: **Red**
   Name: **mnuColorRed**

5. Create a menu item just below the Red menu item with the following properties.
   Text: **Blue**
   Name: **mnuColorBlue**

6. Add the following code to the `mnuColorWhite` `Click` event procedure. This event procedure will change the background color of the form to white and will add a check mark next to the *White* menu item.

```
'Change the background color to white and reset check marks
Me.BackColor = Color.White
mnuColorWhite.Checked = True
mnuColorRed.Checked = False
mnuColorBlue.Checked = False
```

7. Add the following code to the `mnuColorRed` `Click` event procedure. This event procedure will change the background color of the form to red and will add a check mark next to the *Red* menu item.

```
'Change the background color to red and reset check marks
Me.BackColor = Color.Red
mnuColorWhite.Checked = False
mnuColorRed.Checked = True
mnuColorBlue.Checked = False
```

8. Add the following code to the `mnuColorBlue Click` event procedure. This event procedure will change the background color of the form to blue and will add a check mark next to the *Blue* menu item.

```
'Change the background color to blue and reset check marks
Me.BackColor = Color.Blue
mnuColorWhite.Checked = False
mnuColorRed.Checked = False
mnuColorBlue.Checked = True
```

9. Debug the program and verify that the form's background color changes.

10. Stop debugging the program and save your changes. Close the project, but leave Visual Studio 2005 open.

CRITICAL*Thinking*

Modify the **ProfitLoss** program you worked with in Lesson 4. (If you did not complete that project, ask your instructor for project files with which to work.) Your program should include all of the following:

- Menu items that perform the events in each command button.
- A Print menu item that will print a report of the profit or loss. This menu item should not be enabled until the calculate option has been selected.
- Separator bars in the menus, where appropriate.
- Code with appropriate comments.

MULTIPLE FORMS, MENUS, AND PRINTING

REVIEW *Questions*

TRUE / FALSE

Circle T if the statement is true or F if the statement is false.

T F **1.** The objects on an About box cannot be changed under program control.

T F **2.** Splash screens are loaded by a code module that does not have its own form.

T F **3.** Only one line separator may be used on a menu.

T F **4.** Each menu item must have a unique name.

T F **5.** A Click event is triggered when a user chooses a menu command.

MATCHING

Match the correct term in Column 1 to its description in Column 2.

Column 1	Column 2
___ **1.** splash screen	**A.** an object used to help print information
___ **2.** About box	**B.** a window that appears briefly when a program is started
___ **3.** PrintDocument	**C.** a cascading menu used to further organize the items in a menu
___ **4.** separator line	**D.** a line that groups items on a menu
___ **5.** submenu	**E.** a window that opens to provide information on a program

WRITTEN QUESTIONS

Write a brief answer to each of the following questions.

1. What is the difference between the Show and ShowDialog methods for showing a form?

2. What steps must be taken after a form has been created to have the program show the form?

3. How can the program control the appearance of the check mark next to a menu item?

4. What menu in the IDE holds the Add Module option to add a new code module?

5. What menu generally holds the About option on a program?

6. What method is used in a form or code module to shut down another form?

7. How do you access the Menu Designer in Visual Studio 2005?

8. How do you associate a menu with a particular form?

9. What is the default text value for a new menu item?

10. For what is the PrintDocument object used?

SIMULATIONS

Testing and modifying code is an important part of on-the-job training at most companies. It is also the method companies use to evaluate interns for consideration for future full-time employment. As an intern for a programming firm, you often get assigned the task of enhancing code or writing small segments of code. Today you have been asked to do several such jobs, which are outlined below.

JOB 5-1

Your first assignment is to add menu options to an existing program. Open the **Planets** program you worked with in the Critical Thinking activity in Lesson 9. (If you did not complete this activity, ask your instructor for project files with which to work.) Create a File menu with a Print option and an Exit option. Add code to the Print option click event procedure to print the information on the form. Add code to the Exit menu option to shut down the program. Include any necessary comments in the code.

JOB 5-2

Next, you are asked to add a splash screen and an About Box to an existing program developed by one of the full-time programmers.

1. Open the **Factorial** program from your Unit 4 solution files. This is the program that you created in Job 4-2. (If you did not complete this program, ask your instructor for the project files.)

2. Add a splash screen to the program. The splash screen should contain at least the name of the program. Save this form as **frmSplash**.

3. Add code to the project, and make the necessary changes to the project settings so that the splash screen is displayed when the program is run.

4. Create an About Box that contains your name, the name of the program, and an OK button.

5. Use the Menu Designer to add a **Help** menu to the main form.

6. Add an **About** submenu to the Help menu and add the necessary code to display the About Box.

7. Start debugging the program to verify that it works correctly.

8. Stop debugging the program, save the changes, and then close the project.

JOB 5-3

For your last assignment, your internship advisor wants to assess what you have learned about working with forms and including images in a form. Find an image that represents your school. The image may be found in a yearbook, magazine, or other source and scanned to your computer, or you can find an appropriate image on the Internet. Add the image to a form and create menu items (including the Checked property and separator lines, where appropriate). The menu items should do the following:

■ Change the size of the image.

■ Show and hide the image.

■ Change the background color of the form.

■ End the program.

GRAPHICS AND DRAWING

Unit 6

 Estimated Time for Unit 6: 5.5 hours

LINES AND SHAPES

Drawing Objects Using Code

Visual Studio 2005 provides a single Graphic object with a large number of methods that allow a program to draw on a form. A *Graphic object* is a general-purpose drawing surface that may be used with a number of graphical tools in Visual Studio. The methods in the Graphic object use a number of other objects, such as Pen and Brush objects, *Color objects*, and Point objects, to determine the location and characteristics of the objects you draw.

In order to begin working with drawing objects, you must first understand the coordinate system of a form.

Understanding Coordinates

You have used the coordinate system of a form in earlier lessons. The properties like Top and Left that you used to position buttons and images used the coordinate system. The upper-left point on a form has an X-coordinate of zero and a Y-coordinate of zero. The Top and Left properties measure the distance from the top and the distance from the left, respectively.

To use the DrawLine method, you need to think in terms of X and Y rather than Top and Left. For example, a horizontal line might extend from point (50, 100) to point (200, 100), as shown in Figure 15-1. The main difference between the coordinates on a form and the coordinates you have used in geometry is that the origin (0, 0) appears at the upper-left corner rather than in the center of the form. If you understand geometry well, you might want to think of the form as the fourth quadrant of the coordinate plane. There are no negative values of X or Y. As you move toward the bottom of the form, the Y-coordinate value increases. As you move toward the right side of a form, the X-coordinate value increases.

FIGURE 15-1
A Visual Basic form is mapped into a coordinate system

The combination of the X and Y values is called a *Point*. A location can be given using individual X and Y values or by creating and using a Point object.

You will have to specify locations in points for all objects that are drawn using Visual Basic. With the location, you will also have to specify a Pen or a Brush to use to draw the object. A *Pen* is used to draw lines or the outline of a shape. A *Brush* is used to fill shapes or to draw text.

Understanding Pens and Brushes

When a Pen or Brush is created, the programmer specifies the color to use. The color is indicated using the Color structure, which has a large number of colors already defined and named. When you start entering a Color, IntelliSense will provide a drop-down list, like the one in Figure 15-2, to show you the available colors.

FIGURE 15-2
IntelliSense shows a list of available colors

The Pen object also lets you specify how thick the line should be. The following code creates a Pen object that can be used by graphics drawing methods. The Pen is created to draw a thick (5 pixel wide) blue line.

```
Dim penWideBlue As New Pen(Color.Blue, 5)
```

This pen object can be used in a DrawLine method to draw on a form.

Using the DrawLine Method

To use the DrawLine method, you must specify the endpoints of the line you want to draw and the pen you want to use to draw the line.

For example, the following code will use the Pen object shown above to draw a blue line from coordinate (50, 100) to coordinate (200, 100).

```
Dim g As Graphics = Me.CreateGraphics
g.DrawLine(penWideBlue, 50, 100, 200, 100)
```

You can also create a Pen inside the DrawLine statement. The following code creates a new red pen using the default thickness of one pixel to draw a line.

```
g.DrawLine(New Pen(Color.Red), 50, 150, 200, 150)
```

The following Step-by-Step draws a number of lines on a form in response to a mouse Click event.

STEP-BY-STEP 15.1

1. Open Visual Studio 2005 and create a new Visual Basic Windows Application project called **LineSample**.

2. Open the code window, select **(Form1 Events)** from the Class Name drop-down box, if necessary, and select **Click** from the Method Name drop-down list.

3. Enter the following line in the `Click` event handler to create a new graphic object on the form.

```
Dim g As Graphics = Me.CreateGraphics
```

4. Enter the following lines of code to create a number of lines of different colors.

```
g.DrawLine(New Pen(Color.Blue, 2), 100, 100, 150, 100)
g.DrawLine(New Pen(Color.Red, 2), 100, 100, 100, 150)
g.DrawLine(New Pen(Color.Green, 2), 100, 100, 100, 50)
g.DrawLine(New Pen(Color.Orange, 2), 100, 100, 50, 100)
```

5. Start debugging the program to test it. After clicking on the form, you should have four lines of different colors starting from the same location, as shown in Figure 15-3.

FIGURE 15-3
The `DrawLine` method draws four lines on a form

6. Stop debugging, save your work, close the project, and leave Visual Studio 2005 open for the next Step-by-Step.

Drawing Rectangles

Rectangles and boxes can be drawn two different ways. They can be drawn as outlined objects or as filled objects. The DrawRectangle method uses a Pen object and is used to draw the outline of a rectangle. The FillRectangle method uses a Brush object and is used to draw a rectangle that is filled in. There are several types of brushes available, but we will use the SolidBrush object in this lesson. The SolidBrush object is created with a specific color, just as we did with a Pen, but does not have a thickness because it is used to fill an object.

In the last Step-by-Step, we only drew a line. We will handle rectangles a little differently. First, we will create a rectangle in memory. The rectangle is created with an X and Y location for its upper-left corner. Two other parameters will specify the width and height properties of our rectangle in pixels. Remember that a square is only a rectangle that has the same height and width. That is why there is no need for special methods to draw squares.

$\mathcal{S}$ TEP-BY-STEP 15.2

1. Create a new Visual Basic Windows Application project called **BoxSample**.

2. Open the code window, select **(Form1 Events)** from the Class Name drop-down box, if necessary, and select **Click** from the Method Name drop-down list.

3. Enter the following lines of code in the click event handler to create a new graphic object on the form.

```
' Create a new graphic object
Dim g As Graphics = Me.CreateGraphics
```

4. Enter the following lines of code to create a new rectangle object.

```
' Create a new rectangle object
Dim recBox As Rectangle = New Rectangle(50, 50, 100, 100)
```

5. Enter the following lines of code to draw a filled rectangle with the outline of a rectangle over it.

```
' Draw a blue filled rectangle and outline it in red
g.FillRectangle(New SolidBrush(Color.Blue), recBox)
g.DrawRectangle(New Pen(Color.Red, 3), recBox)
```

STEP-BY-STEP 15.2 Continued

6. Start debugging the program to see that it works. When the form is clicked, the program should display a box on the form like the one shown in Figure 15-4.

FIGURE 15-4
An outlined and filled box is displayed

7. Stop debugging, save your work, close the project, and leave Visual Studio 2005 open for the next Step-by-Step.

Once a rectangle object has been created, it can be used as many times as you want within the method where it was created. You can also change the location of the object and its width and height. These changes will not modify any copy of the rectangle that you have already drawn on the screen. They will be reflected in any new rectangles you draw after the property values have been changed. The following code changes the location and size of a rectangle.

```
recBox.X = 60
recBox.Y = 60
recBox.Width = 50
recBox.Height = 150
```

Drawing Ellipses

Like rectangles, circles and ellipses can be drawn either as outlines, using the DrawEllipse method, or as filled objects, using the FillEllipse method. The parameters for the DrawEllipse method are a Pen object, the location of the ellipse, and the width and height of the ellipse. Remember that a circle is an ellipse with the same width and height. The location and size of the ellipse are actually specified as the location and size of a rectangle that would completely hold the ellipse. You can specify your ellipse by giving the X, Y, Width, and Height parameters, or you can use a rectangle that you have already declared as a parameter. The following code draws the image shown in Figure 15-5.

```
Dim recBox As Rectangle = New Rectangle(50, 50, 100, 100)
Dim g as Graphics = Me.CreateGraphics
g.DrawRectangle(New Pen(Color.Black, 3), recBox)
g.DrawEllipse(New Pen(Color.Black, 3), recBox)
```

FIGURE 15-5
A circle inside its defining rectangle

Notice that, on the first line of code, we are creating the rectangle object, and the last two parameters set both the width and the height to 100. That is why the ellipse in Figure 15-5 is actually a circle. If you wanted to draw an ellipse that wasn't a circle, you would simply modify those last two parameters to make the width and height of the rectangle object different.

The FillEllipse method uses the same location and size parameters, but uses a Brush object in place of a Pen object.

STEP-BY-STEP 15.3

1. Create a new project called **CircleSample**.

2. Open the code window, select **(Form1 Events)** from the Class Name drop-down box, if necessary, and select **Click** from the Method Name drop-down list.

3. Enter the following lines of code in the `click` event handler to create a new graphic object on the form.

```
' Create a new graphic object
Dim g As Graphics = Me.CreateGraphics

' Declare a rectangle to use for new ellipses
Dim recCircles As Rectangle = New Rectangle (25, 25, 200, 200)
Dim intIndex As Integer
```

4. Enter the following lines of code to draw a filled ellipse.

```
' Draw a large filled circle
g.FillEllipse(New SolidBrush(Color.Blue), 25, 25, 200, 200)
```

5. Enter the following lines of code to draw a series of circles of decreasing size.

```
' Loop to draw 5 circles of decreasing size
For intIndex = 1 To 5
   g.DrawEllipse(New Pen(Color.Black, 3), recCircles)

   ' Decrease the size of the rectangle the circle will fit
   recCircles.Height -= 25
   recCircles.Width -= 25
Next
```

6. Start debugging the program to verify that, when clicked, it draws a picture like the one shown in Figure 15-6.

FIGURE 15-6
A series of five circles of decreasing size is drawn

7. Stop debugging, save your work, close the project, and leave Visual Studio 2005 open for the next Step-by-Step.

Drawing Polygons

Rectangles, lines, and ellipses are the most commonly drawn shapes, but they are far from the only shapes we might want to use. There are many instances when we may want to draw multisided figures. A general term for a multisided figure is a polygon. A *polygon* is any shape with three or more sides. Triangles and pentagons are two of the more popular polygons that do not have their own specific method. These shapes can be drawn using two general-purpose methods to draw outlined or filled polygons.

The DrawPolygon method takes a Pen as its first parameter. The FillPolygon method takes a Brush as its first parameter. This is very similar to the methods you have used already. The big difference comes in the second parameter. The second parameter for both methods is an array of points.

The array has one element less than the number of sides in the polygon. (Remember also that the array starts counting from zero.) The system will draw from the last point to the first point automatically. The following Step-by-Step uses FillPolygon to draw a triangle on a form.

STEP-BY-STEP 15.4

1. Create a new project called **SimplePolygon**.

2. Open the code window, select **(Form1 Events)** from the Class Name drop-down box, if necessary, and select **Click** from the Method Name drop-down list.

3. Enter the following lines of code in the Click event handler to create a new graphic object on the form.

```
' Create a new graphic object
Dim g As Graphics = Me.CreateGraphics
```

4. Enter the following code to declare a SolidBrush to use to fill the triangle.

```
' Declare a red SolidBrush
Dim myBrush As Brush = New SolidBrush(Color.Red)
```

5. Enter the following code to declare and initialize a three-element array of points.

```
' Create and initialize a three-element array of points
Dim ptCorners(2) As Point
ptCorners(0) = New Point(125, 75)
ptCorners(1) = New Point(200, 200)
ptCorners(2) = New Point(50, 200)
```

6. Enter the following code to draw the triangle.

```
' Draw a triangle from the point array
g.FillPolygon(myBrush, ptCorners)
```

7. Start debugging the program to see that, when clicked, it draws a red triangle on the form, like the one shown in Figure 15-7.

FIGURE 15-7
A filled triangle drawn by `FillPolygon`

8. Stop debugging the program.

9. Save your work, close the project, and leave Visual Studio 2005 open for the next Step-by-Step.

Locating the Mouse

The `MouseDown` event returns a number of useful pieces of information. One important piece of information it returns is the location on the form where the mouse was pointing when the mouse button was pressed. The event object is returned as a variable named e. This variable has an X and Y property; the coordinates hold the location where the mouse was clicked.

The X and Y property can be used in your code as a starting point to draw objects on the form. This will allow your program to draw wherever the user wishes to draw.

Hot Tip

The Button property of the `MouseDown` event object can be compared to `MouseButtons.Left` and `MouseButtons.Right` to determine which button on the mouse was pressed. This allows your program to take different actions depending on the button used.

$\mathcal{S}$ TEP-BY-STEP 15.5

1. Open the **BoxSample** project you created in Step-by-Step 15.2, and then open the code window, if necessary. (If you did not complete this project, ask your instructor for the project files.)

2. Select **(Form1 Events)** from the Class Name drop-down box and **MouseDown** from the Method Name drop-down list.

3. Move the code from the *Form1_Click* event into the *Form1_MouseDown* event handler.

4. Change the line of code that declares the rectangle to use `e.x` and `e.y` in place of the current x and y values. The new line should look like the code that follows.

   ```
   Dim recBox As Rectangle = New Rectangle(e.X, e.Y, 100, 100)
   ```

5. Start debugging the program and click the mouse on the form to verify that a box is drawn at the location of the mouse every time you click it. After several clicks, your form may look something like Figure 15-8.

FIGURE 15-8
Boxes are drawn wherever the mouse is clicked

6. Stop debugging the program.

7. Save your work and leave the project open for the next Step-by-Step.

Once a position is found, it can be used as a starting place for any number of objects. Other objects become defined by their location relative to the starting point. This allows you to build objects that are made up of combinations of lines and shapes.

We can draw a triangle on top of a square to make a simple drawing of a house, for example. The box that is the house will start at the location where the mouse is clicked and be drawn to the right and down from that location. The roof will be drawn to the right and up from the starting location. The following Step-by-Step shows how this is done.

S TEP-BY-STEP 15.6

1. Change the color in the `FillRectangle` method to **BurlyWood** and remove the `DrawRectangle` method statement. Adjust the comments as necessary.

2. Enter the following code to create the `Point` array to draw the roof.

```
' Define a triangle for the roof
Dim ptCorners(2) As Point
ptCorners(0) = New Point(e.X, e.Y)
ptCorners(1) = New Point(e.X + 100, e.Y)
ptCorners(2) = New Point(e.X + 50, e.Y - 50)
```

3. Enter the following code to draw the triangle defined by the `Point` array. Your completed program should look like Figure 15-9.

```
' Draw the roof triangle
g.FillPolygon(New SolidBrush(Color.Gray), ptCorners)
```

FIGURE 15-9
The BoxSample code to draw a house

4. Start debugging the program to verify that it draws a house with a roof similar to the one shown in Figure 15-10 wherever the mouse is clicked.

STEP-BY-STEP 15.6 Continued

FIGURE 15-10
The house that Visual Basic built

5. Stop debugging the program.

6. Save your work and leave the project and Visual Studio 2005 open for the next Step-by-Step.

Clearing the Form

The form can be cleared in two ways. Parts of the form may be cleared by drawing new shapes over existing shapes and using the background color of the form. A second way is to use the Clear method of the graphic object. The Clear method takes as its parameter the color that will be used to replace what is currently on the form. The BackColor property of the form is the color most commonly used for this purpose. The following Step-by-Step adds a clear function for a program.

STEP-BY-STEP 15.7

1. Add a command button to the form and name it **cmdClear**. Set its Text property to **Clear Form**.

2. Add the following code to the Click event handler for cmdClear.

```
' Create a new graphic object
Dim g As Graphics = Me.CreateGraphics
g.Clear(Me.BackColor)
```

3. Start debugging the program and click on the form to draw several houses.

4. Click **Clear Form** to verify that the form is cleared.

5. Stop debugging the program.

6. Save your program and close Visual Studio 2005.

> **Extra for Experts**
>
> By using the value BackColor taken directly from the form, the Clear command will work as expected even if the program changes the form's BackColor when the program is running.

SUMMARY

In this lesson, you learned:

- You can use the DrawLine method to draw a line on a form using Visual Basic code.

- There are two ways to draw most shapes on a form. A Draw method creates an outline drawing of the object. The Fill method creates an object that is filled with a color specified by a brush color.

- A Pen object is created with a color and may also have a line width specified for it.

- Rectangles (including squares) are created using the DrawRectangle and FillRectangle methods. Rectangles are objects that can be declared with a starting point and width and height. Once they are declared, rectangle objects can be used to draw both rectangles and ellipses.

- Ellipses (including circles) are created using the DrawEllipse and FillEllipse methods.

- Once you used a graphic method to draw a line, rectangle, ellipse, or other shape, you cannot manipulate the shape. The graphic methods draw directly on a form.

- Distance and position on a form is measured using coordinates. The upper-left corner of a form has the coordinates (0, 0). All coordinates are positive. As you move toward the bottom of a form, the Y-coordinate value increases. As you move toward the right of a form, the X-coordinate value increases.

- The MouseDown event returns information about the location of the mouse and the button that was used to click on the mouse.

- The Clear method of the graphic object is used to erase the whole form.

VOCABULARY *Review*

Define the following terms:

Brush	Graphic object	Point
Color object	Pen	Polygon

REVIEW *Questions*

TRUE / FALSE

Circle T if the statement is true or F if the statement is false.

T F **1.** There are two ways to create rectangles on forms.

T F **2.** Circles are really ellipses with the same width and height.

T F **3.** A line drawn on a form can be moved by changing its location properties.

T F **4.** A `FillRectangle` method draws the outline of a rectangle.

T F **5.** The `DrawLine` method for drawing lines on a form does not have the ability to set the line's color.

T F **6.** The `DrawEllipse` method draws inside a rectangle.

T F **7.** The optional width parameter in a Pen object specifies the thickness of the line to be drawn.

T F **8.** You can use the `DrawLine` method to draw a box.

T F **9.** The `Color` structure only defines a very small number of colors.

T F **10.** The coordinate system is measured in pixels.

WRITTEN QUESTIONS

Write a brief answer to each of the following questions.

1. How many elements must there be in the Point array used by `DrawPolygon`?

2. What are the parameters for a `DrawLine` method?

3. Which object is used to specify the color in a `FillPolygon` method?

4. What is the default thickness of the line drawn by a Pen object?

5. What are the X- and Y-coordinates of the upper-left corner of a form?

6. What mouse event returns the location of the mouse when it is clicked?

7. What color should be used with the `Clear` command to erase a form?

8. What two different shapes can be drawn using a rectangle object as a parameter?

9. Why are coordinates (25, –10) not valid when positioning an object on a form?

10. What is a general term for a figure with three or more sides?

PROJECTS

PROJECT 15-1

Start Visual Studio 2005 and create a more complete house drawing program. Have the program draw a house where the user clicks the left mouse button and a tree where the user clicks the right mouse button. You may draw your house and trees differently from what is shown in Figure 15-11, but you must have at least two windows and a door on your house. Include a File menu with a Clear and an Exit option.

FIGURE 15-11
Draw a house and trees similar to the ones shown here

PROJECT 15-2

This project creates a program that allows a user to draw various shapes on a form. The program uses a flag variable to keep track of what type of shape the user has selected to draw.

1. Open **DrawShapes** from the **proj15-02** folder in the data files for this lesson.

2. Add the following code for the `mnuShapeBox` menu option to set the check marks and the `intShape` flag for boxes.

```
' Set the check mark in the right place
mnuShapeBox.Checked = True
mnuShapeCircle.Checked = False
mnuShapeTriangle.Checked = False

' Set the value of intShape to zero for boxes
intShape = 0
```

3. Add similar code to the `mnuShapeCircle` and `mnuShapeTriangle` menu `Click` event methods to turn on the check mark and to set the value of `intShape`. The value of `intShape` for a circle is **1** and for a triangle is **2**.

4. Enter code for the `mnuFileClear` option to clear the form.

5. Enter code for the `mnuFileExit` option to exit the program.

6. Enter the following code to the `Form1_MouseDown` event method to draw the shape the user selected from the Shape menu.

```
' Create a graphic object and a SolidBrush
Dim g As Graphics = Me.CreateGraphics
Dim brushBrush As New SolidBrush(Color.Blue)

' If intShape is a zero, draw a box
If intShape = 0 Then
    g.FillRectangle(brushBrush, e.X, e.Y, 50, 50)
End If

' If intShape is a one, then draw a circle
If intShape = 1 Then
    g.FillEllipse(brushBrush, e.X, e.Y, 50, 50)
End If

' If intShape is a two, draw a triangle
If intShape = 2 Then
    Dim ptArray(2) As Point

    ptArray(0) = New Point(e.X, e.Y)
    ptArray(1) = New Point(e.X - 25, e.Y + 25)
    ptArray(2) = New Point(e.X + 25, e.Y + 25)
    g.FillPolygon(brushBrush, ptArray)
End If
```

7. Start debugging the program and verify that the shapes drawn match the checked menu selection.

8. Test the Clear menu option, and then exit the program using the **Exit** menu option.

9. Save the changes to the project and leave the project open.

> **Note**
>
> You may have noticed that when the form is minimized or another window or menu covers it, the program doesn't automatically redraw the graphic objects that were there. We will talk about why this happens, and how to handle it, in the next lesson.

PROJECT 15-3

1. If necessary, open the **DrawShapes** project you modified in Project 15-2.

2. Add a **Color** menu to the right of the Shapes menu.

3. Add four different color options to the color menu.

4. Add the following code under the declaration of `intShape` in the Declarations section of the program.

```
' Create a variable of type Color
Dim clrColor As Color
```

5. Change the line in the Form1_MouseDown event that creates the Brush to use **clrColor** in place of *Color.Blue*. It should look like the following line.

    ```
    Dim brushBrush As New SolidBrush(clrColor)
    ```

6. For each option in the color menu, write a line of code that sets the value of **clrColor** to the color named. For example the line of code for a Red menu option follows.

    ```
    clrColor = Color.Red
    ```

7. In the Form1_Load method, set the value of **clrColor** to one of the colors in your Color menu.

8. Start debugging the program and test it to make sure that it lets you properly change colors and shapes.

9. Stop debugging the program, save the changes to the project, and then close it.

CRITICAL*Thinking*

The MouseUp event returns the same information about the location of the mouse as the MouseDown event does. Create a program that uses this information to draw lines on the form. The line will begin where the mouse is pressed down and will end where it is released. Save the X and Y values of the mouse location when a button is pressed in two form level variables. In the MouseUp event, create a Pen graphic object and use the locations from both the MouseDown and MouseUp events to draw a line that connects the two points.

CASE STUDY—SNAKE GAME

OBJECTIVES

Upon completion of this lesson, you should be able to:

- Run the Snake Game.

- Draw with individual pixels and use the `Paint` event.

- Describe how the Snake Game draws and controls the direction of the snake.

- Describe how the Snake Game code functions.

Estimated Time: 1.5 hours

VOCABULARY

Bitmap object

`GetPixel` method

`Paint` event

Running the Snake Game

The Snake Game that you ran in Lesson 1 is an example of how a simple game can be created in Visual Studio with very little code. Let's run the program again as a reminder of how the game is played.

STEP-BY-STEP 16.1

1. Start Visual Studio 2005 and open **SnakeGame** from the **step16-01** folder in the data files for this lesson.

2. Start debugging the program and play the game at least once to refamiliarize yourself with the game's operation.

3. End the program and close the project. Leave Visual Studio open for the next Step-by-Step.

The Snake Game is based on a very simple principle. A blue line (the snake) grows within a blue box. The user can change the direction in which the snake grows. As long as the user steers the line in a direction that keeps a clear path ahead of the line, the game continues. But if the line crosses itself or hits the blue box, the game ends.

Writing a program like the Snake Game is not difficult. Visual Basic includes a method that allows a single pixel to be changed to a particular color. To draw the growing snake, a loop must repeat until the snake crosses its own tail or hits the blue box. With each iteration of the loop, another pixel is turned blue.

Drawing with Pixels and Using the Paint Event Handler

There are only four Visual Basic features that the Snake Game uses which you have not yet learned. The first is the feature that allows you to create an image and draw it on your form. The second is the method that allows you to draw on an image one pixel at a time. The third is a feature that allows you to retrieve the color of a specific pixel. Finally, there is the Paint event that prevents the graphics you draw from being erased if another window covers the graphics you have drawn.

Creating a Graphic Image

A Bitmap object is an object used to work with images defined by pixel data. Images from files may be loaded into a Bitmap object, but a program can set individual pixels on a bitmap as well.

Bitmap objects may be saved to a file or they may be drawn on a Graphics object. In the SnakeGame program, a Graphics object is the surface on which our image is drawn.

A Bitmap object and a Graphics object are created using Dim statements. The following example uses the CreateGraphics command to create a new Graphic object on the form. The second Dim statement creates a Bitmap object that is 200 pixels wide and 200 pixels high.

```
' Create a Graphics object to use with the game's bitmap
Dim myGraphicObject As Graphics = Me.CreateGraphics
' Create an empty Bitmap object.
Dim myBitmap As New Bitmap(200, 200)
```

The complete bitmap is actually stored in the computer's memory. Only when the image is drawn or painted on the form does it become visible. Using the image from memory in a Bitmap object gives us two advantages. The first is that a complete picture can be drawn in memory bit by bit and then painted all at once on the form. The second is that the memory image can be repainted at any time to recover any part of the image that is lost when the form is covered by another object.

The bitmap image is drawn on the form by using the DrawImage method of the Graphic object. The statement in our example below draws the bitmap in myBitmap at a location 10 pixels over from the left of the form and 10 pixels down from the top of the form. The width and height of the picture are the same as the width and height of the bitmap image that was created.

```
myGraphicObject.DrawImage(myBitmap, 10, 10, myBitmap.Width, myBitmap.Height)
```

The `DrawImage` method can be called directly after any change has been made to the image. A more efficient place for this code is generally in the method that handles the `Paint` event for the form. The `Paint` method is called whenever the form needs to be drawn. This includes such events as part of the form being covered and uncovered, the form being minimized, or the whole form being covered by another application. The program can also create a `Paint` event by using the `Refresh` method. The `Refresh` method tells the system to update an object. Refreshing a form includes painting the controls and images on it.

A form is refreshed using a statement like the one that follows.

```
Me.Refresh()
```

The `Paint` method for this project will look something like the following:

```
Private Sub frmMain_Paint(ByVal sender As Object, _
    ByVal e As System.Windows.Forms.PaintEventArgs) Handles MyBase.Paint _
    myGraphicObject.DrawImage(myBitmap, 10, 10, myBitmap.Width, _
    myBitmap.Height)
End Sub
```

Using the SetPixel Method

The `SetPixel` method of the Bitmap object is an easy-to-use feature that allows you to change the color of individual pixels on a bitmap. `SetPixel` uses the same coordinate system you learned about in Lesson 15. To use `SetPixel`, you identify the pixel using X, Y coordinates and specify a color for the pixel. The next example turns the pixel at point (120, 200) red.

```
myBitmap.SetPixel(120, 200, Color.Red)
```

Even though you might think of `SetPixel` as turning on individual pixels, in reality the method only changes the color of the pixel. It is best for you to think of all the pixels as being on at all times. Many of the pixels are set to the background color, which makes them appear to be off. The `SetPixel` method can be used to change a pixel to a color that is different from the background, or to return the pixel to the background color.

S TEP-BY-STEP 16.2

1. Create a new Visual Basic Windows Application project called **LineDemo**.

2. Set the (Name) property of the form to **frmMain** and set the Text property to **Draw Line**.

3. Add the following code to the (Declarations) section to create a Graphic object and a Bitmap object.

```
' Create a Graphics object to use with the game's bitmap
Dim myGraphicObject As Graphics = Me.CreateGraphics
' Create an empty Bitmap Object.
Dim myBitmap As New Bitmap(200, 200)
```

4. Create a command button on the lower-middle part of the form.

5. Set the (Name) property to **cmdLine** and set the Text property to **Draw Line**.

STEP-BY-STEP 16.2 Continued

6. Add the following code to the `Click` event procedure for the Draw Line command button, to draw a red line one pixel at a time.

```
' Draw a line a pixel at a time
Dim Counter As Integer
For Counter = 50 To 150
    myBitmap.SetPixel(Counter, 50,  Color.Red)
Next Counter
myGraphicObject.DrawImage(myBitmap, 10, 10, _
    myBitmap.Width, myBitmap.Height)
```

7. Start debugging the program.

8. Click **Draw Line**. A red line is drawn, as shown in Figure 16-1.

FIGURE 16-1
Clicking Draw Line draws a red line on the form one pixel at a time

9. End the program, save your work, and leave the project and Visual Studio open for the next Step-by-Step.

Using the GetPixel Method

The `GetPixel` method returns the color structure of a pixel at the specified pixel. The method works hand-in-hand with the `SetPixel` method. Use `SetPixel` to change the color of a pixel and use `GetPixel` to determine the current color of a pixel. For example, the code below stores the color of the pixel at point (120, 200) to the variable `clrPixelColor`.

```
clrPixelColor = myBitmap.GetPixel(120, 200)
```

The color structure includes four components: alpha, red, green, and blue (ARGB). These can be easily compared using a 32-bit ARGB value. The `ToArgb` method is used to convert this structure into a more easily compared integer value. For example, the following code compares the color in a color object with the system-defined Blue color.

```
If (clrPixelColor.ToArgb() = Color.Blue.ToArgb()) Then
```

Handling the Paint Event

The `Paint` event is called whenever an object is resized, covered and uncovered, minimized and then restored, or when the `Refresh` event is called. This event can be used to make sure that the board is redrawn or repainted to prevent losing data from the form. When part of a form is covered and uncovered or minimized and restored, the system does not automatically redraw things that were on the form before it was covered. The `Paint` event is called when those things happen, and it is up to the program to make sure that items are redrawn.

The information about the playing board (i.e., the color of specific pixels) is kept in the Bitmap object that is used with `SetPixel` and `GetPixel`. This bitmap can be drawn on the form at any time to make this information visible to the person playing the game. We will use the `Paint` event to redraw this information.

S TEP-BY-STEP 16.3

1. Start debugging the LineDemo program and click **Draw Line**.

2. Minimize the program and then restore it. You will see that the red line has disappeared. It has not been repainted.

3. From the Code Window in the IDE, select the **(frmMain Events)** option in the Class Name drop-down list, as shown in Figure 16-2.

FIGURE 16-2
The `frmMain` Events option is selected

Select the **(frmMain Events)** option in the Class Name drop-down list

STEP-BY-STEP 16.3 Continued

4. Using the **Method Name** drop-down, as shown in Figure 16-3, select the `Paint` event so that the IDE will create a method to handle this event.

FIGURE 16-3
The `Paint` event is selected

5. Move the `myGraphicObject.DrawImage` method call to the `Paint` event procedure and add the comment **'Redraw the bitmap image**.

6. Add the following code to the end of the `Click` event procedure for the Draw Line command button. The `Refresh` method will force the `Paint` event to be processed so that the line is drawn immediately.

```
' Refresh the screen to show the updated bitmap
Me.Refresh()
```

Your program should look like Figure 16-4.

STEP-BY-STEP 16.3 Continued

FIGURE 16-4
Modified Draw Line code

```vb
Public Class frmMain

    ' Create a Graphics object to use with the game's bitmap
    Dim myGraphicObject As Graphics = Me.CreateGraphics
    ' Create an empty Bitmap Object.
    Dim myBitmap As New Bitmap(200, 200)

    Private Sub cmdLine_Click(ByVal sender As System.Object, ByVal e As System.EventA
        ' Draw a line a pixel at a time
        Dim Counter As Integer
        For Counter = 50 To 150
            myBitmap.SetPixel(Counter, 50, Color.Red)
        Next Counter

        'Refresh the screen to show the updated bitmap
        Me.Refresh()
    End Sub

    Private Sub frmMain_Paint(ByVal sender As Object, ByVal e As System.Windows.Forms
        ' Redraw the bitmap image
        myGraphicObject.DrawImage(myBitmap, 10, 10, myBitmap.Width, myBitmap.Height)
    End Sub
End Class
```

7. Start debugging the program. Click **Draw Line** to verify that the line is drawn.

8. Minimize and restore the program to verify that the line appears automatically when the form is restored.

9. Save your work and close the project, but leave Visual Studio open for the next Step-by-Step.

How the Snake Game Draws the Snake

The snake that appears on the Snake Game is drawn one pixel at a time using SetPixel. When the user clicks one of the direction buttons, the path of the snake changes to reflect the direction the user selected.

Four variables are key to drawing and controlling the snake. The first two variables, intX and intY, specify the point on the form where the next pixel will appear. When the pixel at point (intX, intY) is turned blue, the values of intX and intY are changed to the position of the next pixel. These adjustments to intX and intY are accomplished using two other variables: intXFactor and intYFactor.

The variable intXFactor specifies the number of pixels that are to be added to intX to advance the head of the snake in the X direction. The variable intYFactor specifies the number of pixels that are to be added to intY to advance the snake in the Y direction.

For example, suppose the head of the snake is moving down, as shown in Figure 16-5. When the head is moving down, `intXFactor` is zero because there is no change to the X-coordinate as the snake moves down. The variable `intYFactor` is 1 because each iteration of the loop increases the Y-coordinate by one pixel.

FIGURE 16-5
The snake moves down

In Figure 16-6, the head of the snake is moving to the right. In this case, `intXFactor` is 1 because the X-coordinate increases by one pixel with each iteration of the loop. The Y-coordinate, however, does not change because the movement is horizontal. Therefore, `intYFactor` is zero.

FIGURE 16-6
The snake moves right

Moving the snake up and left requires negative values because the snake is moving toward either the top or left. To move the head of the snake up, the `intYFactor` must be –1. Adding the negative value to `intY` moves the X,Y coordinate nearer to the top of the form. In Figure 16-7, you can see that when `intXFactor` is zero and `intYFactor` is –1, the snake moves up.

FIGURE 16-7
The snake moves up

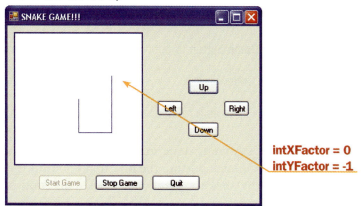

intXFactor = 0
intYFactor = -1

Finally, to move the head of the snake to the left, `intXFactor` must be –1. Figure 16-8 shows the coordinate factors necessary to move left.

FIGURE 16-8
The snake moves left

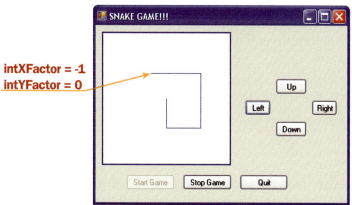

intXFactor = -1
intYFactor = 0

As we analyze the code, you will see how the `intXFactor` and `intYFactor` variables are set to the appropriate values and how the snake is actually drawn.

Analyzing the Snake Game Code

Before we analyze the details of the Snake Game code, let's get an overview of how the program flow is controlled and what each button actually does.

S TEP-BY-STEP 16.4

1. Open the **SnakeGame** project again (from the **step16-01** data files) and, if necessary, open **frmMainForm**.

STEP-BY-STEP 16.4 Continued

2. If necessary, resize the project window to see all seven command buttons.

3. Double-click the **Start Game** button to open the Code window and review the code.

4. Scroll to the top of the Code window.

5. Leave the Code window open as a reference as you read the paragraphs that follow.

The primary work of the game is done in the Start Game button's `Click` event procedure. When the user clicks the Start Game button, the box that contains the snake is drawn, and a loop begins that starts drawing the snake a pixel at a time. This loop continues until one of three things happens:

1. The user runs the snake into a wall or into its tail

2. The user clicks the Stop Game button

3. The user clicks the Quit button

As you will see when we look at the code, the `Application.DoEvents` function allows other events to be processed as the Start Game button's `Click` event procedure is being executed. For example, even though the Start Game button's `Click` event procedure is still being executed, the user can click the Stop Game button to end the game. The `Do Events` function also allows the user to click the direction buttons.

The Up, Down, Left, and Right buttons simply change the `intXFactor` and `intYFactor` variables to change the direction of the snake.

Let's look at the code in detail.

Form-Level Variables

Three form-level variables are required for the Snake Game. First, we need a way to stop the program if the user clicks the Stop Game button. We can declare a Boolean variable named `blnStop` to signal that the user wishes to stop the game. The declaration of the `blnStop` variable is shown here.

```
Dim blnStop As Boolean 'Flag to stop game when user clicks the Stop Game _
    button
```

You will see later in the code how the `blnStop` variable is used to stop the game.

Two more form-level variables are necessary. The `intXFactor` and `intYFactor` variables you learned about earlier must be form-level because the factors will be changed by the direction buttons and used by the Start Game button. By making them form-level variables, the values set by the code for the direction buttons will be available in the Start Game button's `Click` event procedure. The two declarations appear here.

```
Dim intYFactor As Integer
Dim intXFactor As Integer
```

The Start Game Button

As you learned earlier, the primary code for the game is in the Start Game button's Click event procedure. At the heart of the event procedure is a loop. The loop repeats until the snake runs into itself or the wall. The loop will also stop if the user clicks the Stop Game button or quits the program.

Before we look at the details of the loop, let's see what the procedure does before the loop begins.

First, four local variables are declared to be used within this procedure.

```
Dim intX As Integer
Dim intY As Integer
Dim clrSnakeColor As Color = Color.Blue
Dim clrPixel As Color
```

The variables intX and intY are used to keep track of the next pixel that will be turned blue as the snake grows. The variable clrSnakeColor will store the color used to draw the box and the snake. We set this variable to blue. The clrPixel variable will be used to hold information about pixels we will be checking.

The next three lines of code (shown in our next example) take care of some housekeeping before the loop begins. First, the Start Game button is disabled. This is important because we do not want the user to start more than one instance of the game simultaneously. The second line sets the blnStop variable to False. This Boolean variable is set to True if the user clicks the Stop Game button. The third statement makes the picture box invisible until we are ready to use it for the game.

```
cmdStart.Enabled = False  'Disable Start Game button
PictureBox1.Visible = False
DrawBoard()
blnStop = False           'Set Stop flag to false
```

The next lines of code initialize the key variables to prepare for the start of the game. The intX and intY variables are each set to 100. This places the starting point for the snake at point (100, 100). By setting intXFactor to 0 and intYFactor to 1, the snake will initially be heading down the form.

```
intX = 100
intY = 100
intXFactor = 0
intYFactor = 1
```

Now that all of the initial work is done and the variables are initialized, the next step is to draw the box. The DrawBoard method is called to draw a box with a border around it. The game board is drawn by setting each pixel in the bitmap to white, except for those pixels around the edge. The pixels at the top, bottom, and sides are set to clrSnakeColor so that our loop routine will see them as pixels that have already been used.

The Start Game Button's Loop

We are finally ready to analyze the loop. The loop adds one pixel to the snake with each iteration. The intXFactor and intYFactor determine where the next pixel is added. Look at the code that follows. With each iteration of the loop, the SetPixel method draws a pixel in the color of the snake. Then the code immediately increases intX by the value in intXFactor. The code also increases intY by the value in intYFactor. The Refresh method forces the Paint event to fire, redrawing the bitmap to the screen. The DoEvents method makes sure that the Paint event is processed, as well as any button Click events.

```
Do
    ' Wait
    System.Threading.Thread.Sleep(50)

    ' Set the value of the next pixel
    myBitmap.SetPixel(intX, intY, clrSnakeColor)

    ' Calculate the position of the next pixel to draw
    intX += intXFactor
    intY += intYFactor

    ' Force a refresh of the form to call the Paint event handler
    Me.Refresh()

    ' Call DoEvents to make sure interrupts are handled
    Application.DoEvents()

    ' Get the color value of the next pixel
    clrPixel = myBitmap.GetPixel(intX, intY)

    ' If the next iteration of the loop will set a color on a pixel that
    ' is already set, then exit the game
    If (myBitmap.GetPixel(intX, intY).ToArgb() = clrSnakeColor.ToArgb()) Then _
        MessageBox.Show("Game Over", "Snake Game")

    ' Exit the game if a collision has taken place or if the stop button is pressed
Loop Until (clrPixel.ToArgb() = clrSnakeColor.ToArgb()) Or (blnStop = True)
```

Once the board has been drawn, the GetPixel method looks at the color in the next pixel the program would write to and makes sure that it is not already clrSnakeColor. If it is already clrSnakeColor, then the next write would be to either the edge of the board or part of the snake. If the next step would hit the snake or the edge of the board, the game is over. The loop will also end if the user clicks the Stop button, which would change the value of blnStop.

Because the snake will grow too quickly on most computers, a call to System.Threading.Thread.Sleep is used to delay the loop for an instant during each iteration of the loop. Adjusting the value in the Sleep method call will change the speed of the snake. Make the number larger to slow the snake down; make it smaller to speed it up.

Changing the Coordinate Factors

The `intXFactor` and `intYFactor` variables are adjusted through the `Click` event procedures of the four direction buttons. For example, when the user clicks the Right command button, the coordinate factors are set as shown in the following code.

```
Private Sub btnRight_Click(ByVal sender As System.Object, ByVal e As _
    System.EventArgs) Handles btnRight.Click
    intXFactor = 1
    intYFactor = 0
End Sub
```

Because `intXFactor` and `intYFactor` are form-level variables, the new values for these factors will remain as set until one of the other direction buttons changes the values. For the Left command button, the X factor is –1 and the Y factor is 0. For the Down command button, the Y factor is 1 and the X factor is 0. For the Up command button, the Y factor is –1 and the X factor is 0.

Remember, the event loop in the Start Game button's event procedure will not end when the user clicks one of the direction buttons. The direction button only changes the coordinate factors, thereby changing the direction the snake is headed. Once the event procedure above is executed, the Start Game button's event procedure continues looping.

The Stop Game Button

The code for the Stop Game button simply changes the value of `blnStop` to True. If the Stop Game button is pressed while the game is in play, the form-level variable `blnStop` will be changed to True, which will stop the loop.

```
Private Sub cmdStop_Click(ByVal sender As System.Object, ByVal e As _
    System.EventArgs) Handles cmdStop.Click
    blnStop = True
    cmdStart.Enabled = True
End Sub
```

The Start command button is also enabled in this button's `Click` event, to let the user start a new game.

The Quit Button

The Quit button differs from the Stop Game button. The Quit button does more than stop the current game. It ends the program.

```
Private Sub cmdQuit_Click(ByVal sender As System.Object, ByVal e As _
    System.EventArgs) Handles cmdQuit.Click
    blnStop = True
    End
End Sub
```

STEP-BY-STEP 16.5

1. Start debugging the program.

2. Play the Snake Game one more time.

3. End the game and make a list of possible enhancements to the game.

4. Exit Visual Studio 2005 without saving any changes to **SnakeGame**.

SUMMARY

In this lesson, you learned:

■ The Snake Game is an example of a simple game created with Visual Studio 2005.

■ The `SetPixel` method allows you to change the color of individual pixels on a bitmap.

■ The `GetPixel` method retrieves the color of the specified pixel on a bitmap.

■ The `Refresh` method causes the `Paint` event to execute.

■ The `Paint` event handler can be used to redraw objects that are erased when a form is covered or minimized.

■ The Snake Game keeps track of a point on the form where the next pixel will appear as the snake grows.

■ The snake is controlled by two factors. One factor specifies the change in the X-coordinate, and the other factor specifies the change in the Y-coordinate.

■ The direction buttons change the factors that control the direction of the snake. The variables that store the factors are form-level so that multiple buttons can change the value of the factors.

■ The color of the wall and snake are controlled by changing the value of `clrSnakeColor`.

■ The speed of the snake is controlled by adjusting the value in the `Sleep` method call.

VOCABULARY *Review*

Define the following terms:		
Bitmap object	GetPixel method	Paint event

REVIEW *Questions*

TRUE / FALSE

Circle T if the statement is true or F if the statement is false.

T F   1. The SetPixel method turns a specific pixel on or off.

T F   2. GetPixel can be used to determine the color of a specific pixel.

T F   3. The Refresh method causes the Paint event to execute.

T F   4. There is no way to recover objects that are erased when a form is covered and uncovered.

T F   5. If intXFactor is set to 0 and intYFactor is set to 1, the snake will move up.

T F   6. If intXFactor and intYFactor are both set to 0, the snake will continue to move in its current direction.

T F   7. There is no way to change the speed of the moving snake.

T F   8. If the DoEvents statement was removed from the cmdStart_Click event procedure, the direction buttons would not change the movement of the snake.

T F   9. The game can only be stopped by the snake hitting a wall or itself.

T F 10. The Quit button allows the user to end the current game without ending the program.

WRITTEN QUESTIONS

Write a brief answer to each of the following questions.

1. What is the coordinate system of a bitmap object?

2. What method converts a color value to an integer value?

3. What method is used to make a new graphics object on a form?

4. What are the variables intX and intY used for?

5. If intXFactor is set to –1 and intYFactor is set to 0, which direction will the snake move?

6. What effect will a negative X or Y factor value have on the movement of the snake?

7. Why is it necessary to declare the intXFactor and intYFactor variables at the form level?

8. How could we change the starting location of the snake at the beginning of the game?

9. Why is the Start Game button disabled at the beginning of the cmdStart_Click event procedure?

10. What variable is changed by the cmdStop_Click event procedure to stop the game?

PROJECTS

PROJECT 16-1

1. Open the **LineDemo** program that you created in Step-by-Steps 16.2 and 16.3. (If you did not complete this project, ask your instructor for the files.)

2. Change the Text of the command button to **Draw Lines**.

3. Change the Text of the form to **Draw Lines**.

4. Modify the code in the command button's `Click` event so it matches the following.

```
Dim Counter As Integer
For Counter = 50 To 150
    myBitmap.SetPixel(Counter, 10, Color.Red)
    myBitmap.SetPixel(Counter, 35, Color.Black)
    myBitmap.SetPixel(Counter, 60, Color.Blue)
    myBitmap.SetPixel(Counter, 85, Color.Green)
Next Counter
' Refresh the screen to show the updated bitmap
Me.Refresh()
```

5. Close the code window and debug the program.

6. Click **Draw Lines**. Four different colored lines appear on the form.

7. Save the changes to the project, and then close it.

PROJECT 16-2

1. Open the **Snake Game** program (from the **step16-01** data files).

2. Change the value of `clrSnakeColor` to `Color.Red`. (*Hint:* You will have to make the change in both the Start Game `Click` event and in the `DrawBoard` function.)

3. Start debugging the program and start the game. Notice that the border and the color of the snake have changed to red.

4. End the game (if necessary) and save the changes to the project. Leave the program open for the next Project.

PROJECT 16-3

1. Open the **Snake Game** program you worked with in Project 16-2, if it is not already opened.

2. Create a new integer form-level variable called `intWait`.

3. In the `cmdStart_Click` event procedure, set the value of `intWait` to 50 and replace the number in the `Sleep` method call with the `intWait` variable.

4. Create a command button above the Up command button.

5. Set the (Name) property to **cmdSpeed** and the Text property to **Faster**.

6. Add the following code in the button's Click event to toggle the speed at which the snake moves and to change the Text of the command button.

```
If cmdSpeed.Text = "Faster" Then
    intWait = 25
    cmdSpeed.Text = "Slower"
Else
    intWait = 50
    cmdSpeed.Text = "Faster"
End If
```

7. Start debugging the program and start the game.

8. Click **Faster**. Notice that the snake moves faster, and the Text of the command button changes to *Slower*.

9. Click **Slower** to slow the snake down.

10. End the game (if necessary) and save the changes to the project. Leave the program open for the next Project.

PROJECT 16-4

1. Open the **Snake Game** program you worked with in Project 16-3, if it is not already opened.

2. Create a label at the upper-right corner of the form named **lblScore** and set the Text property equal to **0**. Change the BackColor property to **White** using the Web tab. Set the TextAlign property to **MiddleLeft**. Set the AutoSize property to **False** and set the label's Size property to **60, 13**, for a width of 60 pixels and a height of 13 pixels.

3. Create another label to the left of lblScore named **lblScore2** and set the Text property equal to **Score:** (change the TextAlign property to **MiddleRight**). Change the BackColor property to **White**. Your screen should appear similar to Figure 16-9.

FIGURE 16-9
Add two labels as shown here

4. Create a variable named **intScore** in the cmdStart event procedure.

5. Initialize intScore to 0.

6. Add the following code to the main game loop code (just below the code that sets the color to a new pixel) to increment intScore by 1 and set lblScore equal to intScore.

```
' Increment and display the score
intScore = intScore + 1
lblScore.Text = Format(intScore)
```

7. Start debugging the program and start the game. Notice that the more the snake grows, the higher your score becomes.

8. End the game (if necessary) and save the changes to the project. Leave the project open for the next Project.

PROJECT 16-5

Look at the list of possible enhancements to the game that you listed in Step-by-Step 16.5. Choose and implement one of the enhancements, or at least describe how the enhancement might be implemented.

CRITICAL*Thinking*

Create four additional direction buttons that will make the snake move diagonally. You should create a new event procedure for each button that uses the appropriate X- and Y-coordinates. The form layout should look similar to Figure 16-10.

FIGURE 16-10
Add four small diagonal direction buttons

When the snake moves diagonally, it can occasionally cross another diagonal line without ending the game. Try it and see. You may have to try several times before successfully crossing a diagonal line. Can you explain why this is possible?

WEB FUNCTIONALITY AND FORM APPEARANCE

OBJECTIVES

Upon completion of this lesson, you should be able to:

- Use the WebBrowser control on a form.
- Use common methods of the WebBrowser control to navigate to Web pages.
- Set the background image property on a form.
- Use a background image on a form to simulate a skin.
- Use the Open Dialog Box to select a skin file during run-time.
- Change the background image programmatically on a Windows form.
- Use the TransparencyKey property of a Windows form to make irregularly shaped forms.
- Write code to allow a window with no title bar to be moved around on the screen.
- Write code to allow a window with no title bar to be closed.

Estimated Time: 2 hours

VOCABULARY

Open file dialog

Skin

TransparencyKey

WebBrowser control

WebBrowser Control

Visual Studio 2005 contains a **WebBrowser control** that makes it easy to integrate Web browsing capabilities into your Visual Basic Windows Forms. This control gives you access to the basic underlying code that runs the main Microsoft Internet Explorer software. With this control you are able to navigate to Web pages, refresh Web pages, navigate forward and backward, and go to the home page.

Navigate Method

To navigate to a Web page using the WebBrowser control, you would use the Navigate method and pass, as a parameter, the location of the Web site to which you wish to navigate. This code is shown below.

```
WebBrowser1.Navigate("http://www.course.com")
```

Hot Tip

You can find out more about the WebBrowser control on the Microsoft Web site: http://msdn2.microsoft.com/library/2te2y1x6(en-us,vs.80).aspx.

STEP-BY-STEP 17.1

1. Create a new Visual Basic project called **WebBrowser**.

2. Set the (Name) property of the form to **frmMain** and set the Text property to **Web Browser**.

3. Set the Size property of the form to **745**, **560**.

4. Add a TextBox control to the form.

5. Set the Location property of the text box to **12**, **55**; the Size property to **293**, **20**; and the (Name) property to **txtURL**.

6. Add a command Button to the form.

7. Set the Text property of the command button to **Go**; the Location to **311**, **55**; the Size property to **29**, **20**; and the (Name) of the button to **btnGo**.

8. Add a WebBrowser control to the form.

9. Set the (Name) property to **webMain**; the Size property to **685**, **398**; and the Location property to **30**, **97**.

10. Add the following code to the click event procedure for the Go command button.
    ```
    webMain.Navigate(txtURL.Text)
    ```

11. Start debugging the program.

12. Key the value **http://www.course.com** into the text box on the form and click the **Go** command button. The output should resemble Figure 17-1, but the contents of the Web page will likely be different.

STEP-BY-STEP 17.1 Continued

FIGURE 17-1
The WebBrowser control allows Web browsing capabilities inside a form

13. Stop debugging the program, save your work, and leave the project and Visual Basic open for the next Step-by-Step.

As mentioned previously, in addition to the `Navigate` method, the WebBrowser control includes other methods that give the control added functionality. As you know, Web browsers typically allow the user to go to a specified home page, refresh the current page, and move forward and backward through a list of Web sites that have been visited by the user during the current session. These same four functions are offered by the WebBrowser control.

GoHome Method

Browsers typically have a home page that first loads when the browser application is started. The WebBrowser control that is part of Visual Studio 2005 actually uses the same home page that the regular Internet Explorer application uses. If a user has changed the default home page setting inside of Internet Explorer, that same change will be reflected in the WebBrowser control. So, for example, if a user sets his or her home page inside of Internet Explorer to http://www.course.com, then the WebBrowser control will also use http://www.course.com as its home page. To navigate to the home page of the WebBrowser control, use the `GoHome` method as shown in the following code.

```
WebBrowser1.GoHome()
```

Refresh Method

To refresh the page that the WebBrowser control is currently displaying, you can use the `Refresh` method. A user might refresh a page when the content might have changed since the last loading of the Web page. An example of a page that might need to be refreshed would be a weather map or a stock quote. The code used for this method is shown below.

```
WebBrowser1.Refresh()
```

GoForward and GoBack Methods

When a browser is used to navigate a series of Web pages, the browser typically maintains a list of visited pages. Most browsers have a mechanism that allows a user to step forward and backward through the list of visited pages. The WebBrowser control handles this list of visited pages for you. To navigate forward or backward through the list of visited pages, you simply need to call the `GoForward` and `GoBack` methods of the WebBrowser control.

Sample code for these methods is shown below.

```
WebBrowser1.GoFoward()
WebBrowser1.GoBack()
```

STEP-BY-STEP 17.2

1. Add four buttons to frmMain with the values shown in Table 17-1.

TABLE 17-1
Values to enter for Step 1

(NAME)	TEXT	SIZE	LOCATION
btnBack	Back	55, 25	14, 14
btnForward	Forward	55, 25	72, 14
btnRefresh	Refresh	55, 25	131, 14
btnHome	Home	55, 25	190, 14

2. Add the following code to the `Click` event procedure for the btnBack command button.

```
webMain.GoBack()
```

3. Add the following code to the `Click` event procedure for the btnForward command button.

```
webMain.GoForward()
```

4. Add the following code to the `Click` event procedure for the btnRefresh command button.

```
webMain.Refresh()
```

5. Add the following code to the `Click` event procedure for the btnHome command button.

```
webMain.GoHome()
```

STEP-BY-STEP 17.2 Continued

6. Start debugging the program. Your form should resemble the form shown in Figure 17-2.

FIGURE 17-2
The form with the newly created buttons

7. Key the value **http://www.course.com** into the text box on the form and click the Go command button.

8. Click several of the links on the Course Technology Web site, and then test the **Forward**, **Back**, and **Refresh** buttons.

9. Finally, click the **Home** button to return to the home page.

10. Stop debugging the program and leave the project and Visual Basic open for the next Step-by-Step.

Altering the Appearance of Forms

Visual Studio 2005 makes it very easy to create forms with rich functionality. However, unless you modify the standard appearance of the forms, your programs will look unpolished and less professional. Editing the background image of a form and changing the form's normal rectangular shape are two ways to make your form look more interesting and professional.

Using BackgroundImage Property to Simulate a Skin

In computing terms, a *skin* is a custom look and feel that can be applied to an application. Often users can choose from existing skins or create their own skins so that the program has a custom look and feels tailored to the user's preferences. Examples of common programs that use skins include media players and Web browsers. Visual Basic forms do not have a built-in way to handle skins. However, by experimenting with the background image on a form, you can simulate this skinning ability and create forms that look very different from the standard form.

To set the background image of a form during design time, you use the BackgroundImage property of the form. This allows you to use an image as the form background.

S TEP-BY-STEP 17.3

1. If the Properties window is not already visible, select **Properties Window** from the **View** menu.

2. From the drop-down list at the top of the Properties window, select the properties for **frmMain**.

3. Click on the BackgroundImage property, and then click the button to the right of the BackgroundImage property. You should see a window resembling Figure 17-3.

FIGURE 17-3
The Select Resource dialog box

4. Select the radio button labeled **Local resource** and click on the **Import** button.

5. Navigate to the data files for this lesson and select **skin1.jpg**.

6. Click **Open**, and then click **OK**.

7. Start debugging the program. The output should resemble Figure 17-4.

STEP-BY-STEP 17.3 Continued

FIGURE 17-4
A Windows form with a background image applied

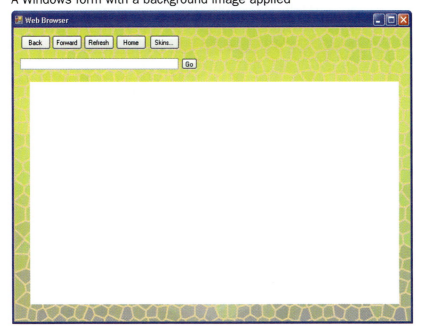

8. Stop debugging the program and leave the project and Visual Basic open for the next Step-by-Step.

Changing Skins at Run-time Using the OpenFileDialog Control

Setting the background image is a good way to make your form look different from the standard Visual Basic form. However, for users to be able to change the background image of the form, they will need a means to change the background image in the final program. And if a user knows how to use a simple image editing program, the user can create his or her own background image for the form.

As you saw from Step-by-Step 17.3, the background image of a form can be a simple image that is saved in one of several common formats, including .jpg, .gif, .tif, .png, and .bmp. To allow users to choose an image while the program is running, we will provide a button which triggers an *open file dialog* box. The user will use the open file dialog box to choose the file that he or she wants to set as the background of the form.

To use an open file dialog box on a form, you would first drag and drop the OpenFileDialog control from the toolbox onto the form. If you do this, you will notice that nothing is actually added to the form itself when you drop the OpenFileDialog control on the form. Instead, an icon representing this OpenFileDialog control appears at the bottom of the Visual Basic window, as shown in Figure 17-5.

FIGURE 17-5
A Windows form with an OpenFileDialog control added

OpenFileDialog control

This icon indicates that the control has been added to the form and is ready for use. To make use of the OpenFileDialog control, you could use the following code.

```
OpenFileDialog1.Title = "Choose a skin file..."
     OpenFileDialog1.Filter = "All files (*.*)|*.*"
     OpenFileDialog1.FileName = ""
```

The first line of code sets the title of the dialog box. The second line indicates the type of file that will be looked for as the default file type. In the case of this code, we are not filtering by any kind of file, but we could have written the code to show only bitmap files, for example. The third line of code defines the name of the file that will be opened. Since we do not want to specify the filename for the user, we will set that property to be an empty string.

To check for the file that the user selected, we want to look at the file after the user clicks the OK button. Then, we want to take the image that the user selected and set it to the background property of the form. To accomplish these steps, we use the following code:

```
If (OpenFileDialog1.ShowDialog() = Windows.Forms.DialogResult.OK) Then
     Me.BackgroundImage = Image.FromFile(OpenFileDialog1.FileName)
End If
```

STEP-BY-STEP 17.4

1. Drag an **OpenFileDialog** control (found in the Dialogs section of the Toolbox) and drop it onto frmMain, then set the (Name) property to **ofdChooseSkin**.

2. Add a command button to the form. Set the (Name) property to **btnSkins**; the Text property to **Skins...**; the Location to **252**, **14**; and the Size property to **55**, **25**.

3. Add the following code to the `click` event procedure of the btnSkins command button.

```
ofdChooseSkin.Title = "Choose a skin file..."
ofdChooseSkin.Filter = "All files (*.*)|*.*"
ofdChooseSkin.FileName = ""
If (ofdChooseSkin.ShowDialog() = Windows.Forms.DialogResult.OK) Then
    Me.BackgroundImage = Image.FromFile(ofdChooseSkin.FileName)
End If
```

4. Start debugging the program.

5. Click the **Skins...** button and navigate to the file named **skin2.jpg** in the data files folder and click **Open**.

6. Click the **Skins...** button again and choose **skin1.jpg**.

7. Stop debugging the program and leave the project and Visual Basic open for the next Step-by-Step.

Using the TransparencyKey

So far, you have given forms a unique appearance by changing their BackgroundImage property and by letting users choose an image while the program is running. To make forms really stand out, you can use the *TransparencyKey* property of the form to make certain areas of the form transparent. The TransparencyKey property allows you to specify a color on the form that will become transparent while the form is running. To use the TransparencyKey property when designing a form, simply set the TransparencyKey property to the desired color in the properties window.

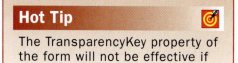

Hot Tip

The TransparencyKey property of the form will not be effective if you have your color resolution set to more than 24-bit color.

STEP-BY-STEP 17.5

1. Set the TransparencyKey property of frmMain to the color **Magenta**. (Note that you may need to scroll to the bottom on the Web tab to find magenta.)

2. Set the BackgroundImage property of frmMain to the file named **skin3.jpg** that is found in the data files.

Note

Even though you selected a .jpg image, the properties window will show System.Drawing.Bitmap as the value for the BackgroundImage.

STEP-BY-STEP 17.5 Continued

3. Start debugging the program. The output should resemble Figure 17-6. (Remember to make sure that your screen resolution is less than 24-bit color.)

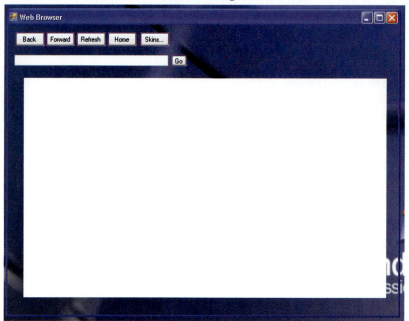

4. Stop debugging the program and leave the project and Visual Basic open for the next Step-by-Step.

Creating Irregularly Shaped Forms Using the TransparencyKey

Although the form you created in Step-by-Step 17-5 is starting to look really interesting, it is still shaped like a regular rectangular Windows form. To make forms that are more irregularly shaped, you can use the TransparencyKey concept and create background images with some transparent parts and some parts that will show up on the form. For example, by using the background image shown in Figure 17-7, you can see that the magenta parts will be transparent while the green portions will be visible to the user.

FIGURE 17-7
A background image that contains the transparent color

Removing the Title Bar and Borders from a Form

Using a background image like the one in Figure 17-7 will certainly help your form look very different from a standard form. However, your form will still have the title bar across the top, as shown in Figure 17-6, unless you explicitly turn it off. The title bar for the form is controlled by the FormBorderStyle property. To turn off the border entirely, set the FormBorderStyle property to None.

S TEP-BY-STEP 17.6

1. Set the FormBorderStyle property of frmMain to **None**.

2. Set the BackgroundImage property of frmMain to the file named **skin4.bmp** that is in the data files folder.

STEP-BY-STEP 17.6 Continued

3. Start debugging the program. The output should resemble Figure 17-8.

FIGURE 17-8
A Windows form with no title bar and transparent regions

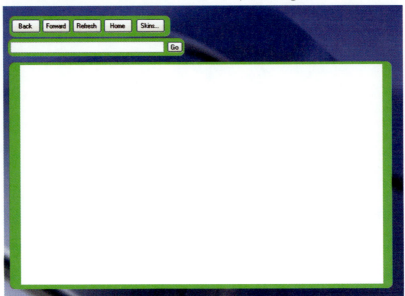

4. Notice that there is no way to move the form around on the screen or to close it.

5. Make Visual Studio the active window and click the **Stop Debugging** button.

6. Leave the project and Visual Basic open for the next Step-by-Step.

Closing and Moving the Form

When running the program during Step-by-Step 17.6, you should have noticed that without a title bar at the top of the form, it is not possible to exit the program without switching back to Visual Basic, nor is it possible to move the form around on the screen. A user would likely become frustrated with this poor user experience. To give the user a way to exit the application, simply add a button to the form and put the following line of code in the button `Click` event handler:

```
Application.Exit()
```

Giving the user a way to move the form around requires a few more lines of code. First, at the top of the form inside the class definition, you need to add code to define a Point. As you learned in Lesson 15, a Point is an object that represents an ordered pair of X- and Y-coordinates that define a single point on a two-dimensional plane. The code used to define the Point is found below.

```
Private offset As Point
```

Next, we need to add the following subroutine.

```
Private Sub frmMain_MouseDown(ByVal sender As Object, ByVal e As_
     System.Windows.Forms.MouseEventArgs) Handles MyBase.MouseDown
offset = New Point(-e.X, -e.Y)
End Sub
```

This routine will be executed whenever the mouse button is pressed down. The routine determines the X- and Y-coordinates of the location where the mouse is pressed down and sets the X- and Y-coordinates of the point named offset to the negative X- and negative Y-coordinates of the current point, respectively. Since the location of the form is measured using X and Y values starting at the top left of the form, this offset value will basically help determine where the user clicked.

Then, if we determine the coordinates of the X and Y point when the user moves the mouse, we can use the offset point to determine where the top-left part of the form should be. To make that determination, we use the following code.

```
Private Sub frmMain_MouseMove(ByVal sender As Object, ByVal e As_
     System.Windows.Forms.MouseEventArgs) Handles MyBase.MouseMove
        If (e.Button = System.Windows.Forms.MouseButtons.Left) Then
            Dim finalPos As Point = Control.MousePosition
            finalPos.Offset(offset.X, offset.Y)
            Me.Location = finalPos
        End If
    End Sub
```

This code first checks to see if the left mouse button was clicked. If it was, then the code declares a new point that contains the X and Y positions of the location of the mouse. Then, it offsets that point equal to the offset point that was created above. Finally, the location of the form is set to the new point. This handles the moving of the form to the new location.

S TEP-BY-STEP 17.7

1. Add a command Button to frmMain.

2. Set the (Name) property of the button to **btnQuit**; the Text property to **Quit**; the Location property to **640, 14**; and the Size property to **75, 23**.

3. Set the BackgroundImage property of frmMain to **skin5.bmp**.

4. Add the following code to the click event procedure for the btnQuit command button.

```
Application.Exit()
```

5. Add the following code inside the class definition, but above the first subroutine.

```
Private offset As Point
```

STEP-BY-STEP 17.7 Continued

6. Add the following code to the form.

```
Private Sub frmMain_MouseDown(ByVal sender As Object, ByVal e As_
    System.Windows.Forms.MouseEventArgs) Handles MyBase.MouseDown
        offset = New Point(-e.X, -e.Y)
End Sub

Private Sub frmMain_MouseMove(ByVal sender As Object, ByVal e As_
    System.Windows.Forms.MouseEventArgs) Handles MyBase.MouseMove
        If (e.Button = System.Windows.Forms.MouseButtons.Left) Then
                Dim mousePos As Point = Control.MousePosition
                mousePos.Offset(offset.X, offset.Y)
                Location = mousePos
        End If
End Sub
```

7. Start debugging the program. The output should resemble Figure 17-9.

FIGURE 17-9
A movable Windows form with a Quit button added

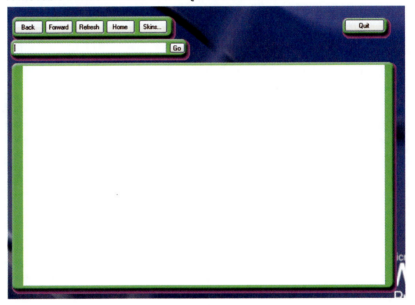

8. Move the form around on the screen by clicking in the green area and dragging the form.

9. Click the **Quit** button to exit the application.

10. Close the project and exit Visual Basic 2005.

SUMMARY

In this lesson, you learned:

■ The WebBrowser control allows you to integrate a simple Web browser into your Visual Basic programs.

■ The `Navigate` method of the WebBrowser control causes the control to load a Web page.

■ The WebBrowser control uses the same home page as Internet Explorer. Using the `GoHome` method causes the home page to load.

■ The `Refresh` method of the WebBrowser control reloads the current Web page.

■ The `GoForward` and `GoBack` methods load pages from the WebBrowser control's history.

■ The BackgroundImage property of a form can be used to set an image as the background of a form.

■ The OpenFileDialog control can be used to allow the user to browse the hard drive and select a file.

■ The TransparencyKey property specifies a color that will be transparent when the program is running.

■ The form border and title bar of a form can be turned off by using the FormBorderStyle property.

■ With no title bar across the top of the form, there is no way for the form to be moved or closed, unless you add code to handle these situations.

■ An offset Point can be used to help track a form's location while it is being moved around the screen.

VOCABULARY *Review*

Define the following terms:

Open file dialog	TransparencyKey	WebBrowser control
Skin		

REVIEW *Questions*

TRUE / FALSE

Circle T if the statement is true or F if the statement is false.

T   F   **1.** The WebBrowser control allows for simple Web browsing inside a form.

T   F   **2.** The WebBrowser control uses the same home page as Internet Explorer.

T   F   **3.** The homepage method of the WebBrowser control is used to navigate to the home page.

T   F   **4.** The BackgroundImage property can be used to set an image as the background of a form.

T   F   **5.** For an image to be used as a form background, it must be a bitmap image.

T   F   **6.** The OpenFileDialog control allows the user to navigate on the hard drive and choose a file.

T   F   **7.** The TransparencyKey property of the form sets the background color of a form to white.

T   F   **8.** To turn off the border and title bar of a form, set the FormBorderStyle to None.

T   F   **9.** Without a title bar, the form has no automatic way to be moved or closed.

T   F   **10.** A Point is an X and Y pair that represents a single point on a two-dimensional plane.

WRITTEN QUESTIONS

Write a brief answer to each of the following questions.

1. What is the main purpose of the WebBrowser control?

2. What image types are able to be used as the background image for a form?

3. What is the purpose of the OpenFileDialog control?

4. What is the TransparencyKey property of a form used for?

5. How can you hide the title bar and border on a form?

6. What code needs to be added to a form to make it moveable if there is no title bar?

7. Describe the process for making an irregularly shaped form.

8. What is the purpose of the BackgroundImage property of a form?

9. What are some common methods of the WebBrowser control?

10. What code needs to be added to a button Click event handler to exit the current application?

PROJECTS

PROJECT 17-1

In this project, you will add a WebBrowser control and four buttons that link to your favorite sites.

1. Create a new Visual Basic project called **Favorites.**

2. Set the (Name) property of the form to **frmMain** and set the Text property to **Favorites.**

3. Set the Size property of the form to **620, 490.**

4. Add a WebBrowser control to the form. If the WebBrowser control automatically resizes to fill the entire form, click the small arrow button in the upper-right corner of the control, and choose **Undock in parent container.** You will need to do this in order to set the size and location properties.

5. Set the (Name) property to **webMain**; the Size property to **486, 432**; and the Location property to **114, 12.**

6. Add four buttons to the left of the WebBrowser controls.

7. Choose four of your favorite Web sites. Give each of the four buttons a (Name) property and Text property that is representative of one of the Web sites.

8. Using the `Navigate` method of the WebBrowser control, add code to the `Click` event procedure for each button that causes the WebBrowser control to load your favorite site.

9. Start debugging the program and test the four buttons.

10. Stop debugging the program, close the project, and leave Visual Basic open for the next Project.

PROJECT 17-2

Many search engines allow you to link directly to the search results by concatenating the search keyword onto a specially formatted Web address. Below are the Web addresses used by Yahoo, MSN, and Google, respectively. The links all show the Web address when searching for the word **computers.**

http://search.yahoo.com/search?p=computers
http://search.msn.com/results.aspx?q=computers
http://www.google.com/search?q=computers

Using this knowledge, create a project that allows a user to enter a keyword in a text box. The user should be able to click a GO button which will load three separate WebBrowser controls on the same form. Each WebBrowser control should show the search results from one of the three search engines listed above.

PROJECT 17-3

Using the methods explained in this lesson, create your own background image that can be used to create an irregularly shaped form. The general steps are as follows:

1. Using Microsoft Paint or another graphics program, create an irregularly shaped object, such as a star or a triangle.

2. Leave the inside of the shape white, but give the background area outside the shape a background color.

3. Save the image as a bitmap file.

4. Create a new project in Visual Basic.

5. Set the TransparencyKey property of the form to match the background color that you used in the image you created.

6. Set the BackgroundImage property of the form to point to the image you created.

7. Set the FormBorderStyle property of the form to **None**.

8. Make sure your screen resolution is set to less than 24-bit color and execute your program to see your form.

9. Customize the form as you wish, adding controls or code to drag the form around.

CRITICAL *Thinking*

One of the nice features of full Web browsers is the ability to send an e-mail to a friend that has a link to a page that you are viewing in a browser. Use the **WebBrowser** project found in the **crit17-01** folder of the data files for this lesson as a starting point. Add a feature that allows a user to click a button to send the current link to a friend. Clicking a button on the main form should launch a second form with text boxes in which to enter the sender's e-mail address, the recipient's e-mail address, the subject of the e-mail, and the body of the e-mail. The text box for the body should show the link that was viewed in the browser when the button was clicked. To actually send the e-mail, you will need access to an SMTP server.

GRAPHICS AND DRAWING

REVIEW *Questions*

TRUE / FALSE

Circle T if the statement is true or F if the statement is false.

T F **1.** Pen objects are used to specify the color for a filled shape.

T F **2.** The thickness of the line drawn by the DrawLine method is always one pixel.

T F **3.** The Paint event procedure is used to redraw graphics that have been erased.

T F **4.** Boxes are drawn with the DrawRectangle method using the same values for height and for width.

T F **5.** The coordinates (0, 0) are assigned to the top-right corner of a form.

T F **6.** The SetPixel method can set the color of a pixel only one time.

T F **7.** The bitmap object measures distance in pixels.

T F **8.** You cannot have negative X and Y location values.

T F **9.** The WebBrowser control allows for simple Web browsing inside a form.

T F **10.** The BackgroundImage property can be used to set an image as the background of a form.

WRITTEN QUESTIONS

Write a brief answer to each of the following questions.

1. What is the difference between the output of a FillEllipse method and a DrawEllipse method?

2. Name two different methods that will take a rectangle object, as location and size information, to draw filled rectangles on another graphics object.

3. What four parameters describe the location and size of a rectangle object?

4. What method is used to draw the outline of a triangle on a graphics object?

5. What method is used to erase the images on a graphics object?

6. How do you specify where the DrawLine method should draw?

7. What event procedure returns a value for a mouse button pressed by the user?

8. What method retrieves the color of the specified pixel?

9. Name and describe five common methods of the WebBrowser control.

10. Describe the steps required to create transparent areas on a form.

PROJECTS

PROJECT 6-1

Write the code necessary to perform the following tasks when a button is clicked.

1. Draw a **red** line 3 pixels wide from **Point (0, 0)** to **Point (40, 100)**.

2. Draw a **yellow** line 5 pixels wide from **Point (200, 200)** to **Point (10, 10)**.

3. Draw a **green** rectangle with its top-left corner at **Point (20, 20)** and a width of **60** and height of **80**.

4. Draw a **black** box with its top-left corner at **Point (10, 10)** and a width of **40** and height of **40**.

5. Draw a **blue** box filled with **blue** color, with its top-left corner at **Point (100, 30)** and a width of **40** and height of **40**.

6. Start debugging the program to verify that it works correctly.

7. Save the changes to the program, then close the solution. Leave Visual Basic open for the next project.

PROJECT 6-2

Create a program that will ask the user to input the height and width of a box, convert the values to points, and draw the box on the form.

1. Open **Size Box** from the **proj06-02** folder in the data files for this unit review.

2. Add code and appropriate comments to the Draw button's click event procedure to:
   A. Declare two integers named `intHeight` and `intWidth`.
   B. Clear the form using the `clear` method.
   C. Set `intHeight` equal to the value in the `txtHeight` text box.
   D. Set `intWidth` equal to the value in the `txtWidth` text box.
   E. Draw a blue box starting at **Point (25, 75)** and ending with (`intWidth`, `intHeight`).

3. Start debugging the program to verify that it works correctly.

4. Save the changes to the program, then close the solution. Leave Visual Basic open for the next project.

PROJECT 6-3

Create a program that will draw the Xs and Os of a Tic Tac Toe game. This program will use some procedures that will draw objects in any picture box. Other parts of the program will tell these procedures which picture box to use.

1. Open **Tic Tac Toe** from the **proj06-03** folder in the data files for this unit review.

2. Double-click on the **New Game** button to open the code window.

3. Add the following code above the cmdNew Click event procedure to clear the graphics from a picture box.

```
Sub ClearBox(ByVal b As PictureBox)
    Dim g As Graphics = b.CreateGraphics
    g.Clear(b.BackColor)
End Sub
```

4. Add the following code to draw a circle inside a picture box.

```
Sub drawO(ByVal b As PictureBox)
    ' Create a graphics object on the picture box
    Dim g As Graphics = b.CreateGraphics

    ' Draw the O inside the box
    g.DrawEllipse(New Pen(Color.Red), 2, 2, b.Width - 7, b.Height - 7)
End Sub
```

5. Add the following code to draw an X in a picture box.

```
Sub drawX(ByVal b As PictureBox)
    ' Create a graphics object on the picture box
    Dim g As Graphics = b.CreateGraphics

    ' Draw the X
    g.DrawLine(New Pen(Color.Black), 2, 2, b.Width - 7, b.Width - 7)
    g.DrawLine(New Pen(Color.Black), 2, b.Height - 7, b.Width - 7, 2)
End Sub
```

6. Add the following code to the general declarations section at the top of the program.

```
' Variable to keep track of whose turn it is
Dim blnPlayer As Boolean
```

7. Add the following code inside the box_Click procedure to call a drawing procedure depending on which player clicked the picture box.

```
' Check the Boolean variable to see whose turn it is
' Pass the object that was clicked to one of the drawing procedures
If blnPlayer Then
    drawO(sender)
Else
    drawX(sender)
End If
```

8. Add the following code to switch the player.

```
' Change the player for the next click
blnPlayer = Not blnPlayer
```

9. Add code to the Exit menu item to end the program.

10. Start debugging the program to verify that it works correctly.

11. Save the program, then exit Visual Basic.

> **Note** ☑
>
> This event procedure handles Click events for all of the picture boxes on the form.

SIMULATIONS

You are an entry-level Visual Basic developer at a stock brokerage firm. Your assignment is to write some simple programs to help your coworkers analyze stock.

JOB 6-1

Create a program that will prompt the user for the name and stock symbol of a stock and the high and low of the stock for three consecutive days. The program should graph the information using lines to connect the highs and dots to draw the lows. The stock name should appear at the top of the graph, followed by its symbol in parentheses.

1. Open **Stock Watch** from the **job06-01** folder in the data files for this Unit Review.

2. Double-click the **Graph** button to open the code window.

3. Scroll through the code for the Graph button. Notice that the code consists of a series of nested If statements that verify whether valid data has been entered in each of the text boxes.

4. Locate the comment that reads *Create the title on the graph and display it*. Below the comment, add the following code to place the stock name and symbol at the center of the graph.

```
lblTitle.Text = txtName.Text & " (" & txtSymbol.Text & ")"
lblTitle.Visible = True
```

5. Locate the comment that reads *Get coordinates for Day1 High*. Below the comment, add the following code to get the X and Y values of the stock's high for each day.

```
intXCoordinate1 = lblDay1Graph.Left
intYCoordinate1 = 205 - Val(txtDay1High.Text) * 3 / 2

'Get coordinates for Day2 High
intXCoordinate2 = lblDay2Graph.Left
intYCoordinate2 = 205 - Val(txtDay2High.Text) * 3 / 2

'Get coordinates for Day3 High
intXCoordinate3 = lblDay3Graph.Left
intYCoordinate3 = 205 - Val(txtDay3High.Text) * 3 / 2
```

6. Locate the comment that reads *Draw line connecting Highs*. Below the comment, add the following code to draw a red line connecting each day's stock high.

```
g.DrawLine(New Pen(Color.Red), intXCoordinate1, intYCoordinate1, _
    intXCoordinate2, intYCoordinate2)
g.DrawLine(New Pen(Color.Red), intXCoordinate2, intYCoordinate2, _
    intXCoordinate3, intYCoordinate3)
```

7. Locate the comment that reads *Graph Day1 low*. Below the comment, add the following code to get the X and Y values of the stock's low for each day and draw a blue dot at each point.

```
intXCoordinate1 = lblDay1Graph.Left - 5
intYCoordinate1 = 205 - Val(txtDay1Low.Text) * 3 / 2

'Get coordinates for Day2 low
intXCoordinate2 = lblDay2Graph.Left - 5
intYCoordinate2 = 205 - Val(txtDay2Low.Text) * 3 / 2

'Get coordinates for Day3 low
intXCoordinate3 = lblDay3Graph.Left - 5
intYCoordinate3 = 205 - Val(txtDay3Low.Text) * 3 / 2

g.DrawLine(New Pen(Color.Blue), intXCoordinate1, intYCoordinate1, _
    intXCoordinate1 + 10, intYCoordinate1)
g.DrawLine(New Pen(Color.Blue), intXCoordinate2, intYCoordinate2, _
    intXCoordinate2 + 10, intYCoordinate2)
g.DrawLine(New Pen(Color.Blue), intXCoordinate3, intYCoordinate3, _
    intXCoordinate3 + 10, intYCoordinate3)
```

8. Add code to the Exit menu item to end the program.

9. Start debugging the program to verify that it works correctly.

10. Save the program, then close it. Leave Visual Basic open for the next Job.

JOB 6-2

Create a simple application that will use the WebBrowser control to load a remote Web page of financial information based on a stock symbol.

1. Create a new Visual Basic 2005 project called **StockBrowser**.

2. Set the (Name) property of the form to **frmMain** and set the Text property to **Stock Browser**.

3. Set the Size property of the form to **745, 560**.

4. Towards the top of the form, add a text box with a (Name) property of **txtStockSymbol**.

5. Next to the text box, add a button with a (Name) property of **btnSubmit** and a Text property of **Look Up Stock**.

6. Add a WebBrowser control with a (Name) property of **webMain**; a size property of **712, 465**; and a location property of **13, 49**.

7. Double-click the button and add the following code to the button `Click` event procedure.

```
webMain.Navigate("http://finance.yahoo.com/q?s=" + txtStockSymbol.Text)
```

8. Start debugging the program, enter the stock symbol **MSFT** in the text box, and click the button.

9. Close the program, then exit Visual Studio 2005.

ASP.NET

Unit 7

Estimated Time for Unit: 6 hours

INTRODUCTION TO ASP.NET

What is ASP.NET?

Up to this point you have been developing "desktop" applications that must be installed on a user's computer before they will run. That is, if you want someone to use your application, you would have to distribute the .exe file that is created when you compile your program. This is not always convenient or practical. But with so many people now having access to the Internet, many companies and individuals are now choosing to write software that runs inside a Web browser. *ASP.NET*, short for Active Server Pages .NET, is the technology that allows you to build applications that will run in a user's Web browser. For ASP.NET applications, the user does not install any files on their personal computer. Instead, they use a Web browser and navigate to a Web site where your application is stored.

ASP.NET itself is not technically a language; it is a technology. ASP.NET applications can be written in many languages, including Visual Basic, C#, or J#. Many of the same concepts that you have learned about Visual Basic in this book can be used to create ASP.NET Web applications.

Creating a New Web Project

Creating a new ASP.NET project, or Web Project, in Visual Studio 2005 is very similar to the process you used to create desktop applications. After starting Visual Studio 2005, simply select New Web Site from the File menu. You will then see a dialog box similar to the one shown in Figure 18-1. From this dialog box, you have the option of choosing the type of project, the storage location and path of the project, and the language for the project. Your New Web Site dialog box may vary depending on the components of Visual Studio 2005 that have been installed on your computer.

FIGURE 18-1
New Web Site dialog box

Once the new Web site is created, Visual Studio will create a main default file for you named Default.aspx. This file is itself a Web page and is sometimes referred to as a *WebForm* to distinguish it from a form that is found in a desktop application. (Forms in desktop applications are sometimes referred to as *WinForms*.) With the new default form created, you are now ready to create a Web page by dragging and dropping controls much like you do for desktop applications.

S TEP-BY-STEP 18.1

1. Start Visual Studio 2005 and choose **New Web Site** from the **File** menu.

2. When you are presented with the New Web Site dialog box, choose **ASP.NET Web Site** as the template type if necessary.

3. From the drop-down list of locations, select **File System**. Next to the location drop-down list, enter the path on your local computer where you want your files to be stored. An example might be *C:\Visual Studio Projects\WebSite1*. In this case, *WebSite1* is the name of the project that will be created in the Visual Studio Projects folder.

STEP-BY-STEP 18.1 Continued

4. From the drop-down list of language choices, select **Visual Basic**.

5. Click **OK**. Select **Designer** on the **View** menu to open the Design view. Your development environment should now resemble Figure 18-2, although your window layout may be slightly different.

FIGURE 18-2
A new ASP.NET Web Project

6. In the main window, with the Default.aspx tab highlighted, key **Hello World**. Your screen should now resemble Figure 18-3.

FIGURE 18-3
A page with Hello World written on it

STEP-BY-STEP 18.1 Continued

7. From the **File** menu, choose **Save Default.aspx** or click the **Save** button on the Standard toolbar.

8. Click the **Start Debugging** button. You will be presented with the dialog box shown in Figure 18-4.

Note ✅

Debugging information is written onto the screen and could sometimes present users with information about the code that could pose a security vulnerability. Therefore, debugging is turned off by default, and you must explicitly agree to turn it on.

FIGURE 18-4
Debugging Not Enabled dialog box

9. If necessary, choose the option labeled **Modify the Web.config file to enable debugging** and click **OK**. Your computer should now launch the default Web browser on your machine and display the Web page that you just created. Your browser should resemble Figure 18-5.

STEP-BY-STEP 18.1 Continued

FIGURE 18-5
A Web page with Hello World written on it

10. Click the **Close** button in your Web browser to return to Visual Studio 2005. Leave Visual Studio 2005 and the current Web site file open for the next Step-by-Step exercise.

Hot Tip

If you were to look in the WebSite1 folder, you would see a web.config file. This file is a configuration file that can be used to store information related to the Web site, such as the user name and password needed to connect to a database or the address of a mail server.

ASP.NET Development Server

While completing the steps for Step-by-Step 18-1, you may have noticed that after you clicked the green triangle to start the project, a small icon appeared on your Window's taskbar. The icon is shown in Figure 18-6.

FIGURE 18-6
ASP.NET Development Server notification icon

This icon lets you know that the *ASP.NET Development Server* is now running on your machine. The ASP.NET Development Server is a lightweight Web server that is built into the Visual Studio 2005 product. As previously noted, one major difference between desktop projects and ASP.NET projects is that desktop projects run directly on the end user's machine, while

ASP.NET projects actually run on a Web server. To view your ASP.NET pages, the user must navigate to a Web site with a Web browser. Using a separate Web server to review a project would be inconvenient while you are building the project. The ASP.NET Development Server allows you to have a small Web server running on your machine when you are developing your Web site.

When you have completed your development process, you will need to move your pages to a full-fledged Web-hosting environment, for example a Windows 2003 Server running Internet Information Server. One reason for this is that the ASP.NET Development Server does not allow remote users to visit the pages you are developing. That is, other computers on your network cannot navigate to your computer to see your pages.

Also note the URL or Web address shown in Figure 18-6 (i.e., http://localhost:1249/WebSite1). In our example, the first part of the address (*http://localhost*) tells the Web browser to look at the local machine to find the pages. The *1249* part of the URL indicates a port number. The ASP.NET Development Server automatically loads your Web pages on a random port. Typically, a full-fledged Web server would host the Web pages on port 80 on a machine. Having the development server choose a random port allows the ASP.NET Development Server and a full-fledged server to be running on the same machine if necessary. The final part of the URL is the name of the project that you are currently working on, in this case *WebSite1*.

Structure of an ASP.NET Project

While working with desktop applications, you became accustomed to the idea that for any single form in Visual Basic, you can choose to view the design elements (Design view) or the Visual Basic code (Code view). Ultimately, the code and the design elements were stored in a single file that ended in the extension .vb.

ASP.NET projects have a slightly different structure. You must work with three different views when dealing with ASP.NET projects: the Design view, the Code view, and the Source view. The Design and Code views are very similar to the views used in developing desktop applications. The Design view allows you to drag and drop controls from the Toolbox onto the Web page. When you double-click a button or other control in the Design view or choose to view the code, you see the Visual Basic code that is run "behind the scenes."

The ASP.NET project view that is not present in desktop applications is the *Source view*. Recall that the ASP.NET pages that you are creating will eventually be displayed in a Web browser. Although Web technologies have evolved rapidly over the past few years, most Web sites ultimately present *HyperText Markup Language (HTML)* code that is interpreted by the Web browser. Each time you drag and drop a control from the Toolbox in an ASP.NET project, Visual Studio displays the control in the Design view and also generates code for you in the Source view. For example, Figure 18-7 shows the source that was automatically created for you when you completed Step-by-Step 18.1.

FIGURE 18-7
Source view for the Default.aspx page

The source code shown in Figure 18-7 is not technically pure HTML code, but instead is declarative code that represents the items that will be shown on the Web page. When a user makes a request of the Web page via a Web browser, the Web server examines the .aspx page, pulls in any Visual Basic code it needs from the DLL, and then combines the logic from the Visual Basic code and the declarative code to output pure HTML that can be viewed in the Web browser.

In addition to the extra view, another main difference between desktop applications and ASP.NET projects is the way in which the different views are stored. As mentioned above, when creating desktop applications, the code and the design elements were stored in a single file that ended in the extension .vb. Unlike desktop applications, however, ASP.NET applications store these two views in separate files. In the example you created in Step-by-Step 18.1, you created a page called *Default.aspx*. The Source and Design views are stored in this file, but the actual Visual Basic code is stored in a separate file named *Default.aspx.vb*. This second file that ends in .vb is often called the *codebehind file*. Once the ASP.NET project is compiled, all of the .vb codebehind files are compiled into one or more *Dynamic Link Library* files *(DLL)* instead of an executable file.

STEP-BY-STEP 18.2

1. In the Design view, click after the words *Hello World*, and press **Enter** two times.

2. From the Toolbox, drag a label and drop it under the *Hello World* text.

3. In the Properties Window, set the (ID) property of the label to **lblMessage** and the Text property of the label to an empty string. (Clear the text that is already there.)

4. Next to the label, add a button. Set the (ID) property of the button to **btnSubmit** and the Text property to **Click Me**.

5. Double-click the button to view the code. Visual Studio should create the button `click` event handler code for you.

6. Inside the event handler, add the following code.

```
lblMessage.Text = "You clicked the button!"
```

STEP-BY-STEP 18.2 Continued

7. Start debugging the project. Your default Web browser should launch, and your output should be similar to that of Figure 18-8.

Note ☑️

When you click the button, you may see a dialog box warning you about sending information to a local intranet. If you see this warning, click Yes and submit the information.

FIGURE 18-8
The output of Step-by-Step 18.2

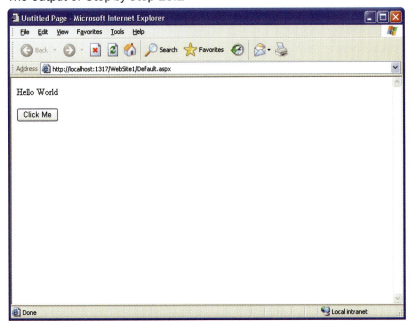

8. Click **Click Me** in the browser. Your screen should now resemble Figure 18-9.

STEP-BY-STEP 18.2 Continued

FIGURE 18-9
The Web browser view after the button is clicked

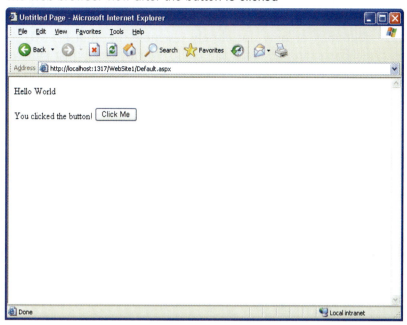

9. While still in your Web browser, view the source of the Web page. (In Internet Explorer, choose **Source** from the **View** menu.) Your output should resemble Figure 18-10.

FIGURE 18-10
The HTML source code actually rendered in the Web Browser

```
<!DOCTYPE html PUBLIC "-//W3C//DTD XHTML 1.0 Transitional//EN"
"http://www.w3.org/TR/xhtml1/DTD/xhtml1-transitional.dtd">

<html xmlns="http://www.w3.org/1999/xhtml" >
<head><title>
        Untitled Page
</title></head>
<body>
        <form name="form1" method="post" action="Default.aspx"
id="form1">
<div>
<input type="hidden" name="__VIEWSTATE" id="__VIEWSTATE"
value="/wEPDwUKLTE2MjY5MTY1NQ9kFgICAw9kFgICAQ8PFgIeBFRleHQFF1lvdS
BjbGlja2VkIHRoZSBidXR0b24hZGRkGL1/566SLVmnMPQvl6ES/0cWNOE=" />
</div>

    <div>
        Hello World<br />
        <br />
        <span id="lblMessage">You clicked the button!</span>
        <input type="submit" name="btnSubmit" value="Click Me"
id="btnSubmit" /></div>

<div>

        <input type="hidden" name="__EVENTVALIDATION"
id="__EVENTVALIDATION"
value="/wEWAgK2zorZAgLCi9reAxCNaRfOHcOCv0Ou08yFHohCoadK" />
</div></form>
</body>
</html>
```

10. Close the project, and then close Visual Studio 2005.

Source View vs. HTML Output

Recall that the Source view in Visual Studio shows the code representation of the items that you have added to the ASP.NET Web page. If you compare the source code view of the Default.aspx page created in Step-by-Step 18.2 with the HTML output in Figure 18-10, you will see how the source code may or may not closely resemble the final HTML code that is interpreted by the browser. For example, since the Hello World text is just simple text, it appears almost identical in the Source view and the final HTML output. The button, however, is different. In the Source view, we see the following line of code:

```
<asp:Button ID="btnSubmit" runat="server" Text="Click Me" />
```

When you view the HTML output, the code that creates the button looks like the following:

```
<input type="submit" name="btnSubmit" value="Click Me" id="btnSubmit" />
```

Visual Basic and the Web server do the work of this conversion for you. You only need to know how to use the controls from the toolbox.

ASP.NET Compilation Options

You may have noticed that we did not formally compile any code in the Step-by-Step examples in this Lesson. When writing desktop applications, debugging a project will automatically build the project for you and provide error messages should your code contain errors. In desktop applications, you can build applications manually by choosing to build your project from the Build menu. ASP.NET projects are similar to desktop projects in that you may build them manually by using the Build menu, or they will be built automatically when you start debugging. In addition to these scenarios, ASP.NET projects also have the ability to be compiled at run time when the user requests the Web page. That is, if you make a change to the Visual Basic code and do not compile the changes in Visual Studio, the first time a user accesses the page, the Web server will detect the changed code and compile it for the user before providing the page. The first user to navigate to the changed page may see a slight delay in the response time for the page while the page is being compiled.

SUMMARY

In this lesson, you learned:

- ASP.NET stands for Active Server Pages .NET.
- ASP.NET is a technology that allows you to build Web-based programs.
- ASP.NET applications run in a Web browser, and the user must navigate to a Web site to use the applications.
- ASP.NET projects can be written in a variety of languages, including Visual Basic.
- ASP.NET Development Server is a lightweight Web server that allows you to develop Web applications on your own machine.

- ASP.NET Development Server allows only the local computer to have access to the pages that are created on a computer.

- ASP.NET pages are separated into three views: Design, Source, and Code. The Design and Source views are visible from the pages ending in .aspx. The code for the pages is stored in a separate file ending in .vb.

- In ASP.NET projects, the code from the codebehind pages is compiled into a single DLL file.

- The HTML that is generated by a Web server may look very different from the Source view seen in Visual Studio 2005.

- ASP.NET projects can be compiled manually or automatically when a user visits the Web page.

VOCABULARY *Review*

Define the following terms:

ASP.NET	Dynamic Link Library (DLL)	Source view
ASP.NET Development Server	Hypertext Markup Language	WebForm
Codebehind File	(HTML)	WinForm

REVIEW *Questions*

TRUE / FALSE

Circle T if the statement is true or F if the statement is false.

T F 1. Desktop applications and ASP.NET applications are identical.

T F 2. ASP.NET is short for Application Server Pages .NET.

T F 3. Visual Basic is the only language that can be used to create ASP.NET pages.

T F 4. A WinForm is another name for a Web page.

T F 5. Visual Studio comes with a built-in Web server.

T F 6. ASP.NET applications have a view called a Source view.

T F 7. ASP.NET Web sites compile all the code into a single executable file.

T F 8. Codebehind files can contain the Visual Basic code.

T F 9. The Source view contains the actual HTML that a Web browser will read.

T F 10. If a Web site has not been compiled, the first user that accesses it will cause the site files to compile.

WRITTEN QUESTIONS

Write a brief answer to each of the following questions.

1. What are some differences between ASP.NET applications and desktop applications?

2. What are at least three languages in which ASP.NET applications can be written?

3. What is the purpose of the ASP.NET Development Server?

4. What is the process for creating a new Web site using ASP.NET?

5. What are the three views in an ASP.NET application, and what can you see in each view?

6. Describe the ways an ASP.NET project might be compiled.

7. Explain why the Source view in Visual Basic and the HTML source are different.

8. In what ways are creating desktop applications, and Web applications similar in Visual Studio 2005?

9. Why must Web pages be moved from the ASP.NET Development Server to a full-fledged Web server before Internet users can access them?

10. What is the difference between a WebForm and a WinForm?

PROJECTS

PROJECT 18-1

In this project, you will create a simple Web page and use some of the properties of the Label control that you have likely used before.

1. Start Visual Studio 2005 and choose **New Web Site** from the **File** menu.

2. Create a new Web site named **LabelTest**. (To name the site, simply save it to a folder with the name that you choose.)

3. On the Default.aspx page that is created for you, switch to the Design view and add a label from the Toolbox.

4. Set the (ID) property of the label to **lblTest.**

5. Double-click on the form somewhere in the open space away from the label; Visual Basic will switch to the Code view and create the `Page_Load` event handler for you. This is the code that will be run when the page is first loaded.

6. Enter the following code in the `Page_Load` event handler.

```
lblTest.BackColor = Drawing.Color.Chartreuse
lblTest.BorderStyle = BorderStyle.Dashed
lblTest.BorderColor = Drawing.Color.Blue
lblTest.BorderWidth = 2
lblTest.ForeColor = Drawing.Color.White
lblTest.Font.Size = 24
lblTest.Font.Bold = True
lblTest.Text = "This is a label control!"
```

7. Click **Start Debugging** and verify that the **Modify the Web.config file to enable debugging** option is selected. Click **OK**.

8. Examine the output of the label control, then close the Web browser and close the project.

PROJECT 18-2

In this project, you will create a simple Web page that uses labels and buttons.

1. Start Visual Studio 2005 and choose **New Web Site** from the **File** menu.

2. Create a new Web site named **ButtonTest**.

3. Add three buttons to the Default.aspx page that was created for you. Key **Enter** between each of the three buttons.

4. Set the (ID) property of the buttons to **btnHide**, **btnGrow**, and **btnChange**.

5. Set the Text property of the buttons to **Hide**, **Grow**, and **Change** to match each (ID).

6. Double-click **btnHide** and add the following code to the `Click` event handler.

```
btnHide.Visible = False
```

7. Double-click **btnGrow** and add the following code to the `Click` event handler.

```
btnGrow.Height = 100
btnGrow.Width = 300
```

8. Double-click **btnChange** and add the following code to the `Click` event handler.

```
btnChange.Text = "Text changed"
btnChange.BackColor = Drawing.Color.Blue
btnChange.BorderStyle = BorderStyle.Groove
```

9. Click **Start Debugging** and verify that the **Modify the Web.config file to enable debugging** option is selected. Click **OK**.

10. When the page loads in the browser, click each button and examine the results.

11. Close the Web browser and close the project.

PROJECT 18-3

In this project, you will create a simple Web page that uses a loop and a label to write text to the screen.

1. Start Visual Studio 2005 and choose **New Web Site** from the **File** menu.

2. Create a new Web site named **LoopLabel**.

3. Add a label and a button to the Default.aspx page that was created for you. Key **Enter** between each item.

4. Set the (ID) property of the label to **lblMessage** and the Text property to an empty string.

5. Set the (ID) property of the button to **btnSubmit** and the Text property to **Submit**.

6. Double-click **btnSubmit** and add the following code to the Click event handler.

```
Dim i As Integer
      For i = 10 To 1 Step -1
          lblMessage.Text += "T minus " + i.ToString() + "<BR>"
      Next
      lblMessage.Text += "Blastoff"
```

7. Click **Start Debugging** and verify that the **Modify the Web.config file to enable debugging** option is selected. Click **OK**.

8. When the page loads in the browser, click the button and examine the results.

9. Close the Web browser and close the project.

> **Hot Tip**
>
> In Step 6, the ToString method is used to convert the integer value to a string so that it may be displayed inside the label on the page. The <BR> code is the HTML value that represents a line break. The break forces any text which might be written to the label after the break to appear on the next line.

CRITICAL *Thinking*

This lesson introduced you to the basics of ASP.NET programming. It also pointed out some of the main differences between Web applications and desktop applications. Think about other differences and similarities between WebForms and WinForms. Use a common search engine to find additional differences and similarities. Your brainstorming and searching does not need to be limited to ASP.NET technology. Rather, compare and contrast the general concepts of Web-based programming. Record all your answers and submit them to your instructor.

WEBFORMS AND CONTROLS

Recall from Lesson 18 that WebForms or Web pages are the units that make up an ASP.NET application. In Lesson 18, you created a couple of simple WebForms using labels and buttons, controls that you had already used in desktop applications. In this lesson, we will examine additional controls that you have used before and see how they can be used in ASP.NET projects. Specifically, we will look at the use of images, text boxes, radio buttons, and check boxes, all of which you used earlier in this book. Additionally, we will introduce and demonstrate the Hyper Link control.

Adding WebForms to an ASP.NET Project

Before we examine the different controls that can be added to a WebForm, it is helpful to understand how to add WebForms to an existing project. Recall from Lesson 18 that when you make a new ASP.NET Web site, Visual Basic automatically adds a page called *default.aspx*. Typically, a Web site will be made up of numerous WebForms that will be linked together, and the default.aspx page will be the first one that users see when they visit your Web site. Adding pages to a site is fairly straightforward. At the top of the Solution Explorer, you will see the name of your currently open project. When you right-click on the project name, you will see a context menu that offers many options, including Add New Item. See Figure 19-1.

FIGURE 19-1

A menu showing many of the common options for working with a Web site

After clicking Add New Item, you will see a dialog box similar to the one shown in Figure 19-2. You will see from the dialog box that many file types can be added to this project. To add a new WebForm, make sure Web Form is selected from the list of template options, give the file a new name, and click Add. The new file will open in design mode and be ready for you to use.

FIGURE 19-2

The Add New Item dialog box

Images

When creating desktop applications in Lesson 3, you used a PictureBox control to add images to a form. ASP.NET applications have an analogous control called the *Image control*. To use the control, simply drag and drop the control onto a WebForm and set the ImageURL property to point to the image file that will be used. To use an image in an ASP.NET application, the image will need to reside inside the ASP.NET project. The common practice is to create an images folder inside the application and add existing images to that folder. Once the images have been added to the application, you can point the Image control at the image.

STEP-BY-STEP 19.1

1. Start Visual Studio 2005 and choose **New Web Site** from the **File** menu.

2. Create a project named **WebFormControls** and select a location on the file system to store your project.

3. Close the **Default.aspx** file that was automatically created for you by selecting **Close** from the **File** menu.

4. Add a new WebForm named **image.aspx**. To do so, right-click on the project name in the Solution Explorer, then select **Add New Item**. Next, choose **Web Form** from the list of item types and name the file.

5. Right-click on the project name (the item that includes the path) in the Solution Explorer and select **New Folder**. Name the folder **images**.

6. Right-click on the newly created **images** folder in the Solution Explorer and choose **Add Existing Item**. Navigate to the file named **rainier.jpg** located in the **step19-01** folder in the data files and click **Add**.

7. Switch to Design View if necessary, then drag and drop an Image control onto the **image.aspx** WebForm.

8. Right-click on the Image control and select **Properties**.

STEP-BY-STEP 19.1 Continued

9. Click the ellipsis button next to the ImageURL property, and you will see a dialog box resembling Figure 19-3.

10. Select the **images** folder and the image named **rainier.jpg**.

11. Click **OK**.

12. In the Solution Explorer, right-click on **image.aspx**, and select **View in Browser**. If prompted to save the changed file, do so. Your output should resemble Figure 19-4.

STEP-BY-STEP 19.1 Continued

FIGURE 19-4
The resulting Web page showing the Image control

13. Close the Web Browser, but leave Visual Studio 2005 open for the next Step-by-Step exercise.

Text Boxes

As was the case with desktop applications, text boxes are used to give the user an area in which to enter content. Since most ASP.NET applications allow users to enter data, you will use text boxes quite often. After dragging a new *Text Box control* to a WebForm, it is important to set the (ID) property of the form. As with desktop applications, we prefix the name of text boxes with *txt*. In addition to the (ID) property, another property that is used often is the TextMode property. This property determines whether the text box will be in single-line mode, multiple-line mode, or password mode. In the next Step-by-Step exercise, you will see each of these modes.

Extra for Experts

If you look at the value of the ImageURL property in Step-by-Step 19.1 after you have selected the image, you will see that it has a tilde (~) in front of the image path. The tilde represents the "root" of the application. That is, the tilde tells the server to look at the lowest level of the application and then look for a folder called images.

STEP-BY-STEP 19.2

1. Using the existing WebFormControls project, add a new WebForm named **textbox.aspx**.

2. From the Toolbox, drag and drop three Text Box controls onto the WebForm. Press **Enter** after adding each one.

3. Set the (ID) properties of the three text boxes to **txtSingle**, **txtMulti**, and **txtPassword**, respectively.

4. Set the TextMode property of the txtSingle text box to **SingleLine** if necessary.

5. Set the TextMode property of the txtMulti text box to **MultiLine**.

6. Set the TextMode property of the txtPassword text box to **Password**.

7. Click on the lower sizing handle of the multiline text box and drag it until it is **72** pixels tall.

8. In the Solution Explorer, right-click on the **textbox.aspx** page and select **View in Browser**. Save your work if you are prompted to do so.

9. In the first text box, key **single-line text box**.

10. In the second text box, key **This is a multiline text box, and the text spans the lines.**.

11. In the third text box, key **password**. Your output should now resemble Figure 19-5.

FIGURE 19-5
Three different types of text boxes

12. Close the Web Browser, but leave Visual Studio 2005 open for the next Step-by-Step exercise.

Radio Buttons

As you learned earlier in this book, radio buttons are used when you need to present a list of options from which the user is only allowed to select one. In ASP.NET applications, you will notice that the Toolbox has the Radio button control that you have used before. In addition, there is also a *Radio Button List control*. Both of these controls work in similar ways, but since radio buttons are most often used in groups, ASP.NET has added the Radio Button List control to make working with multiple radio buttons a little easier. For instance, when using the Radio Button List control, it is a little easier to write the code to determine which button a user selected.

Radio buttons actually will have two different values, each of which is stored in a different property. To retrieve the text that is associated with the value that a user chose, you would use the SelectedItem property. To retrieve the "behind the scenes" value that is associated with a radio button, you would use the SelectedValue property.

Before using the Radio Button List control in a project, you should be familiar with the idea of common tasks for a control. When you drag and drop some controls onto a WebForm, a small window will pop up next to the control listing common tasks that you might expect to perform with that control. Figure 19-6 shows the *common tasks menu* for a Radio Button List control.

Hot Tip

The preface typically used for a Radio Button List control is *rbl*.

FIGURE 19-6
The common tasks for a Radio Button List control

Notice from Figure 19-6 that some of the items are blue text followed by an ellipsis. Clicking one of these items typically launches a dialog box or wizard that allows you to control the settings of the radio button. Another item from the common tasks list is check boxes. Using the common tasks will change the properties of the code for you automatically. In the case of the common task list for the Radio Button control, Choose Data Source allows you to bind the list of items in the control to a database or other data store. The Edit Items common task allows you to specify which items show up in the radio button list. Finally, the Enable AutoPostBack check box tells the page that each time a user changes the radio button, the results should be sent back to the server and the page reloaded.

S TEP-BY-STEP 19.3

1. Using the existing **WebFormControls** project, add a new WebForm named **radiobuttons.aspx**.

2. Add a Radio Button List control to the WebForm.

3. From the list of common tasks that appears, choose **Edit Items**. You will see a dialog box that resembles Figure 19-7.

FIGURE 19-7
The ListItem Collection Editor dialog box

4. In the ListItem Collection Editor, click **Add** to add a list item for the radio button list. After the item has been added, you may edit the properties.

5. In the rightmost side of the dialog box, for the Text property, key **Small**. The Value property, when selected, will automatically be set to the text *Small*, but change it to the value **7.00**.

6. Repeat steps 4 and 5 to add the following text and value property pairs: **Medium 8.00**, **Large 9.00**.

7. Click **OK**.

8. Set the (ID) property of the Radio Button List to **rblSizes**.

9. Underneath the radio button list, add a label and a button.

10. Set the (ID) property of the label to **lblMessage** and the text property to an empty string.

11. Set the (ID) property of the button to **btnSubmit** and the text property to **Submit**.

STEP-BY-STEP 19.3 Continued

12. Double-click the **Submit** button and add the following code to the button `click` event handler.

```
lblMessage.Text = "You selected the radio button " & _
rblSizes.SelectedItem.ToString() & " which has a value of " & _
rblSizes.SelectedValue.ToString() & "."
```

13. Right-click on the **radiobuttons.aspx** page in the Solution Explorer and choose **View in Browser**. Save your work if you are prompted to do so.

14. Select different radio buttons and click **Submit** to examine the output. Your output should resemble Figure 19-8.

FIGURE 19-8
The output of the radiobuttons.aspx page in the browser

15. Close the Web browser, but leave Visual Studio 2005 open for the next Step-by-Step.

Check Boxes

In Lesson 8, you learned that check boxes are often used to ask a user a yes-or-no question. Check boxes can also be used when you want to give users a series of options and let them choose all of the options from the list that apply. For example, you might present the user with a list of foods and have the user check off all the foods he or she has tried.

In desktop applications, you used the Check Box control. For ASP.NET applications, you have the additional ***Check Box List control***. Much like the Radio Button List control, the Check Box List control was designed to make it easier to work with a group of check boxes at one time. Also, like the Radio Button List control, the Check Box List control will show you a list of common tasks when you add it to a WebForm.

Since users can choose more than one option presented to them, determining which values were selected in a Check Box List is a little more involved than determining the single option chosen in a Radio Button List. To determine the values that a user selected, you must loop through each of the items in the Check Box List

Hot Tip

The preface typically used for a Check Box List control is *cbl*.

and determine if that particular item was selected. If it was, then you can use the Text or Value property to retrieve the information you need from the Check Box List item.

STEP-BY-STEP 19.4

1. Using the existing **WebFormControls** project, add a new WebForm named **checkboxes.aspx**.

2. Add a Check Box List control to the WebForm and set the (ID) property to **cblStates**.

3. Using the **Edit Items** common task, add the following text value pairs to the Check Box List.

TEXT	VALUE
Texas	TX
Washington	WA
Arizona	AZ
Louisiana	LA

4. Add a label under the Check Box control that has a Text property of **Select all the states that you have visited**. Set the (ID) property of the label to **lblMessage**.

Hot Tip

If the Edit Items common task menu is not visible, click the small arrow at the upper-right of the Check Box List control to make it visible.

5. Add a button with the (ID) property of **btnSubmit** and a Text property of **Submit**.

6. Double-click the **Submit** button and add the following code to the button click event handler.

```
lblMessage.Text = "You have visited: "
Dim i As Integer
For i = 0 To cblStates.Items.Count - 1
    If cblStates.Items(i).Selected Then
        lblMessage.Text = lblMessage.Text & cblStates.Items(i).Text & ", "
    End If
Next
```

7. View the page in the Web browser and experiment by selecting different check boxes and clicking the **Submit** button. Your output should resemble Figure 19-9.

STEP-BY-STEP 19.4 Continued

FIGURE 19-9
The output of the checkboxes.aspx page in the browser

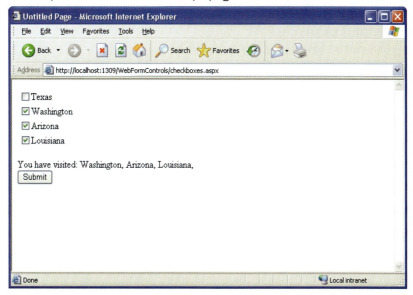

8. Close the Web browser, but leave Visual Studio 2005 open for the next Step-by-Step.

Hyper Links

As you are probably aware, one of the most beneficial features of Web sites is the ability to create links between your own pages or to other Web sites. To create links, also called hyperlinks, in ASP.NET projects, you can use the *Hyper Link control*. Like other controls, you set the (ID) property and the Text property for the Hyper Link control. In addition, you will need to set the NavigateURL property. This property can have the value of a local page or a remote Web site.

Hot Tip

The preface typically used for a Hyper Link control is *hlk*.

STEP-BY-STEP 19.5

1. Using the existing **WebFormControls** project and the existing WebForm named **checkboxes.aspx**, add a Hyper Link control underneath the Submit button.

2. Set the (ID) property to **hlkMyPage** and the Text property to **Visit the radio button page**.

STEP-BY-STEP 19.5 Continued

3. In the Property Window, click the ellipsis next to the NavigateURL property. You will see the Select URL dialog box, as shown in Figure 19-10.

FIGURE 19-10
The Select URL dialog box

4. From the rightmost side of the dialog box, double-click on the file named **radiobuttons.aspx**.

5. View the page in the Web browser and click the link. You should be redirected to the radio buttons page.

6. Close the Web browser, the project, and Visual Studio 2005.

SUMMARY

In this lesson, you learned:

■ Many of the controls used in desktop applications can be used for ASP.NET applications.

■ An easy way to add a new WebForm to a project is to right-click on the project name in the Solution Explorer.

■ The Image control is used in ASP.NET projects to add images to WebForms.

■ The ImageURL property of the Image control is what indicates the image to be loaded in the Image control.

■ Text Box controls in WebForms work very much like they do in desktop applications—allowing users to enter data into them.

■ Text boxes can be set in single-line mode, multiline mode, and password mode. The Radio Button List control allows users to choose one of many options presented.

■ Each radio button has text that is displayed to the user and some value that is bound to the radio button behind the scenes.

- You can use the SelectedItem or SelectedValue property to get the values from a Radio Button List control.

- The common tasks menu is presented when you add certain controls to a WebForm.

- The common tasks provide shortcuts to some of the things you are likely to do with the control.

- The Check Box List control allows you to present the user with many options from which they may select more than one. To determine which values from a Check Box List control have been selected, you will need to loop through each item and check the selected property.

- The `Hyper Link` control is used to create links from an ASP.NET page to another page or another Web site.

VOCABULARY *Review*

Define the following terms:

Check Box List control	Hyper Link control	Radio Button List control
Common tasks menu	Image control	Text Box control

REVIEW *Questions*

TRUE / FALSE

Circle T if the statement is true or F if the statement is false.

T F **1.** Individual pages that make up an ASP.NET project are known as WebForms.

T F **2.** Many of the controls used in desktop applications can also be used in ASP.NET applications.

T F **3.** The Text Box control is used to add a list of options from which the user may choose only one.

T F **4.** The ImageURL property of the Text Box control points to the image that should be loaded.

T F **5.** Radio Button List controls are used in situations in which users can choose one option from a list of options.

T F **6.** The common tasks menu presents a list of common things you might do with a control.

T F **7.** The steps used to determine the value for Radio Button Lists and Check Box Lists are identical.

T F **8.** The Hyper Link control allows you to build links to other pages in your site.

T   F   **9.** A Text Box control can be used to allow users to enter data.

T   F   **10.** A radio button has a value that is displayed to the user and one that is bound to the control behind the scenes.

WRITTEN QUESTIONS

Write a brief answer to each of the following questions.

1. Describe the process of adding a new WebForm to a project.

2. What is the purpose of the ImageURL property of the Image control?

3. List the three modes that a Text Box control might have and describe when you might use each one.

4. What are the similarities between the Radio Button List control and the Check Box List control?

5. What are the differences between the Radio Button List control and the Check Box List control?

6. What is the difference between the SelectedItem property and the SelectedValue property of a Radio Button List control?

7. Explain the purpose of the common tasks menu.

8. Describe how you can get the selected values from a Check Box List.

9. What is the importance of the NavigateURL property of the Hyper Link control?

10. List the prefixes you might use when naming each of the following controls: Image control, Text Box control, Radio Button List control, Check Box List control, and Hyper Link control.

PROJECTS

PROJECT 19-1

Using the same **WebFormControls** project that you created in the Step-by-Step exercises in this lesson, turn the default.aspx page into a menu of hyperlinks that point to all the other pages that you created. Your menu page will have four hyperlinks.

PROJECT 19-2

In this project, you will create the Web-based equivalent of the project you worked on in Step-by-Step 6.1 in Lesson 6. This project will calculate the amount of money in a savings account.

1. Open Visual Studio 2005 and create a new Web site named **SavingsCalculator**.

2. In the **Default.aspx** page, using labels, text boxes, and buttons, re-create the form as it is shown in Figure 6-5 in Lesson 6. You may omit the Exit button.

3. Set the (ID)s of the text boxes to **txtAmount, txtInterest,** and **txtYears**.

4. Set the (ID) of the label that displays the total amount saved to **lblMessage** and set the Text property to **Amount in savings $**.

5. Set the (ID) of the calculate button to **btnSubmit**.

6. Double-click the **Calculate** button; Visual Basic will create the button `Click` event handler for you.

7. Inside the button `Click` event handler, add the following code.

```
Dim myYears As Short
myYears = Val(txtYears.Text)

lblMessage.Text = Fix(Val(txtAmount.Text) * (1 + (Val(txtInterest.Text) _
/100)) ^ myYears).ToString()
```

8. View the page in a Web browser and key the following values: Amount deposited **1500**, interest rate **8%**, and number of years **15**.

9. Click the **Calculate** button to ensure that the program works properly.

10. Close the Web browser and the project, but leave Visual Studio 2005 open.

PROJECT 19-3

In this project, you will create a small WebForm that presents users with a list of potential computer-related jobs that might interest them.

1. Open Visual Studio 2005 and create a new Web site named **JobList**.

2. On the **default.aspx** page, add a Check Box List control to the WebForm and set the (ID) property to **cblJobs**.

3. Using the **Edit Items** common task, add the following text value pairs to the check box list.

TEXT	VALUE
Architect	Architect
Database Administrator	Database Administrator
Programmer	Programmer
Project Manager	Project Manager
Systems Analyst	Systems Analyst
Web Developer	Web Developer

4. Add a label under the Check Box control that has a Text property of **Select all the jobs that interest you**. Set the (ID) property of the label to **lblMessage**.

5. Add a button with the (ID) property of **btnSubmit** and a Text property of **Submit**.

6. Double-click the submit button and add the following code to the button `Click` event handler:

```
lblMessage.Text = "You selected: "
Dim i As Integer
For i = 0 To cblJobs.Items.Count - 1
    If cblJobs.Items(i).Selected Then
        lblMessage.Text = lblMessage.Text & cblJobs.Items(i).Text & ", "
    End If
Next
```

7. View the page in the Web browser and experiment by selecting different check boxes and clicking the **Submit** button.

8. Close the Web browser and the project, but leave Visual Studio 2005 open.

PROJECT 19-4

In this project, you will create a small WebForm that is similar to the program you created in Lesson 9, in which you calculated a user's weight on different planets.

1. Open Visual Studio 2005 and create a new Web site named **PlanetWeight**.

2. On the **default.aspx** page, add a text box to capture the user's weight. Set the (ID) of the text box to **txtWeight** and add a descriptive label in front of the text box.

3. Below the text box, add a **Radio Button List** control to the WebForm and set the (ID) property to **rblPlanets**.

4. Using the **Edit Items** common task, add the following text value pairs to the radio button list.

TEXT	VALUE
Mars	.38
Jupiter	2.64
Saturn	1.15
Pluto	.04

5. Add a label under the Radio Button List control that has a Text property of **no text**. Set the (ID) property of the label to **lblMessage**.

6. Add a button with the (ID) property of **btnSubmit** and a Text property of **Submit**.

7. Double-click the **Submit** button and add the following code to the button click event handler:

```
Dim sngCurrentWeight As Single
sngCurrentWeight = Convert.ToSingle(txtWeight.Text)

Dim sngPlanetFactor As Single
sngPlanetFactor = Convert.ToSingle(rblPlanets.SelectedValue)

Dim sngPlanetWeight As Single
sngPlanetWeight = sngCurrentWeight * sngPlanetFactor

lblMessage.Text = "Your weight would be " + Convert.ToString(sngPlanetWeight)
```

8. View the page in the Web browser and experiment by selecting different radio buttons and clicking the **Submit** button.

9. Close the Web browser and Visual Studio 2005.

CRITICAL *Thinking*

In this lesson, you learned to use several of the common controls that are used to capture data from a Web site user. In one of the exercises, you looked at the Text Box control that had a Text Mode property set to password. When using this Text Mode, the text that is keyed by the user is masked so that others viewing the same computer can not see the value keyed. This text mode is commonly used for values like passwords or credit card information that need to remain secure. While the Password text mode does obscure the data in a text box, the value is actually not secure as it travels from the user's Web browser to the Web server that is hosting the Web page. If someone were to intercept the data in transit, they could actually see the secret value.

To keep the data secure in transit, we would need to use Secure Sockets Layer (SSL) technology. Using the Internet, research SSL technology to find out, in general, how it works. Write a one-page summary of your findings and submit it to your instructor.

CASE STUDY
PIZZA ORDER FORM

The Task

As a consultant hired by Mountain Top Pizza, you have been asked to create an online order form for its customers. You will begin by creating a simple form that takes the customer information. You will then add to the form so that it can accept order information and print the order confirmation to the screen. In creating this form, you will utilize many of the controls you experimented with in the last lesson and will learn about form validation.

Creating the Simple WebForm

The first step in creating the online order form is to create a new Web site containing a WebForm. First, you will create a basic page, with a banner image at the top, to hold the form elements.

STEP-BY-STEP 20.1

1. Start Visual Studio 2005 and choose **New Web Site** from the **File** menu.

2. Create a Web site named **PizzaOrderForm** and select a location on the file system to store your project.

3. Using the **Default.aspx** file that was automatically created, change to the Design view if it is not already visible.

4. Add a new folder named **images** to your project.

5. Add the file named **MountainTopBanner.jpg** to the images folder you just created. The image can be found in the **step20-01** folder in the data files.

6. On the WebForm, add an Image control and set the ImageURL property to the **MountainTopBanner.jpg** file.

7. Below the banner image, key the following text: **Please fill out the form below. The fields in bold are required. Please allow 30 minutes for delivery.**.

8. At the top of the properties window, select **DOCUMENT** from the drop-down list to set the properties of the overall document.

9. Set the Title property of the document to **Mountain Top Pizza**.

10. View the page in a Web browser. Your output should resemble Figure 20-1.

FIGURE 20-1
The basic WebForm with the banner

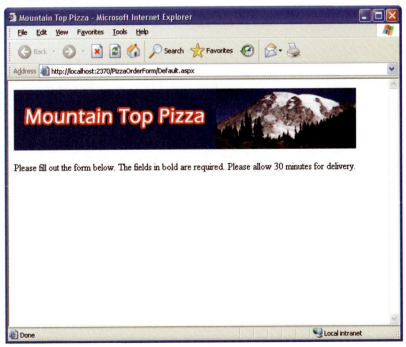

11. Close the Web browser, but leave Visual Studio 2005 open for the next Step-by-Step exercise.

Adding the Customer Information Fields

Now that you have the basic form in place, you will need to provide the user with form elements to enter his or her personal information. The management at Mountain Top Pizza wishes to collect first name, last name, e-mail address, address, city, state, zip, and phone number. At this point, the management does not want to collect credit card information online, so the customers will have to pay when the pizza is delivered. You will create a simple two-column table to hold labels and text boxes to collect this information.

S TEP-BY-STEP 20.2

1. Using the **Default.aspx** page that you created in the last Step-by-Step, click under the text you keyed, press **Enter** if necessary, and then select **Insert Table** from the **Layout** menu.

2. Select the radio button for **Custom**, if necessary, and select eight rows and two columns for the table.

3. Click **OK**.

4. In the first column, add labels in each cell, and then set the text property of each so that the user will see **First Name**, **Last Name**, **E-mail**, **Address**, **City**, **State**, **Zip**, and **Phone**.

5. Across from each label in the second column, add a text box. Prefix the ID of each text box with **txt** and name the boxes to match the label (e.g., **txtFirstName**, **txtLastName**, etc.).

6. View the page in a Web browser. Your output should resemble Figure 20-2.

FIGURE 20-2
The pizza order form with the customer fields

7. Close the Web browser, but leave Visual Studio 2005 open for the next Step-by-Step exercise.

Adding the Pizza Information Fields

Thus far, you have added elements to the form that will capture the user's basic contact information. Now you will need to add form elements to capture the order information. You will add a radio button list to allow users to choose a pizza size. You will use a second radio button list to allow users to choose a crust type. Finally, you will use a check box list to allow users to select one or more toppings. Both the radio button list and the check box list will make use of the Value property to store pricing information for the customer's choices.

STEP-BY-STEP 20.3

1. Using the **Default.aspx** page that you created in the last Step-by-Step, select the last row of the table that contains the customer information.

2. From the **Layout** menu, choose **Insert Row Below**.

3. Repeat the previous step three more times until you have added a total of four new rows.

4. In the first new row, add a label that reads **Pizza Sizes** in the first column and a radio button list in the second column.

5. Name the radio button list **rblSizes**, and set the Text and Value properties according to the table below. The Text property will be shown to the user. The Value property will be used to calculate the cost of the pizza.

TEXT	VALUE
Small	6
Medium	7
Large	8
Extra Large	9

6. In the next row, add a label for **Crust Type** in the first column and a radio button list named **rblCrustType** in the second column.

STEP-BY-STEP 20.3 Continued

7. The radio button list properties should be set up according to the table below. The Text property will be shown to the user. The Value property will be used to calculate any additional cost of the pizza. In our example, *Thin* or *Original* crust do not add to the cost of the pizza, but *Thick* crust pizza is one dollar extra.

TEXT	VALUE
Thin	0
Original	0
Thick	1

8. In the next row, add a label for **Toppings** in the first column and a check box list named **cblToppings** in the second column.

9. The check box list properties should be set up according to the table below. The Text will be presented to the user; the Value property will calculate the additional cost of each topping.

TEXT	VALUE
Pepperoni	.50
Sausage	.50
Beef	.50
Mushrooms	.25
Peppers	.25

10. In the last row in the first column, add a button named **btnSubmit** and set the Text property to **Place Order**.

STEP-BY-STEP 20.3 Continued

11. View the page in a Web browser. Your output should resemble Figure 20-3.

FIGURE 20-3
The bottom half of the order form with fields for pizza information

12. Close the Web browser, but leave Visual Studio 2005 open for the next Step-by-Step exercise.

Adding Validation Controls

Now you have a form to accept information about the user and the pizza that the user wishes to order. You still need to write the Visual Basic code that will show the user a confirmation screen. But before you do that, it would be helpful to add some validation controls. *Validation controls* are used to validate user input. For example, you might want to make sure that a user has specifically filled out certain form fields or that the input they have entered matches a certain format. Visual Basic has some built-in controls, known collectively as validation controls, that make it easy to perform validation.

Required Field Validator

To deliver the pizza, we certainly have to know the user's address. So the address would be considered a required field. Visual Basic has a built-in control, known as the *required field validator*, that allows you, as the developer, to specify which fields are required. To use this control, you drag the control from the validation section of the Toolbox and drop it next to the form element that you want to have required. You will need to set three properties of this control. First, use the ErrorMessage property to indicate the message that will be shown to the user if they do not fill out the form element. Then set the ControlToValidate property of the required field validator to point to the control that you want to require. Finally, a property named Display is used to control how the validator will be displayed. If you set the display property to Static, the required field validator will take up room in the form even if it is not currently visible on the screen. When set to Dynamic, the validator will only take up room on the form if it is visible to the user.

STEP-BY-STEP 20.4

1. Using the **Default.aspx** page that you created in the last Step-by-Step, drag the **RequiredFieldValidator** control from the Validation section of the Toolbox onto the form below the text box with the ID **txtAddress**.

2. Set the ID property to **rfvAddress**.

3. Set the ErrorMessage property to **Please supply a delivery address.**.

4. Set the ControlToValidate property to **txtAddress**.

5. Set the Display property to **Dynamic**.

6. Since your text at the top of the form indicates that required fields will be in bold text, set the Font Bold property of the label for Address to **True**.

7. View the page in a Web browser, and click the **Place Order** button without filling out any of the form fields. Your output should resemble Figure 20-4.

FIGURE 20-4
The required field validator indicating the error message to the user

8. Close the Web browser, but leave Visual Studio 2005 open for the next Step-by-Step exercise.

Regular Expression Validator

Another type of validation control provided by Visual Studio 2005 is the *regular expression validator*. This type of validation step can check user input by comparing it to an expression that defines what values are valid for a certain type of input. For example, e-mail addresses are only valid if the address is in the form of user@servername.domainname. That is, there has to be a user name before the @ symbol, followed by the server name and domain name, separated by a period. Regular expressions make it easy to check complex validation rules like this one. Visual Basic has many built-in regular expression validators. As with the required field validator, when working with this validator you will need to set the ErrorMessage, ControlToValidate, and Display properties. Additionally, you need to need to set the property named ValidationExpression. This property tells Visual Basic what kind of data you are trying to validate. Visual Basic has a built-in list of expressions for you to choose from, or you can write your own.

S TEP-BY-STEP 20.5

1. Using the **Default.aspx** page that you created in the last Step-by-Step, add a regular expression validator below the text box with the ID **txtEmail**.

2. Set the ID property to **revEmail**.

3. Set the ErrorMessage property to **Please make sure your e-mail address is in the proper format.**.

4. Set the ControlToValidate property to **txtEmail**.

5. Set the Display property to **Dynamic**.

6. Next to the ValidationExpression property, click the ellipsis button to show the Regular Expression Editor.

7. Scroll down, if necessary, and select **Internet e-mail address** and click **OK**.

STEP-BY-STEP 20.5 Continued

8. View the page in a Web browser, and enter **user@sitecom** as the e-mail address. Submit the form. Your output should resemble Figure 20-5.

FIGURE 20-5
The regular expression validator indicating the error message to the user

9. Close the Web browser, but leave Visual Studio 2005 open for the next Step-by-Step exercise.

Presenting the Confirmation Screen

Now that you have created all the form elements, you will write the code that extracts the values input by the user on the form and displays them back to the user in a confirmation screen. In a real-world Web application, you would also likely store the user order in a database. To complete the code that shows the user's order, you must first understand two more topics: the panel control and page postbacks.

The Panel Control

The *panel control* is a control that is used to group together other controls. By grouping controls inside a panel control, you can programmatically alter the entire set of controls as a group. For example, using the Visible property of the panel control, you could hide or show a collection of other controls. For our pizza order form, we will place all the controls that make up the order form inside a panel and all of the controls that make up the confirmation screen inside a second panel. We will then programmatically hide and show these controls at the appropriate time. The panel control can be added to a Web form by dragging and dropping it from the Toolbox like other controls. When adding a panel to an existing page that already has content, it is often easier to switch to Source view and add the panel in the code because it is easier to designate which parts of the existing content will be inside the panel.

STEP-BY-STEP 20.6

1. Using the **Default.aspx** page that you created in the last Step-by-Step, switch to the Source view if it is not already visible.

2. Towards the top of the code, below the <asp:Image> tag, key the following: **<asp:Panel runat="server" ID="pnlPizzaForm">**.

3. After you key the text, Visual Basic will automatically add the closing code of </asp:Panel> for you. Move the closing tag to the bottom of the page, just above the </DIV> element.

Note

After step 3, the last lines of code in the file should look like the following:
```
</asp:Panel>
</div>
</form>
</body>
</html>
```

4. After the </DIV> code that you just moved your closing tag above, key the following text: **<asp:Panel runat="server" ID="pnlConfirm">**. Again, Visual Basic will add the closing panel code for you.

5. Switch back to Design view, and you will see a visual representation of the panel `pnlConfirm` that you added at the bottom of the form.

6. At the top of the panel, add a label with a Text property of **Order Confirmation** and a Font Bold property of **True**.

7. Next, add eleven labels that will hold the values that the user input. Set the ID property of each label to match each of the form elements (i.e., **lblFirstName**, **lblAddress**, etc.) and set the Text properties to match the data (i.e., **First Name**, **Address**, etc.).

8. Finally, add a new label in the panel that will hold the total calculated cost. Set the Text property to **Total Cost $** and the ID property to **lblTotalCost**.

STEP-BY-STEP 20.6 Continued

9. View the page in a Web browser. Your output should resemble Figure 20-6.

FIGURE 20-6
The form showing both panels

10. Close the Web browser, but leave Visual Studio 2005 open for the next Step-by-Step exercise.

Page Postbacks

In ASP.NET, when a Web page is submitted (for example, when a button on the page is clicked), the default mechanism submits the data from the page back to itself. This process is called a *page postback*. Postbacks make it easier to extract form data, but they can also cause problems if not handled properly. For example, if a form element, such as a radio button list, has a selected item by default, each time the page reloads, that selected item is automatically selected. So unless you check for the postback, then the value that the user selected would be replaced with the default value.

Fortunately ASP.NET has a built-in mechanism for checking for postbacks. A simple check for a postback might look like the following:

```
If Page.IsPostBack Then
     'do something
  Else
     'do something else
  End If
```

Typically this check for the postback occurs inside the *page load subroutine* that is run when the page is loaded. The page load subroutine will be automatically generated for you if you double-click in the Design view of a form. For our pizza form, we will use the postback check that is run on page load to hide and show the proper panels.

S TEP-BY-STEP 20.7

1. Using the **Default.aspx** page that you created in the last Step-by-Step, switch to the Design view if it is not already visible.

2. Double-click on the WebForm outside of the table, and Visual Studio should generate the `Page Load` event handler for you.

3. Add the following code inside the page load event handler:

```
If Page.IsPostBack Then
     pnlPizzaForm.Visible = False
     pnlConfirm.Visible = True
  Else
     pnlPizzaForm.Visible = True
     pnlConfirm.Visible = False
  End If
```

4. View the page in a Web browser. Notice that you only see the form and not the confirmation screen.

5. Fill out the form and click the **Place Order** button. You should see the confirmation screen, although the values from the form will not yet be shown.

6. Close the Web browser, but leave Visual Studio 2005 open for the next Step-by-Step exercise.

The Code for the Confirmation Screen

Now that you have the structure in place to handle the presentation of the form and the confirmation screen, you will need to add the code that actually takes the user values and displays them in the confirmation panel.

In Lesson 19, you learned techniques to extract the selected value from text boxes and radio button lists. You also learned how to loop through the items of a check box list to see what values were selected. We will use these same ideas to populate the labels on the confirmation screen.

To calculate the total cost of the pizza, we need to add up the cost of the size, the crust, and all of the selected toppings. In each case, we stored the price information inside the Value property of the control that is used to display the options.

The final code that will be executed when the user clicks the Place Order button is shown below:

```
Dim intTotalCost As Decimal
   Dim i As Integer

   lblFirstName.Text += txtFirstName.Text
   lblLastName.Text += txtLastName.Text
   lblEmail.Text += txtEmail.Text
   lblAddress.Text += txtAddress.Text
   lblCity.Text += txtCity.Text
   lblState.Text += txtState.Text
   lblZip.Text += txtZip.Text
   lblPhone.Text += txtPhone.Text
   lblPizzaSizes.Text += rblSizes.SelectedItem.ToString()
   lblCrustTypes.Text += rblCrustType.SelectedItem.ToString()

   intTotalCost += rblSizes.SelectedValue
   intTotalCost += rblCrustType.SelectedValue

   For i = 0 To cblToppings.Items.Count - 1
   If cblToppings.Items(i).Selected Then
   lblToppings.Text = lblToppings.Text & cblToppings.Items(i).Text &","
   intTotalCost = intTotalCost + Convert.ToDecimal(cblToppings.Items(i).Value)
   End If
   Next

   lblTotalCost.Text += intTotalCost.ToString()
```

The first part of the code basically extracts the values from the text boxes and radio button lists and concatenates the existing text of the confirmation label with the value entered by the user. Then the code loops through the check box list and extracts the selected toppings' Text and Value properties. Finally, the code outputs the total cost that was calculated.

STEP-BY-STEP 20.8

1. Using the **Default.aspx** page that you created in the last Step-by-Step, switch to the Design view if it is not already visible.

2. Double-click on the **Place Order** button and Visual Basic should generate the button `click` event handler for you.

STEP-BY-STEP 20.8 Continued

3. Inside the event handler, add the following code:

```
Dim intTotalCost As Decimal
   Dim i As Integer

   lblFirstName.Text += txtFirstName.Text
   lblLastName.Text += txtLastName.Text
   lblEmail.Text += txtEmail.Text
   lblAddress.Text += txtAddress.Text
   lblCity.Text += txtCity.Text
   lblState.Text += txtState.Text
   lblZip.Text += txtZip.Text
   lblPhone.Text += txtPhone.Text
   lblPizzaSize.Text += rblSizes.SelectedItem.ToString()
   lblCrustTypes.Text += rblCrustType.SelectedItem.ToString()

   intTotalCost += rblSizes.SelectedValue
   intTotalCost += rblCrustType.SelectedValue

   For i = 0 To cblToppings.Items.Count - 1
   If cblToppings.Items(i).Selected Then
   lblToppings.Text = lblToppings.Text & cblToppings.Items(i).Text &","
   intTotalCost = intTotalCost + Convert.ToDecimal(cblToppings.Items(i).Value)
   End If
   Next

   lblTotalCost.Text += intTotalCost.ToString()
```

4. View the Web page in a browser. Fill out the form and make sure all the user data is displayed on the confirmation screen.

5. Close the Web browser and close Visual Studio 2005.

SUMMARY

In this lesson, you learned:

- User controls can be used to create a WebForm to capture data.

- Validation controls are used to validate user input.

- The required field validator is used to specify that a form element is required for form submission.

- The ErrorMessage property of the required validator is used to specify the message that the user will see if the form element is not filled out.

- The ControlToValidate property of the required validator is used to specify the control that will be required.

- The Display property of the required validator is used to specify how the validator will be laid out on the screen.

- The regular expression validator is used to validate more complex data like e-mail addresses or phone numbers.

- The regular expression validator has a property named ValidationExpression which defines the regular expression that will be used to validate the data.

- The panel control is used to group together other controls so that the group can be treated as an individual unit.

- A postback is when a form posts data back to itself.

- The page load subroutine is run when the ASP.NET page is loaded in the browser.

VOCABULARY *Review*

Define the following terms:

Panel control	Page postback	Required field validator
Page load subroutine	Regular expression validator	Validation controls

REVIEW *Questions*

TRUE / FALSE

Circle T if the statement is true or F if the statement is false.

T   F   **1.** WebForms can be used to capture user data.

T   F   **2.** Validation controls are used to make sure the page loads properly.

T   F   **3.** The required field validator is used to specify which form elements are required on a form.

T   F   **4.** The ErrorMessage property of the required field validator specifies the message that a user will see if the form element is not filled out.

T   F   **5.** If you set the Display property of the required field validator to Static, the validator will only take up room on the screen if the message is displayed to the user.

T   F   **6.** The regular expression validator works by comparing user input to an expression that determines the valid values for the field.

T   F   **7.** The ValidationExpression property of the regular expression validator specifies the regular expression to be used for the comparison.

T   F   **8.** The panel control allows controls to be grouped together and treated as a group.

T   F   **9.** When data is submitted from a form, it is submitted to another WebForm by default.

T   F   **10.** The Page.IsPostBack method is a built-in way to check for postbacks.

WRITTEN QUESTIONS

Write a brief answer to each of the following questions.

1. What are validation controls used for?

2. What kind of validator would be used to make sure the user supplied a first name?

3. What kind of validator would be used to make sure the phone number matches the format (XXX) XXX – XXXX?

4. What is the purpose of the ControlToValidate property of the regular expression validator?

5. Explain the difference between the Static and Dynamic options for the Display property of the required field validator.

6. What is the purpose of the panel control?

7. Which property of the panel control can be used to hide and show the panel?

8. What is a page postback?

9. Write some sample code that checks for page postbacks.

10. Where is the check for the page postback typically done?

PROJECTS

PROJECT 20-1

In this lesson, you learned how to add and use required field validators. Start Visual Studio 2005 and open the **PizzaOrderForm** Web site that was created in the Step-by-Steps. Add additional required field validators so that all of the following fields are required:

- First Name
- Last Name
- E-mail
- City
- State
- Zip
- Phone

Use appropriate error message text for each validator.

PROJECT 20-2

Using the principles learned in this lesson, add two additional regular expression validators to the pizza order form (which you edited in Project 20-1) to make sure that the phone number and zip code are in the proper format. You should find built-in expressions for each of these.

PROJECT 20-3

Many times, when there are multiple validation controls on one form, it is difficult for the user to easily see all the errors at one time—especially on longer forms. Visual Basic provides a Validation Summary control that shows all of the errors in one place.

1. Open Visual Studio 2005 and open the **PizzaOrderForm** Web site that you have been working with in this lesson, if necessary.

2. In the empty table cell next to the Place Order button, drag and drop a validation summary control from the Toolbox.

3. View the Web page in a browser and submit the form without filling in any fields. Notice the validation summary at the bottom of the form, near the button.

4. Close the project and close Visual Studio 2005.

CRITICAL*Thinking*

In this lesson, you learned how to use regular expressions. In step 7 of Step-by-Step 20.5, you selected a regular expression to validate Internet e-mail addresses. When you selected this item from the regular expression dialog box, the expression `\w+([-+.']\w+)*@\w+([-.]\w+)*\.\w+([-.]\w+)*` was added as the ValidationExpression. Research regular expressions on the Internet to determine how they work and then explain what the parts of this regular expression mean.

ASP.NET

REVIEW *Questions*

TRUE / FALSE

Circle T if the statement is true or F if the statement is false.

T   F   **1.** A WebForm is another name for a Web page.

T   F   **2.** If a Web site has not been compiled, the first user that accesses it will cause it to crash.

T   F   **3.** The Source view contains the code representation of the controls that are added to a WebForm.

T   F   **4.** Many languages, including Visual Studio, can be used to create ASP.NET pages.

T   F   **5.** The text box is used to capture user input, such as first name, last name, etc.

T   F   **6.** A radio button list is used when the user should be presented multiple choices from which they can choose more than one.

T   F   **7.** Hyperlinks can only be used when linking to external Web pages.

T   F   **8.** Validation controls are used to validate user input.

T   F   **9.** When data is submitted on a WebForm, it posts back to itself.

T   F **10.** The Panel control is used to match the user input with a regular expression.

WRITTEN QUESTIONS

Write a brief answer to each of the following questions.

1. List some similarities between ASP.NET applications and desktop applications.

2. Name the two file extensions you have used when creating WebForms in ASP.NET.

3. What is the purpose of the Design view in Visual Studio 2005?

4. What property of the check box list contains the items that are shown to the user on the screen?

5. Describe how you can get the selected values from a radio button list.

6. When should the Password setting for the TextMode property of the text box be used?

7. What type of validation control could be used to ensure that a user entered a social security number in a format like the following: XXX-XX-XXXX?

8. What type of validation control can be used to make sure that a user entered a password?

9. How can a panel be used to hide several controls at one time?

10. What is the purpose of the ValidationExpression property of the regular expression validator?

SIMULATIONS

You are a Web developer working for a computer company. Your company wants to entice prospective customers to provide useful information by offering a contest in which the winner can choose from a series of prizes. Your company wishes to collect the customer's contact information, programming language preferences, and his or her choice of prizes. Your company will then follow up with e-mail or phone calls to each of the potential customers and draw for the winner. The contest is only open to residents of the United States.

JOB 7-1

First, create a WebForm that will capture the user's basic contact information, including first name, last name, e-mail address, street address, city, state, zip, and phone number. All of the fields should be required, and you should use regular expression validators to validate the e-mail address and U.S. phone number.

1. Create a new Web site project named **Contest**.

2. Add two panels to the **Default.aspx** page. Name the panels **pnlForm** and **pnlThanks**.

3. Inside pnlForm, add labels and fields for first name, last name, e-mail address, street address, city, state, zip, and phone number.

4. Add required field validators on each of the fields. Use appropriate error messages.

5. Add regular expression validators on the e-mail address and phone number fields.

6. Add a button to pnlForm that will cause the page to be submitted.

7. In pnlThanks, add a thank you message to the user for entering the information.

8. Add code in the page load event that hides the form and shows the thank you message on postback.

9. View the page in the browser and make sure it works properly.

10. Close the browser, but leave this Web site open for the next job.

JOB 7-2

To enter the contest, users must enter the programming languages they use and the gift they would like if they win the contest. In this job, you will add form elements to support those questions.

1. Open the **Default.aspx** page from the Web site you created in the previous job, if it is not already open.

2. Inside pnlForm and underneath the text box for phone, add a check box list that allows the user to choose one or multiple options from the following choices: **Visual Basic**, **J#**, or **C#**. The check box list should have a label that asks users to check all the programming languages that they use.

3. Add a radio button list asking the user to choose a gift option. The options are **Television**, **Cellular Phone**, or **Mp3 Player**.

4. View the page in the browser and make sure it works properly.

5. Close the browser, but leave this Web site open for the next job.

JOB 7-3

Now that you have created the form that will capture the user information, you will need a way to get this information back to the company so that a winner may be chosen. You will have the Web page e-mail all the information.

The basic code used to send e-mail from a Web page is the following:

```
Dim mlmEmail As MailMessage = New MailMessage(From, To, Subject, Body)
Dim client As SmtpClient = New SmtpClient("smtp.domain.com")
client.Send(mlmEmail)
```

In the code above, `From`, `To`, `Subject`, and `Body` should be replaced by variables that hold the e-mail information. To send all the order information, you could concatenate all the user input into one variable that represents the body. Also, the SMTP server needs to be changed to one that you can send mail through. Ask your instructor for help with the SMTP server.

CAPSTONE SIMULATION

You work for Adelphia Bank as a Visual Studio developer. One of the services that the bank offers is home loans for its customers. Often, potential home buyers wish to get an idea of the approximate monthly payment required for a new home.

Adelphia bank wants to assist customers in the home-buying process by creating two forms that will help them answer the question of how much the monthly payment would be for a given loan amount. Adelphia Bank would like you to create two forms to help users get this information. One form will be a Web-based form that users can access via the bank's existing Web site. The second form will be used internally by bank employees for those users who might not want to use the Web site or might not have Internet access.

Both forms will capture the user's basic contact information as well as the information about the loan needed to calculate the monthly payments.

When you are finished, the Windows application form should resemble Figure C-1, while the Web-based form should resemble Figure C-2.

FIGURE C-1
The Windows form that will be used by bank employees

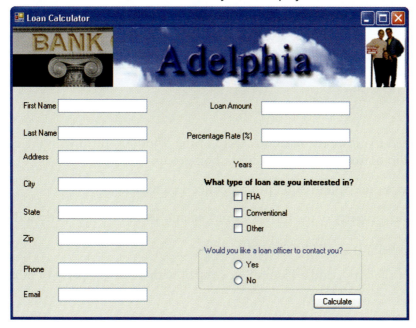

FIGURE C-2
The Web-based form that will be used by customers

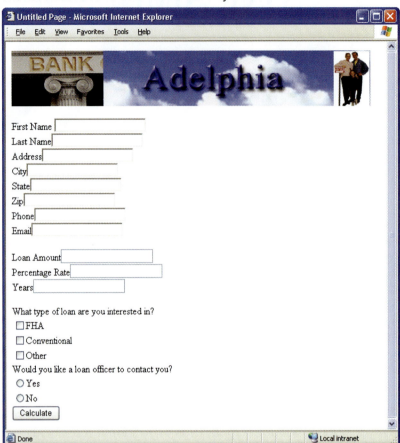

Both forms should check for required fields, calculate the payment amount, and display the payment amount to the user.

The formula for calculating the monthly payment for a loan is as follows.

```
Payments = Loan Amount x monthly interest rate / (1-(1+monthly interest _
    rate)^-total number of payments
```

ACTIVITY C-1

First, you need to create the basic structure of the Windows form with the company banner, text boxes, a radio button group, and a check box group.

1. Create a new Visual Studio 2005 project called **LoanCalculator**.

2. Set the (Name) property of the form to **frmMain** and set the Text property to **Loan Calculator**.

3. Set the Size property of the form to **608, 460**.

4. At the top of the form, add a PictureBox control with a Size property of **602, 89**.

5. Set the Image property of the PictureBox control to point to the file named **Adelphia.jpg**, which can be found with the data files for this capstone simulation.

6. Add labels on the form for the following elements: **First Name, Last Name, Address, City, State, Zip, Phone, E-mail, Loan Amount, Percentage Rate**, and **Years**.

7. Next to each label, add an appropriately named text box that will be used to collect the data identified by each label.

8. Add a label with a Text property of **What type of loan are you interested in?** using MS Sans serif, Bold, 8.

9. Under that label, add three check boxes with properties set according to Table C-1.

TABLE C-1
Values to enter for Step 9

(NAME)	TEXT
chkFHA	FHA
chkConventional	Conventional
chkOther	Other

10. Add a group box control with a Text property of **Would you like a loan officer to contact you?** using a blue font.

11. Inside the group box, add two radio buttons with properties set according to Table C-2.

TABLE C-2
Values to enter for Step 11

(NAME)	TEXT
rdoYes	Yes
rdoNo	No

12. Under the group box, add a button with a (Name) property of **btnCalculate** and a Text property of **Calculate**.

13. Start debugging the program. Your output should resemble Figure C-1.

14. Stop debugging the program and leave the project and Visual Studio 2005 open for the next Activity.

ACTIVITY C-2

Next, you need to add code to make sure that the user has entered the required fields. All of the contact information is considered required, as are the fields for loan amount, rate, and number of years. Since Windows forms do not have required field validator controls like WebForms, you will need to use If Then statements to manually check that these fields are not left blank. If any fields are left blank, the user should be presented with an error message, and the payment amount should not be calculated. You will use a Boolean variable to track whether or not any fields have failed validation.

1. Double-click the **Calculate** button so that the button Click event procedure will be automatically created.

2. At the top of the event procedure, add the following code.

```
Dim strErrorMessage As String = "The following errors were found:" + vbCrLf
Dim blnShowErrorMessage As Boolean = False
```

3. Next, add the following code.

```
If txtFirst.Text = "" Then
    strErrorMessage += "First Name missing" + vbCrLf
    blnShowErrorMessage = True
End If
```

4. Repeat the pattern of code from step 3 another ten times so that you have code that checks each of the required fields. In each case, make sure you change the text box name and the error message that will be presented to the user.

5. Underneath the last If Then statement, add the following code.

```
If blnShowErrorMessage = True Then
    MessageBox.Show(strErrorMessage)
        strErrorMessage = ""
Else
    'Code to calculate Payments
End If
```

6. Start debugging the program.

7. Intentionally leave some of the fields blank and click the **Calculate** button. Make sure the error messages are displayed.

8. Stop debugging the program and leave the project and Visual Studio open for the next Activity.

ACTIVITY C-3

Now you need to add code to actually calculate the payments based on the data the user entered.

1. Double-click the **Calculate** button so that you can see the code that has been created thus far.

2. At the top of the event procedure, add the following code underneath the existing variable declarations.

```
Dim sngMonthlyInterestRate As Single
Dim curMonthlyPayment As Decimal
Dim strMonthlyPayment As String
Dim sngNumberOfPayments As Single
```

3. At the bottom of the event procedure, find the following line of code.

```
'Code to calculate Payments
```

4. Replace that line of code with the following code (be sure to use the names of your text boxes).

```
sngNumberOfPayments = CDbl(txtYears.Text) * 12
sngMonthlyInterestRate = CDbl(txtRate.Text) / 1200
curMonthlyPayment = CDbl(txtLoanAmount.Text) * sngMonthlyInterestRate / _
    (1 - (1 + sngMonthlyInterestRate) ^ (-sngNumberOfPayments))
strMonthlyPayment = Format(curMonthlyPayment, "$######.00")
MessageBox.Show("The monthly payment is: " + strMonthlyPayment.ToString())
```

5. Start debugging the program.

6. Fill out all the required fields and enter values of **118000, 6.25**, and **30** in the text boxes for loan amount, rate, and years, respectively.

7. Make sure the monthly payment reported is *$726.55.*

8. Stop debugging the program and close Visual Studio.

ACTIVITY C-4

For the next phase of this project, you need to create the basic structure of the WebForm with the company banner, text boxes, a radio button list, and a check box list.

1. Create a new Visual Studio Web site called **LoanCalculator**.

2. At the top of the **Default.aspx** page, add an Image control with a Height property of **89** and a Width property of **602**.

3. In the Solution Explorer, right-click on the Web site name, choose **Add Existing Item**, and add **Adelphia.jpg** to this Web site (the one showing the drive letter). (The image is found with the data files for this capstone simulation.)

4. Set the ImageURL property of the Image control to point to the file named **Adelphia.jpg**.

5. Add a panel to the form with an (ID) property of **pnlForm**.

6. Add labels in the panel for the following elements: **First Name, Last Name, Address, City, State, Zip, Phone, E-mail, Loan Amount, Percentage Rate**, and **Years**.

7. Next to each label, add an appropriately named text box that will be used to collect the data identified by each form.

8. Add a label with a text property of **What type of loan are you interested in?**.

9. Under that label, add a check box list with an (ID) property of **cblLoanType**.

10. Add the following three items to the check box list: **FHA, Conventional, Other**.

11. Add a label with a Text property of **Would you like a loan officer to contact you?**.

12. Under that label, add a radio button list with an (ID) property of **rblContact**.

13. Add the following two items to the radio button list: **Yes, No**.

14. Under the radio button list, add a button with an (ID) property of **btnCalculate** and a Text property of **Calculate**.

15. Save the page and view it in a Web browser. Your output should resemble Figure C-2.

16. Close the Web browser, but leave the project and Visual Studio open for the next Activity.

ACTIVITY C-5

Now you need to add required field validators to make sure that the user has entered the required fields. All of the contact information is considered required, as are the fields for loan amount, rate, and number of years.

1. Add required field validators to the following text boxes, making sure to enter an appropriate message for each: First Name, Last Name, Address, City, State, Zip, Phone, E-mail, Loan Amount, Percentage Rate, Years.

2. Save the page and view it in a Web browser.

3. Intentionally leave some of the fields blank and click the **Calculate** button. Make sure the error messages are displayed.

4. Close the Web browser, but leave the project and Visual Studio open for the next Activity.

ACTIVITY C-6

In the last phase of this project, you need to add code to actually calculate the payments based on the data the user entered. Additionally, you need to add a second panel in which to display the payment information.

1. Below the existing panel, add a new panel with an (ID) property of **pnlThanks**.

2. Inside pnlThanks, add a label with an (ID) property of **lblMessage** and a Text property of **Thanks**.

3. Below lblMessage, add another label with an (ID) property of **lblPayment** and a Text property of **Your monthly payment is:**.

4. Double-click the **Calculate** button so that the button `Click` event procedure will be created for you.

5. At the top of the event procedure, add the following code.

```
Dim sngMonthlyInterestRate As Single
Dim curMonthlyPayment As Decimal
Dim strMonthlyPayment As String
Dim sngNumberOfPayments As Single
```

6. Next, add the following code (using your text box names).

```
sngNumberOfPayments = CDbl(txtYears.Text) * 12
sngMonthlyInterestRate = CDbl(txtRate.Text) / 1200
curMonthlyPayment = CDbl(txtLoanAmount.Text) * sngMonthlyInterestRate / _
    (1 - (1 + sngMonthlyInterestRate) ^ (-sngNumberOfPayments))
strMonthlyPayment = Format(curMonthlyPayment, "$######.00")
lblPayment.Text += strMonthlyPayment.ToString()

    lblMessage.Text += txtFirst.Text + "," + vbCrLf

    If rblContact.SelectedItem.ToString() = "Yes" Then
        lblMessage.Text += "A loan officer will contact you about a loan."
    End If
```

7. While in Design view, double-click on the form somewhere outside of the panel. This action will automatically create the `Page load` event procedure for you.

8. Inside the page load event procedure, add the following code.

```
If Page.IsPostBack Then
    pnlThanks.Visible = True
    pnlForm.Visible = False
Else
    pnlThanks.Visible = False
    pnlForm.Visible = True
End If
```

9. Save the page and view it in a Web browser.

10. Fill out all the required fields and enter values of **118000**, **6.25**, and **30** in the text boxes for loan amount, rate, and years, respectively. Also, choose either Yes or No for the question that asks if you want a loan officer to contact you.

11. Make suse the monthly payment reported is *$726.55*.

12. Close the Web browser and close Visual Studio 2005.

GLOSSARY

A

About box A dialog box that might include information like a registration number, version number, copyright, and information about the developer of the software.

Alphanumeric Text data that can include letters or numbers.

Array A data structure that allows you to refer to a series of variables by the same name and to use a number, called an index or subscript, to tell them apart.

ASP.NET The technology that allows you to build applications that will run in a user's Web browser.

ASP.NET development server A lightweight Web server that is built into the Visual Studio 2005 product that allows you to have a small Web server running on your machine when you are developing your Web site.

Assignment operator Assigns the result of the expression on the right of the operator to the item on the left of the operator.

AutoSize property A property that causes an object to resize to fit the contents of the Text property of an object.

B

Bitmap object An object used to work with images defined by pixel data.

Boolean data type A data type that holds the values True or False.

Brush A graphic object used to fill shapes or to draw text.

C

Case-sensitive Capitalization of key words and other elements of the code is critical. Visual Basic 2005 is not case-sensitive, but some other languages are.

Check box list control A control designed to make it easier to work with a group of check boxes at one time.

Check boxes Allow the program to ask the user a Yes or No question or to turn an option on or off.

Codebehind file The file, separate from the file that stores design elements, in which actual Visual Basic code is stored.

Color object An object that sets the color for drawing.

Command button A standard pushbutton control.

Comment Explanations of program actions that are included with the code. Comments are used to create internal documentation for a program.

Common tasks menu Provides short cuts to some of the things you are likely to do with a control.

Component tray An area at the bottom of the design window where nonvisual items appear. Once a control has been added to the component tray, you can select the component and set its properties as you would any other control on the form.

Concatenation Appends one string to the end of another.

Conditional operator Used to compare two values and return a value of True or False.

Control The command buttons, text boxes, scroll bars, and other objects that make up the user interface.

D

Decimal data type A data type specifically designed to be precise in calculations involving money.

Declaring To set up a memory location and specify what you want to call the variable and what data type you want the variable to have.

Do Until loop An iteration structure that repeats the statements until a certain condition is True.

Do While loop An iteration structure that repeats the statements while a certain condition is True.

Double data type A general decimal data type for numbers that may exceed 38 digits.

Dynamic Link Library (DLL) file A file that holds the compiled code from an ASP.NET project.

E

Element An individual value in an array.

Enabled property A property that makes a control inactive but still visible.

Endless loop A loop in which the condition that stops the loop from repeating never becomes True.

Error handler Code that executes when an error is detected.

Error trapping The process of interrupting the normal chain of events that occurs when an error is encountered and substituting your own code.

Event An action, such as a mouse click, that can cause the program to react.

Event-driven The computer is constantly waiting for the user to take some action with the mouse, keyboard, or other device.

Event procedure A subroutine that responds to an event.

Exceptions Problems that occur during run-time. An attempt to divide by zero is one common run-time problem that causes an exception.

Exponentiation The raising of a number to a power.

F

Fix function Returns a truncated number.

Flowchart Uses symbols and shapes connected by lines to illustrate the steps of a program.

Focus The object that is currently active is said to have the focus.

For Next loop A loop specifically designed for repeating a block of code a specific number of times.

Form The object that holds the buttons, boxes, and other objects that make up the program's user interface.

Form-level variable A variable that can be used by any subroutine in a form.

G

GetPixel method A method that returns the Color structure of a pixel at the specified pixel. The method works hand-in-hand with the SetPixel method.

Global variable A variable that can be used in any routine in any form in a project.

Graphics object A general purpose drawing surface that may be used with a number of graphical tools.

GroupBox control A container control that can be used to define groups of controls.

H

Hard-coded Information that is entered directly into the source code and cannot change; similar to literals.

Hyper Link control Used to create links from an ASP.NET page to another page or another Web site.

Hypertext Markup Language (HTML) Code that is interpreted by a Web browser.

I

If statement Allows you to execute specified code when the result of a conditional expression is true.

Image control Used in ASP.NET projects to add images to WebForms.

Index The number that identifies a specific element of an array.

Initialization list A list of initial values loaded into an array.

Integer A whole number; a number with no fractional part.

Integer division   Returns only the whole number portion of the division of integers.

Integrated Development Environment   A program that includes tools for creating, testing, and running computer programs.

Internal documentation   Consists of written explanations of subroutines, variables, and code sections that are included inside the program.

Iteration structure   The code required to create a loop.

L

Label control   Used to hold text that describes objects on the form.

Line-continuation character   Tells the compiler to skip to the next line and treat the text there as if it were a part of the previous line.

ListBox control   A control that enables you to display a list of items to the user.

Literals   Values that are keyed directly into source code; similar to hard-coded.

Load event   An event that is triggered when an object loads.

Local variable   A variable that can only be used in the subroutine that declares it.

Logical operators   Used with True and False values and can be used to combine several comparisons into one statement.

Loop   A method that executes a group of statements a number of times.

Lower bound   The smallest index value that can be used to access an element of an array.

M

Menu   A list of related items that can be selected to cause an event.

Menu Designer   A tool that helps you build menus for your programs.

Message   The information sent to an object method asking it to perform some activity.

Method   A function associated with an object that is used to change a property or take some other action.

Modal form   A form or dialog box that must be dismissed before you can continue working with the application.

Modeless form   A form or dialog box that can stay on the screen and be moved behind other forms in a project.

Modulus   Returns the remainder of integer division.

N

Nested If statement   An If statement inside another If statement.

Not operator   An operator that can be used to reverse the current status of the properties.

O

Object data type   A data type that can hold any type of data.

Objects   The pieces that make up a Visual Basic 2005 program, such as windows, command buttons, text boxes, and scroll bars.

One-way selection structure   A program structure in which the decision is to go "one way" or just bypass the code in the If statement.

Open File Dialog   A dialog box that allows the user to browse for a file to open.

Operators   Symbols that perform specific operations in Visual Basic 2005 statements.

Option group   A number of radio buttons contained inside a GroupBox control.

Order of operations   The rules that determine the order in which mathematical operations are performed.

P

Page load subroutine   Code that runs when an ASP.NET page is loaded.

Page postback   When data from an ASP.NET page is submitted back to itself.

Paint event   An event called whenever an object is resized, covered and uncovered, minimized and then restored, or when the Refresh event is called.

Panel control   A control used to group together other controls.

Parallel array Arrays of the same length in which each element in one array is related to an element in the second array with the same index value.

Pen Used to draw lines or the outline of a shape.

Pixel The smallest dot on a screen that the computer can address.

Point The combination of the X and Y values used to locate a graphics object.

Polygon Any shape with three or more sides.

PrintDocument object A collection of prewritten programming code that allows you to communicate with the printer.

Project A collection of files that make up a Visual Basic 2005 program.

Properties The characteristics of an object that describe how it looks and functions.

Properties window A window that holds a list of an object's properties and their values. It is used to set and change the properties of an object.

R

Radio Button List control Allows users to choose one of many presented options.

Radio buttons Similar to check boxes except that they always appear in groups, and only one button in the group can be selected at a time.

Regular expression validator Checks user input by comparing it to an expression that defines what values are valid for a certain type of input.

Required field validator Used to specify that a form element is required for form submission.

Run-time error An error that occurs while a program is running.

S

Scope Refers to the reach of a variable; a variable's scope indicates which procedures can use the variable.

Select Case statement Lets you set a variable to test and then list a number of cases that you want to test against that variable.

SelectionLength property Sets the number of characters to be selected and highlighted in a textbox.

SelectionStart property Indicates the position of the first character to select and highlight in a textbox.

Separator bars A graphical line that separates groups of commands within the same menu.

Single data type A general decimal data type for numbers that will not exceed 38 digits.

Skin A custom look and feel that can be applied to an application.

Snap lines Colored lines that appear to help you line objects up with one another.

Software development tool A tool that allows you to create programs.

Solution A collection of one or more projects.

Solution Explorer Allows you to see the forms and files that make up your program.

Source view The view that displays the programming code.

Splash screen A window that appears briefly when a program is started to identify the program.

Standard toolbar Holds icons representing a standard set of commands.

Step keyword Used to cause the loop counter to count by an increment other than one.

String A data type that holds text information.

String literal Text that is hard-coded in a program.

Submenu A menu that appears beside a command in a menu in order to provide organization within a menu.

Subroutine A section of program code that executes a specific action.

Subscript Another term for the index of an array.

T

Tab order The order in which objects get focus when the user tabs from object to object.

Text Box control Allows users to enter text into a WebForm or a WinForm.

Text boxes The fields placed on dialog boxes and in other windows that allow the user to enter a value.

Toolbox The collection of tools that allows you to add objects (controls) to the forms you create in Visual Basic 2005.

TransparencyKey A property that allows you to specify a color on the form that will become transparent while the form is running.

Truncation Removes everything to the right of the decimal point.

Two-way selection structure A program structure in which one block of code is executed if the specified conditions are True, or another block of code is executed if the specified conditions are False.

U

Unary minus Performs negation, which means making a positive value negative or making a negative value positive.

Upper bound The largest index value that can be used to access an element of the array.

V

Val function Takes numbers that are in a text format and returns a numeric value that can be used in calculations.

Validation controls Controls used to validate user input.

Variable A named location in memory that is used to store information.

W

WebBrowser control A control that makes it easy to integrate Web browsing capabilities into your Visual Basic Windows Forms.

WebForm A form created in a Web application.

WinForm A form created in a Windows desktop application.

Z

Zero-based array An array in which the index of the first element is zero.

INDEX